FORTY YEARS OF PSYCHIC RESEARCH

FORTY YEARS

OF

PSYCHIC RESEARCH

A Plain Narrative of Fact

By

HAMLIN GARLAND

112616

BOOKS FOR LIBRARIES PRESS
FREEPORT, NEW YORK

First Published 1936
Reprinted 1970

STANDARD BOOK NUMBER:
8369-5281-2

LIBRARY OF CONGRESS CATALOG CARD NUMBER:
70-114877

PRINTED IN THE UNITED STATES OF AMERICA

PREFACE

In this volume I have brought together in chronological order all of the outstanding experiments which I conducted as an investigator of spiritualistic phenomena. Much of this material is drawn from official reports, letters and addresses, but has been rewritten for the first time into a plain narrative of fact. It is as exact as my dated records, supplemented by my memory, can make it. The names of psychics are mainly fictional.

As a man of seventy-five, it seemed advisable that this chronicle should be put into definite form while yet I am able to revise and proof-read it. The method is substantially the same as that which I employed in "Afternoon Neighbors" and "Companions on the Trail." It is my psychic log-book, as "Roadside Meetings" and its companions form my literary log-book.

All phenomena described in these pages are presented as something I saw, heard, felt and weighed, and are given, for the most part, without regard to any prejudice. If these supernormal events are illusory, then all the events of my life are illusory. They happened and I recorded them. I leave the reader to draw his own conclusions concerning their significance.

CONTENTS

CONTENTS

FORTY YEARS OF PSYCHIC RESEARCH

CHAPTER ONE

ON SPECIAL DETAIL

I

In 1891, I was an aspiring young writer with an attic study in Boston, a novelist holding a keen interest in positive science. As a student of Herbert Spencer I counted myself an agnostic and an evolutionist, but among my most loyal friends at this time was B. O. Flower, a mystic, and editor of the *Arena,* the leading radical magazine of that day.

As a young man of about my own age—that is to say, thirty-one—Flower was my generous advocate. He had already published a number of my articles and stories, a fact which indicates his belief in me—as a fictionist at least. That he was a spiritualist I well knew, but we had never argued the matter. Like myself he was a student of Darwin, and had a special regard for Alfred Russel Wallace, who, though one of the leading evolutionists, had written in support of the spiritualistic hypothesis.

One day as we were chatting in his office Flower said to me: "A group of us are about to organize an American psychic society with central office here in Boston. Nominally, there is an American branch of the English society, but actually the organization consists of one man, Hodgson, the resident secretary, who does very little but draw his salary. We are determined on an organization which shall do something in the way of experimental research. We want you to come in as one of the directors."

Surprised and somewhat amused by this request, I protested that I didn't know a thing about such matters and that my mind ran toward the positive sciences.

"That's just why we want you," replied Flower. "You are young, logical in your thought, and a close observer. Furthermore you are not bereaved as so many people are who go into this work. You are not a mourner. You can approach an experiment with unprejudiced mind. We need a youth of your positive character. I am also asking Professor Dolbear of Tufts College to serve with us. He is a physicist and an inventor, and the author of a book on matter and motion. He and you will offset Minot J. Savage and Allen, who are already committed to the spirit side of the question as I am. Rabbi Schindler, who is inclined to the negative side, has also consented to act and we shall have, I hope, one or two other men of science. Our secretary, Ernest Allen, will edit the journal which we intend to publish."

Up to this time I had given very little thought to this "dark side of the moon," although in my youth I had listened to stories told by my father, in which he described my mother as a young girl acting the part of a medium. In his report my grandfather's house in southern Wisconsin, during the early fifties, had been the stage of a series of singular dramas, in which my mother, a girl of ten or twelve, and her brother Franklin, a child of five, had been chief actors.

"Settlers came from all parts of the country to hear mysterious raps and see tables move without apparent cause. Chairs would follow Isabelle up the stairs, and Frank, a little shaver who couldn't read or spell a word, wrote on slates long messages full of cuss-words and obscene threats. It was this development in Frank's case which led your grandfather McClintock to stop it all. 'It is the work of the devil,' he declared."

In confirmation of all this one of my aunts, a gentle, lovely character, said, "Yes, these forces made my life a hell for two years."

With these stories in mind and with a natural curiosity as to the facts I said to Flower: "I will come on the board of directors if Dolbear does. I know something of his work as a professor of physics and, if he is disposed to investigate, I'll follow along with him."

Pleasantly excited by the vista which this connection opened out before me, I was careful to stipulate that my duties on the committee should not interfere with my work as a writer. "I will give my afternoons and evenings to investigations, but my mornings must not be disturbed."

To this Flower agreed, and a few days later I met the directors and was introduced to them.

The president of the society, Minot J. Savage, was a scholarly and highly respected Unitarian clergyman whom I had often heard speak and whom I greatly admired. Rabbi Solomon Schindler, another sceptical member of the board, was one of the best known Jewish speakers in Massachusetts, a sturdy, scholarly man

of German birth. The Reverend Ernest Allen, who
acted as secretary, was a blond, smiling, curly-haired
man of about my own age. Although fairly committed
to the spirit hypothesis he remained (as I soon discovered) a very keen investigator. He had an orderly mind
and was given to making numbered precise statements
of his theories.

Amos Emerson Dolbear, professor of physics at Tufts
College, was a typical Yankee, thin, keen-eyed, quick-
spoken, and dryly humorous. In physique and the cut
of his beard he suggested "Uncle Sam." He confessed
that his experience with metaphysical phenomena had
been slight but that he was willing to give a certain
amount of time to investigation.

In my presence, Flower smilingly said to Dolbear,
"We are depending on you and Garland and Rabbi
Schindler to counteract the credulity of Dr. Savage,
Allen, and myself."

Dolbear's eyes twinkled as he replied: "I shall approach the doings of spooks as I would investigate any
other alleged happenings in the physical universe. I'll
serve the society to the best of my ability."

This remark led Dr. Savage to name Dolbear and me
as a special committee on physical phenomena, and in
preparation for my duties I spent several days at the
library going over the records of the English society.

I was surprised to find many concise and unbiased
reports of scientific experiments with Old World mediums. Up to this time I had read only a few copies of
badly printed spiritualistic weeklies whose editors were
in effect paid advocates. Their articles had bored me.
They smelled of darkened back-parlors, and their ex-

tended comment often took the form of prolix essays in which spiritualism was a divine revelation, an assault on traditional Christianity. In short, spirit converse in America seemed to be still in the stage which had aroused Emerson's disgust and Hawthorne's grave doubt.

"Whatever the facts about mediumship, it is unfortunate in its historians," I remarked to Flower when I saw him next. "I find that many of its advocates are savage critics of the established order. American authors for the most part keep clear of it. Howells touched upon it adversely in his 'Undiscovered Country' and Henry James has dealt with some of the dubious practices of mediumship; but their approach has been thus far entirely fictional rather than scientific."

"It is not a question of a medium's social standing," replied Flower. "It is a question of fact. Observation is not enough. Read Alfred Russel Wallace and William Crookes. Their approach to the subject was purely scientific."

II

Opportunities for experiment offered almost immediately. The Boston papers having announced the formation of our society, letters began to come to our secretary each presenting a psychic mystery and requesting aid in its solution. Many of the letters were badly written on cheap stationery, but they all gave evidence of sincerity and a genuine desire for help.

One report which I recall rather clearly, especially interested Dolbear. It came from Virginia and described a haunted well in which, as one peered down it, one could see faces on the water, faces not accounted for at the curb. This was so amply authenticated that Dolbear agreed to go down and look into it. Several other agitated citizens wrote of strange happenings in their homes, noises, shifting furniture and the like, and asked my committee to come and investigate. "You'll see tables rock and chairs slide without discoverable cause," they declared.

In brief, I became aware almost in a day of an amazing world of hidden outlaw forces, a world in which miracles were everyday occurrences. On reading these letters it seemed possible for me to step at once into this region of the unaccountable. It was at my door— or just across the street.

While Dolbear went to Virginia to inspect the magic well, Allen, our secretary, and I took train to a nearby city with intent to examine a young girl in whose presence, it was reported, tables heaved and chairs squeaked as if some invisible person were seated there.

As this was a typical case, I shall describe it in some detail:

The family was intelligent and industrious. Its members were all laborers in near-by shops. The father, a man of middle age, was notably pious. The home was plain, the furniture threadbare but well kept by the mother, who was the housekeeper. The daughter, a girl of eighteen, was a shoe-hand; the brother, a few years older, was a skilled mechanic. All the members of the family accepted the tappings on the walls and the movement of small objects as the work of a dead boy. "It is his way of letting us know that he is still among us," the mother explained.

At this point some reader is certain to ask the question: "Why do spirits rock chairs and lift tables?"

The spiritualist says: "Because by such unaccountable movements of familiar objects, attention is drawn to them and wonder is awakened." And certainly the movement of a pair of scissors with no one touching them provokes thought and leads to experiment.

At the invitation of the family, we took our seats at the plain dining table with our hands laid flat upon it. A small rocker which had been the little boy's favorite seat stood on the floor a little back of my chair. The medium, a large, slow-spoken, pleasant girl, sat beside me.

After the room was darkened the mother began to sing one of the hymns which "Robbie" particularly liked, and within a very few minutes the table began to heave, and soon after this the little rocker, which I could dimly see, creaked and moved as if some one were veritably sitting upon it. Slowly, by slight impulses, it slid up to me and at last rested against my knee. After a pause as if to gather strength it began to climb, and by painful effort, after several trials, succeeded in reaching and resting upon my elbow. It almost attained the top of the table, but fell as if exhausted.

These motions were followed by rappings which answered questions—one rap meaning "no" and three raps "yes." The mother talked to the invisible as to her little son. The girl said: "Robbie likes to play tricks on us. Don't you, Robbie?" And a fusillade of raps responded.

As I sat facing the window (the shade of which was only partly drawn) I could see the heads of passing workmen, and in the silences between our songs I could hear the sounds of feet on the pavement. Here in vivid contrast were the prosaic facts of everyday life in the street and the room in which a mother was communing with an invisible, intangible son.

The members of this family were so serious of purpose and so happy in their faith that I had no desire to question it in their presence. There was nothing evidential in the sitting, nothing to make a report upon, but, recalling my father's stories of my mother's similar mediumship, I felt in this circle something of the same religious awe with which my uncles and aunts had approached the sittings in my grandfather's pioneer cabin fifty years before.

III

Soon after this trip to Lowell, one of our members, the principal of a high school in Jamaica Plain, related to me the story of an experiment which he had recently made, and his statement gave me a new angle on "clairvoyance."

He said: "Professor Wilton, one of my friends, principal of a school in Forest Hills, had been testing with me the ability of a certain medium who claimed to read sealed letters, and we had both been deeply impressed by the man's candor as well as by his astounding success in reading our questions even when enclosed in sealed envelopes. Not entirely satisfied, however, we agreed to try again, using every precaution against opening and resealing the envelopes.

"That night I prepared another letter for this test, but on the following morning I was shocked to learn that Wilton had died in his bed of heart disease. His family asked me to come over at once.

"This I did, and as I entered his study I noticed on his desk an envelope of the sort we had planned to prepare, and the thought came to me, 'Here is a perfect test! No living person knows what is in this envelope.' I put it in my pocket and a few days later took it to the medium, together with another sealed letter which I had myself prepared.

"The psychic read mine quickly and correctly, holding it to his brow with his eyes closed. I then gave him my friend's letter. After pressing it against his forehead a few moments he said: 'I can't read this message. It is the writing of a dead man. If you will have it read by anyone—anywhere in the world—*I* will read it but I can't do it now. It must be in the mind of some living person before I can lay hold upon it.' Since then I have tried it with other clairvoyants and none of them can read it."

This story, which I give from memory, provoked thought along new lines. To my friend I said, "Your test seems to prove that the wall between the living brain and the dead mind is a very real barrier."

My interest in clairvoyance and psychometry began that day, and although my committee work was mainly along physical lines I found that metaphysical elements were present in every problem. Each medium presented several types of phenomena.

The first case of "independent slate writing" which I examined emphasized this fact. The medium was the wife of a skilled workman whose home was in Roxbury. They were both young and unschooled in the laws of matter as well as of spirit communication, and in awe of the strange power which they had developed. "We want to understand it. We are scared by it."

As a novelist, I was interested in these young people and quite willing to let them demonstrate their power in their own way. The medium, who was hardly more than a child, looked up to me as an official investigator, a person of wide experience in such matters, and I made no attempt to undeceive her.

After telling me how he had discerned his wife's mediumship, the husband bound a pair of hinged school slates together with a strong cord, and handed them to me. "You hold one end of them, and Mary will hold the other," he said.

Taking position in the center of the room under a gas chandelier in full burning, the girl and I stood facing each other with the husband a few feet away. There was no table between the medium and myself. All was in the light. Candid, natural, but tense, the girl seemed to wait for a message, her head turned a little as if listening.

Suddenly the slates began to twitch from side to side. My hands are large and strong, and I put forth my strength in an effort to stop this movement. Thereupon the slates began to twist with amazing force, and a grinding noise developed. The movement became so furious that I feared the slates might be broken, and yet the medium's small hands did not show strain. She was apparently awed and at the same time gratified.

When I opened the slates I found a dozen lines of writing as if done by several different hands, but the messages had no relationship to me.

The young husband then said, "We have had over twenty different kinds of writing."

He showed me these scripts, but as I had not seen them done I could not take them into account. For some reason which I do not now recall, I made no formal report of this sitting. The medium had every appearance of sincerity, but I could not accept her testimony; and the possibility of invisible writing weakened the test.

At this time many materializing sittings similar to those Howells had described in "The Undiscovered Country" were going on in the lodging-house district of Boston, in the back-parlors of stately mansions, homes which had long since fallen into the hands of indigent landladies. Sunday evenings offered scores of these séances, several of which I shared. All were of the same general character.

A dark cabinet or curtained alcove filled one corner of a room whose windows were always heavily curtained. The auditors were seated in a half-circle facing the cabinet. The psychic—or her manager—usually made a short speech on the subject of spirit-return. At the close of this the lights were turned out and the audience sang a hymn.

The first voice to be heard was often that of a red Indian who announced himself with a whoop: "Me big chief—guide to white squaw." But I observed that for all their grunts and rumblings, these redskins had the vocal peculiarities of the medium and used a highly conventionalized dialect.

During one of these performances I sat very close to the cabinet and on its right, so that when a "spirit form," a tall woman clothed in white, came from the cabinet I was able to see behind the gleaming veil the checked gown, which I had observed she wore when she entered the cabinet.

This was a typical case of materialization. No opportunity for testing the phenomena was offered to me although others were allowed to shake hands with the dimly visible figures.

At another séance of this character the medium, a very large woman (who shook the floor as she walked), spoke with a strong German accent, and all the phantasms—even the American Indian guide—caused the floor to creak and each one addressed me with an amusing mixture of broken English and illiterate German. In this sitting as in many others, no one was able to call my name. Whatever their other powers might be, these spirits were not clairvoyant. Not one of them discovered that I was a research officer of the American Psychical Society.

Nevertheless in some of these sittings the inexplicable happened. I was puzzled by certain mysterious lights which flashed from the cabinet, lights which did not seem to illumine the faces of the sitters nor to define the walls of the room. These flashes of white light left on me the impression of a door opening into a glowing chamber. Each was rectangular in form, a block of intense radiance of the same power at the bottom as at the top, which lasted but an instant.

In the effort to detect the fraudulent items in these performances, I read widely in the literature of exposure; but much of this confident news-reporter testimony was offset by the testimony of Editor Flower and by certain phenomena which I had myself observed.

"Some of these phenomena are genuine," I said to Flower, "but they are so mixed with trickery that I can not report on them."

IV

In the intervals of my writing, I continued my study of telekinesis (movement of objects without contact), and the production of phantasms, for my lecture tours carried me into many towns and enabled me to see and test many mediums. Dolbear, as a professor, had few opportunities to coöperate. "My will is good, but my work at a college keeps me tied down," he explained.

During a brief stay in Chicago, I carried out several very puzzling experiments with slate writing, which profoundly interested me. They were such simple, compact, and far-reaching tests.

One extremely valuable séance took place in the humble West Side home of a Chicago psychic, a middle-aged woman with a cheerful smile and uncultivated Western accent. The room was well lighted and the hour midday. As we held somewhat similar political views we were almost instantly "in rapport" as the medium called it. Her actions like her words were homely and candid. Admittedly farm-bred, she made no pretense toward necromancy in dress or speech.

"I just know I can do it—that's all I know," she declared.

While distinctly on her guard, she made a favorable impression on me, and the phenomena, so far as I could discover, were without subterfuge. It is true that I used the slates which she furnished me; but at no point was there opportunity for substitution, and before each test I examined them with care. Nevertheless I secured on these slates answers to all the questions which I had written on slips of paper while she was out of the room.

While waiting for the writing to appear, she told me that she and her sister could produce painting on a sheet of cardboard while it was held by a sitter above his head. "I don't know how we do this—I only know that the paintings come just like I tell you. We believe the spirits do it. Spirits of artists."

The messages which appeared on my slates were in answer to my questions but were vague and of no value.

All the mediums I studied at this time were careful to keep me at more than arm's length; and yet the more I saw of them and the more I heard of their "undiscovered country" the more readily I granted the claim that something worthy of careful study was at the bottom of their phenomena. I resolved to humor them, sympathize with them—and watch!

At Flower's suggestion I went to Onset Bay in July of that year—1892. This was a seashore resort which, like "Lily Dale" in New York, was almost entirely given over to spiritualists and spiritualistic programs. It was an amazing assembly. On doorposts of small cabins and pinned to the flaps of tents were signs which announced "Slate Writer," "Materializing Medium," "Clairvoyant," "Psychometrist," "Fortune Teller," and "Healer," but (to be quite fair) I found the campers a genial, kindly lot, homely and weather-beaten.

Nearly all of those I met were familiar New England types; even the magicians were of homespun character. I could not imagine any necromancy in the spaces of these small tents and flimsy cottages. It was all pleasantly humdrum.

At the door of one of these tents, I paid my dollar and had my slates written upon. In another I heard "spirit voices," but I did not attend any of the "developing circles." They were outside my committee work. I talked with several elderly folk who had come down from the farm to hear the voices of their beloved dead, and found them so happy in their faith that I had not the heart to oppose it. They were all serenely confident that their dead were sharing with them the pleasure of this summer outing. "The air is just full of loved ones," they exultantly assured me. "They meet with us as we meet with them."

While making no formal report, I discussed this colony with Flower, whose eyes shone with amusement at my description. "Wouldn't you like to get their religion?" he asked.

"Assuredly—but my faith must be built on the rock of scientific experiment."

"Is there any such rock?" he demanded. "We take the so-called facts of science on faith. What theory explains all the facts of larvae turning into butterflies? What is the cocoon but a dark cabinet? It's only an hypothesis after all—something to work with. Until very recently only two hypotheses were possible: one that all the phenomena were fraudulent, or that they were the work of spirits. There is now a third hypothesis. Certain investigators now claim that they are caused by forces we do not understand. I am not asking you to become a spiritualist. I am only asking you and Dolbear to examine, with open minds, the cases we send to you."

One day as Dolbear and I were discussing our experiences I said, "Have you ever had anything inexplicable happen to you?"

"Never but once," he replied with a twinkle in his keen blue eyes. "One morning as I awoke and lay dozing, gazing at the ceiling, I saw a cloud of vapor form above my head—and while I wondered and waited, an open hand came out of it and reached down toward me as if wishing to grasp one of mine. Thinking it an optical illusion, I reached up and grasped it. It was *solid!* With a yell I leaped out of bed and watched it disappear. That is my one *contact* with a spook. If the senses of touch and sight are worth anything, I saw and clasped a living hand. But with all that I won't swear that it was not an illusion."

CHAPTER TWO

THREE SLATE-WRITING MEDIUMS

I

Shortly after my acceptance of this commission, I went to Washington to do some literary work, and while there I learned that the city had several psychic practitioners of wide renown and I met several enthusiastic patrons of these "magicians." One of these devotees whose home I visited was an old German physician who insisted on a minute examination of his records. His library drawers were filled with scores of slates, each of which bore a message from Napoleon, Washington, Lincoln, Shakespeare, or some other equally celebrated personality.

I confess that it was a bit surprising to find Socrates and Julius Caesar writing messages in commonplace English for the benefit of an elderly citizen of Washington, but the good doctor had no doubts. "I haf received dese messages unter dese gonditions," he declared.

The very mystery of their origin confirmed his belief in their authenticity, and he took vast pride in the advice of Lincoln and Napoleon. We spent several hours going over these communications, which were on

a very high level indeed. There was something touching in the doctor's wish to have me share his convictions.

At this point I must say that the outstanding fact
of all the spirit testimony which I had thus far col-
lected, was its uniformity of method and the small
value of its results. From the *Banner of Light* I gathered that séances in Paris, London, and Chicago all followed the same procedure and reported the same outcome. No matter in what tongue the spirits spoke,
their voices rose from the same conditions. For the
most part they were produced in the dark and addressed
themselves to an awed circle of credulous sitters, many
of whom were not only elderly but bereaved and longing for a message from those who had passed on into
silence. There were a few exceptions, however. Some
investigators reported phenomena obtained in the light
and under careful control.

Certain of the conditions, however, led me to distrust these reports; other accounts seemed reasonable
and logical. "Manifestly we can not expect to find
ghosts on the dusty highway nor can we catch spirit
messages in the turmoil of city streets," I wrote to
Flower. "I am willing to grant that one must step aside
into some quiet corner in order that the subjective side
of life may manifest, but so much of all this testimony
is dubious that I lose patience with it. I am amazed,
however, at the widespread belief in spirit return."

While in Washington (on another errand) I met a
government official who had been a reader of the *Arena*
from the beginning and was a member of our psychical
society. He was himself deeply interested in scientific

research and had joined our membership with especial approval of our purpose. In our first interview he said: "I have in my own household a medium of remarkable powers. She is my niece, a girl of about sixteen years of age. I would like to have you see and test her phases."

Having high regard for his character and his judgment, I went to his home and met the girl. I found her pleasingly normal in appearance. In her speech and manner she was just an attractive schoolgirl, and yet she was able, so her uncle declared, to make a table float in the air, and to produce mysterious lights and spectral hands.

Without much confidence in the outcome I followed the girl into the parlor and took a seat opposite her at a small round stand, whose top was about twenty inches in diameter. No one else was in the room, and a gas fixture was burning directly over our heads. Placing our hands on the table top we waited, and almost immediately it began to move. After rocking about on its legs for a few moments it began to rise.

"Stand up!" I commanded.

The girl did as I requested, and with both of us standing and only the tips of our fingers touching its top, the table rose completely from the floor and hung about twenty inches above the carpet. Pressing down upon it I felt it resist as if it were floating on some thick resilient liquid. It oscillated under my hands as if the power were applied from below, and at its exact center.

"Please step back from the table as far as you can," I then said.

The girl did as requested, and I could plainly see that both her feet were on the floor. The entire front of her dress was visible. Nothing of her person touched the table, except the tips of her fingers. There was no doubt in my mind at the moment. The table was being lifted by an unknown force and was held suspended in the air for a minute, possibly longer. I had ample time for observation.

We then placed a flat-stringed instrument on the table and turned out the light. The room was not wholly dark. I could dimly perceive the girl's hands. Under these conditions the instrument was softly played while small twisting, pointed flames of brilliant color rose from the medium's shoulders and floated toward the ceiling. At all times her arms were faintly visible.

This performance had evidential value, for I believed the girl to be honest—a belief to which the levitation of the table gave support. Nevertheless I did not include the playing of the instrument in my official report. "The room was dark and I had no control of the psychic's hands," I wrote to Flower. "The levitation of the table was in the full light."

On the following day a very curious confirmation of the girl's claim to abnormal powers took place. Scheduled to address a woman's club, I was seated on the platform of a small hall when Miss Brown, my medium, came in and took a seat in the front row of chairs. Soon after, while listening to the secretary's announcements, I heard a soft tapping sound which came apparently from Miss Brown's chair. Upon meeting my glance she flushed deeply and bowed her head, evidently greatly embarrassed by the comment of those seated near her. Some were irritated, others amused. At last the girl rose and went away.

She told me afterwards that she often heard these sounds on her desk at school. "I wish they wouldn't do it," she plaintively said; "they embarrass me terribly. They tap on my bed at night but I don't mind that, if they would only let me alone at school. I don't like to be made conspicuous that way."

I had no further sittings with her, and she passed out of my knowledge.

One of the best known Washington psychics at this time was a man whom I shall call Kelly, who had a performance which some observers considered a brazen piece of legerdemain while others called it inexplicable. I had several sittings with Kelly and, while I was warned against him as a trickster, I could not discover any precise deceit. His "act" was profitable. He owned a comfortable home and was well regarded by his neighbors.

He produced "independent writings" for those who wished them, but his especial performance was more dramatic. Placing three chairs in a row across one corner of his library, he asked two of his sitters to take seats beside him. In front of them and himself he then drew a dark thick curtain which concealed his body and the bodies of his experimenters up to their chins. Behind this curtain and close beside his chair he placed a guitar and a bell. His left wrist was grasped by the sitter next to him and his right hand grasped that of the other sitter.

Under these conditions with both of his hands controlled, as I recall them, I saw (while sitting in the light) swift hands flickering above the curtain. I heard bells ring and I saw the guitar rise in the air while being played upon as if by the use of two hands. I could not conceive how he could free both hands and play his instrument without detection.

While I was the observer a clumsy right hand came through the curtain and wrote on a pad which I held for it. The fingers of this hand were puffy and short but mobile. A little later the guitar climbed to the top of the curtain and peered over at me. It was played upon, so the sitters declared, at the precise moment that Kelly's hands were fully controlled. During two later séances I sat behind the curtain while the guitar was played. I could account for only one hand.

I regarded this at the time as an entertainment, and I am writing of it now largely from memory. My feeling then was one of amusement, but I am now able to record the fact that this man continued for half a lifetime to earn his living in this way.

II

During '92 and '93 I was almost constantly on the road, speaking on literary subjects for clubs and schools, and in almost every city to which I was called, "trumpet mediums," "slate writers," and "diviners" offered their services. For the most part I distrusted their explanations, but their phenomena were often baffling.

Slate writing especially interested me. Having read many expositions of how this trick was done, I was alertly on my guard against substitutions and the use of invisible ink. That slates could be chemically prepared and invisible writing developed, I had no doubt, but Alfred Russel Wallace's statement that he had *dictated* what was to appear on the slates *after the slates were in his hands,* profoundly influenced me. I resolved to apply this test. Giving little attention to the inconclusive messages which came, I hoped each time for a supreme test of the method.

One of the most convincing of my experiences came during a visit to Chicago in 1892. Old Mr. McVicker, the famous theatrical manager, was an open advocate of the spirit hypothesis, and one day while he and I and James A. Herne the actor-dramatist were lunching together, the subject of mediumship came up, and McVicker said, "I know a West Side medium who is able to produce writing on a slate under the bottom of a goblet filled with water—you should see her."

"Why under a goblet of water?" demanded Herne.

"For the reason that most people go to a medium expecting to witness a miracle. We all want messages to come hard, that is to say under conditions impossible to ordinary people. We argue that the dead being free from the limitations of earthly life should be able to manifest their presence in direct opposition to what we call natural law. Hence we insist on their writing on locked slates and reading sealed letters. The poor psychics are forced to grant these tests. So far as my experience goes—and it covers a good many years— I have found most of them honest. Go and see this woman—she's a wonder."

With his recommendation in mind I went at once to the address he had given.

I found this wonder-worker occupying a humble little apartment far out on the ugly West Side. There was nothing occult in her home. She received me at the door and led me to a sunny, plainly furnished back parlor. Taking a seat at a small table covered with a strip of cloth, she asked me to sit opposite her.

She was a plump, humorous, Kansas woman of forty-five, very like my mother's neighbors in Dakota.

"I know you," she said. "You're a writer for the *Arena*. We both voted for General Weaver."

I set this down in order that the reader may sense the commonplace surroundings of this "sibyl" and the friendly basis on which we operated. We were both without the slightest nervous tension. There was nothing oriental or fictitious about Mrs. Simpson, she was just a humorous, freckled, hard-working village house-wife.

After a short discussion of some of my articles (which she heartily approved) she filled a long-stemmed goblet with water and placed it on a slate which I had previously examined to see that it was devoid of writing. Balancing the slate and the glass on the palm of her right hand, she slowly and carefully passed it under the table. She then said: "Put your hand under mine. I want you to help steady the slate."

"Why put the slate under the table?" I asked.

"Because the forces work better out of our sight. They don't like to write when anyone is looking at them."

As we now sat my right hand was under hers which was spread beneath the slate, while her other hand was in full view. Furthermore, as she was sitting sidewise to the table, I could see both of her feet. The room had a southern exposure and was very light. Together we held the slate in such wise that the goblet brimming with water just touched the under side of the table.

As we waited I asked questions. "Did you devise this test?"

"No. It was given to me by my guides."

"I like the precautions you have taken, but in addition I should like to *dictate* what is to be written. I'd like to do it now while the goblet is resting on the slate. If your guides will write one word at my dictation, it will end all talk of prepared slates, and the like."

"They will do better than that," she briskly replied. "They will take something out of our conversation as we go along. Will that answer your purpose?"

"Perfectly."

A moment later I felt a slight movement in the slate and the faint sound of a scribbling pencil.

"They have written," the psychic said, and slowly withdrew the slate.

As she brought it carefully to the top of the table *I saw writing under the foot of the goblet,* and upon reading these words I found that they had in very truth been taken from our talk. I recognized them as words I had uttered after the slate had been passed under the table. How they were written under that water-filled glass, I could not imagine. Accusations claiming prepared or substituted slates have no weight in this case.

"That was a fine test," I said. "Let's try again."

Again we tried, and again the forces met the test successfully. I was not yet satisfied. "Now let me dictate *the exact words* to be written after the slate and goblet are under the table and upheld by our united palms."

"I will ask them," she said, and sat for a few moments, her head bent as if listening to voices inaudible to me. At last she said, "They will try."

The goblet of water was again set on the slate, and after it was under the table I said, "Ask them to write the name 'William Dean Howells' beneath the bottom of the glass."

Almost instantly I felt a distinct vibration in the slate. The power did not come through the psychic's hand, which remained motionless under mine. The force appeared independent of us both.

While the scratching of the pencil was going on, I could detect no slightest motion of the psychic's fingers, and my hand, which is large, covered hers completely. Her left hand was in full view on the top of the table and her feet were both plainly visible.

Suddenly the writing stopped, and with an embarrassed smile the psychic said, "They don't know how to spell the middle name."

I spelled it for her, and a few moments thereafter, a tapping on the top of the table—not on the slate—announced the completion of the task.

As she again drew the slate from under the table, and before she had touched the goblet with her other hand, I bent over to see what had happened.

The water in the glass remained undiminished and *under the round foot of the goblet* I read the name "William Dean Howells"—and what was most unaccountable of all was the fact that the power, after writing the middle word "Dean" which came to the limit of the space covered by the goblet, had dropped down a line in order that the word "Howells" should remain under the glass.

The powers had not only met my test, they had written the words I had dictated, entirely within the circle of the hollow base of the goblet. It is of no value to say that the slate was juggled. It was not.

From the point of view of the spiritualist, this performance was "on a low plane," but to me it was of high significance. It was in fact a more decisive test than that which Alfred Russel Wallace imposed. It met all objections.

To say that the psychic wrote those words with her fingernail on the under side of the slate, is absurd, for my spread hand covered hers. Furthermore she could not turn the slate over without spilling the water in the goblet. That the power came from her and not from a spirit, seemed probable, but I regarded it as supernormal. All the conditions were mine, devised to make trickery impossible. It had nothing to do necessarily with the return of the dead—but it was a "facer."

Whatever the character of the forces, I absolved the psychic from any deception.

III

Soon after this wholly inexplicable experiment, I returned to Boston, and almost immediately thereafter Flower asked me to go with his wife to test a medium who lived in Roxbury. On this occasion I took my own slates, ordinary folding school slates; but whether they were used or not is of no value, for here again I dictated what was to be done *after* the slates were under my hands.

It was about two o'clock, and the sitting took place in a sunlit room with no one but Mrs. Beach, Mrs. Flower, and myself present.

Placing my folded slates on the table, I put my right hand on one corner of them and asked Mrs. Flower to place hers on the corner nearest her. I then addressed the psychic: "Alfred Russel Wallace, the great scientist, in one of his tests caused the word 'Constantinople' to be written *after* the slates were under his hands. I am eager to duplicate his test."

The psychic smiled and said (just as the Chicago psychic had done), "I don't believe they know how to spell that word."

"Very well. I'll be content with anything—a straight line an inch long drawn on these slates while under our hands, will be of the highest value."

After listening for a moment to the invisibles she smilingly retorted, "They say it is hard to draw a straight line."

"Very well. Draw a crooked one," I replied. "Draw a zigzag line like a stroke of lightning, or have them draw a circle—draw it in yellow."

I wish to emphasize these several changes in my concept in order to show that no previous arrangement took place. "Whatever the results, they can not be arranged," I said to Mrs. Flower.

The psychic said no more. She fell silent and appeared to concentrate. Meanwhile, Mrs. Flower and I remained with our hands on the folded slates. Mine were not lifted for a single instant—that I declare. The psychic did not touch the slates. She remained seated on the opposite side of the table and a few feet away from it. Her hands were folded in her lap. She seemed relaxed, confident, thoughtful.

We all waited patiently. The room almost as homely as the Chicago woman's parlor was without the slightest suggestion of conjuring, but no machinery concealed or otherwise could effect this test for I had requested a definite result to be wrought while the slates were under our hands.

At last we heard a tapping, and the psychic brightened as if in pleasurable relief. "It is done!" she exclaimed with a note of exultation in her voice.

I opened the slates myself and there, drawn in yellow crayon, was a small circle with a zigzag line like a flash of lightning crossing it exactly as I had dictated it, and under Mrs. Flower's hand in the other corner of the slate was a painting of a gayly colored bunch of pansies, a tribute to her name. Quietly, modestly, the medium had met my test!

Several sentences in differing script were on the slates, but they were of the usual sort, vague greetings which meant little. They were the kind of messages which could have been written beforehand, but *that circle had been drawn after my hands were on the slates* and strictly in accordance with my dictation. It was a definite, complete, and triumphant victory for the invisibles.

That I was profoundly affected by this test I am willing to admit, but that it raised in me a belief in spirit agency, I must deny. It was in keeping with all

that I had read of the Fourth Dimension, as tremendous
in its implications as the spirit hypothesis.

It is all on record, for I went at once to the hall
where the Psychic Society was in session, and there made
a detailed report of it, a report which was afterward
printed in the *Journal*. In conclusion I wrote: "This
confirms some Japanese experiments as well as those
of Alfred Russel Wallace and it has created in my mind
a conviction that the work of other mediums which I
once believed to be fraudulent, may have been equally
genuine."

This experience must not be passed over as a slight
one, for it has in it the basic mystery of matter in its
relation to mind. "Nothing is so deceptive as our
senses," says Richet, "but they are all we have."

The more I pondered this test, the deeper its implications went. It was performed in harmony with
my will. It was not as planned by the psychic. She
said she had never before met exactly this test, and she
rejoiced in the outcome, just as the Chicago woman
had done.

She seemed not related to the phenomena in any direct way. She must have been the agent, however, for
neither Mrs. Flower nor I had demonstrated power in
that direction. So far as I knew, I might assist in such
a test, but I could initiate nothing.

At this same meeting Rabbi Schindler, himself a
doubter, related his experience. He reported that he
had obtained on a slate hung on the chandelier beyond
the psychic's reach, an answer *in German* to a question
in Hebrew. "The answer was in German with Hebrew

characters," he added. His report and mine may be found in the *Psychical Review* of 1892.

The most disturbing fact about these performances was their stark simplicity. These women had no confederates—no mirrors, no trapdoors, no specially constructed tables. They operated amid prosaic surroundings. They were not shrewd people—they were comparatively simple unlettered folk, earning a few dollars by sitting in their parlors and working miracles apparently without effort on their part.

They were a confiding lot—once they came to believe in my sincerity of intent they lent themselves to my experiment readily, and my attitude toward those I had doubted changed. I began to think along new lines, lines which Dolbear in his new book had projected—"All matter is motion."

He was himself a prophet. He anticipated the wireless telephone and the radio. He listened to my reports respectfully but made no comment other than to say, "I hope some such experiences may come my way."

CHAPTER THREE

TRUMPET VOICES

I

Notwithstanding my deepening interest in psychic matters, I kept my researches subordinate to my work as a novelist and lecturer. My talks on "Local Color in Fiction" and other literary and esthetic subjects were in occasional demand, and, as the *Arena*, which made frequent mention of the activities of the American Psychic Society, referred to me as one of its officers, I began to encounter, at the close of my addresses, auditors who were much more interested in me as an investigator than as a man of letters.

In almost every town I visited, mediums introduced themselves to me and offered their services often without pay, for they had somehow gained the impression that I would be fair in my judgments of them. In this they were right, for it was my policy to study, not to expose them.

Late in December of 1892 I found myself in Santa Barbara filling a lecture date which my father's brother, Addison Garland, a resident in the city, had arranged. With little interest in matters occult he was a man of thought and quite ready to sponsor one of my literary addresses.

In the early afternoon preceding my lecture, a young woman called upon me at my uncle's house and at once said: "I am what they call a trumpet medium. I live in a village about ninety miles away, over the range. I am a reader of the *Arena* and I know of your work for the American Psychical Society. I have come down to have you test my powers. My guides told me to come. They assured me that you will make the best use of my mediumship."

This young psychic interested me. Her name was not Smiley, but I shall call her that. She was a pale, dark-eyed little woman of about my own age, refined in manner and plainly of higher type than any of the mediums I had hitherto met. "Could you give me a test sitting here tonight after my lecture?" I asked. "I am going to Los Angeles tomorrow to begin a series of literary addresses, and a late sitting here is my only chance to test your powers."

She consented to do this, and at the close of my lecture came to my uncle's house, bringing her trumpet, a long tin cone of simplest construction. Unfortunately, a tremendous tropical rain was lashing against the windows and roaring through the trees, and for that reason (or some other) the sitting was a failure. No voice came from the trumpet and nothing stirred in the room but ourselves.

Mrs. Smiley was disappointed, and so was my uncle. I laid our failure to the influence of the storm, but she went away sadly dejected. "I have come so far and accomplished nothing," she said disconsolately.

On the following morning as I entered the car for

Los Angeles, I was greatly surprised to find the little medium there.

She explained her change of plan. "Last night after I went to my hotel my guides came to me and told me to go with you to Los Angeles. They said that you would arrange some sittings there. They promise important results from such sittings."

"It is only fair to say, Mrs. Smiley, that my committee has no funds, as yet, with which to pay for your services or your expenses, and I can not afford personally to pay your usual fees."

"I have no usual fees," she answered. "I am not a professional medium in that sense. I am only an instrument in the hands of my guides."

"Tell me about yourself. How did you discover these powers—and how long have you acted as an 'instrument'?"

"I've been devoted to this work ever since a child. My father was a convinced spiritualist, and when I was about nine years old strange things began to happen in our house. My parents didn't know what to make of it: They thought demons had taken possession of our home. Dishes were broken, the chairs overturned— everything movable shifted about. It was all like the work of a 'poltergeist,' as some writers call it now. Everywhere I went raps followed me, and small objects moved when I passed near them. My schoolmates refused to sit beside me. The mysterious taps on the books and on benches terrified them and greatly embarrassed me.

"Finally my father decided that I was the cause of all this rumpus and made me sit regularly for development.

I didn't like to do this but he insisted, and when he began to get messages from the other side all my relatives said to me, 'It is your duty.'

"They used to tie me and confine me in every way, experimenting with me for hours at a time. It was all very tiresome to me, but I couldn't help myself. I was only a child of ten or twelve, and I was overborne. I have been devoted to the work ever since.

"After my father died, my gift was a great comfort to me as well as to my mother for I got messages from him. I brought consolation to all my friends, many of whom were able to hear the voices of their relatives who had passed on. After my little daughter went away, I was glad of my gift. She comes to me almost every night. I can hear her voice, and she takes care of me when I am in trance."

There was no doubting the sincerity of the little woman's faith; her face and voice were honest. I asked, "Does your daughter speak to you directly?"

"Yes; sometimes she speaks from the air, but generally her voice comes through the trumpet when I sit in the dark. My guides also use the trumpet."

"What do you mean by 'voices'? Do they sound like the voices of people you knew?"

"Yes, they are just as real as any voices."

"You believe that they *are* the voices of your dead?"

She spoke firmly. "I *know* they are. If I didn't believe that, I would be desolate. For over thirty years these voices have been a part of my daily life. They mean more to me than I can tell."

Perceiving in her a clear-sighted and candid spiritualistic practitioner, I spent all the hours of this ride to

Los Angeles in an attempt to get at the heart of her mystery. "What is your condition when these voices are speaking? Are you clearly awake?"

"Not always. Sometimes I hear what is said, at other times I know nothing of the messages. Often I am in a deep trance."

"Are you conscious of leaving your body when objects are being moved about the room?"

"Yes, I often have the feeling of floating about in the air. It sometimes seems as if I were suspended a few feet above and a little to one side of my material body, to which I am always attached by a shining thread. I often see my body lying there, and I know what goes on around me; but it all appears dim, like things in a dream. It is hard to explain what I mean, but I seem to be in two places at once."

"Do you ever perceive a physical connection between yourself and your sitters? Do they help in the production of phenomena?"

She hesitated a moment before replying. "Yes, I sometimes see little shining threads going out from me and from each one of the persons in the circle. These threads meet in the center and twine themselves around the trumpet or pencil. I know that I draw power from my sitters—some aid more than others."

"You say you sometimes go away into the spirit world —tell me of that."

Her face and voice became wistful as she replied: "Sometimes I go to a far-off bright region. Often I have no wish to come back, but there is always a little white ribbon which unites my wandering spirit with my body and holds me fast. Once when I had resolved not to return, that band of light began to tug at me; and although the thought of leaving my daughter and my parents, who were with me in that bright place, almost broke my heart I yielded and came back to life on earth. It was cheerful and lovely in the spirit land, and I hated to come back to a life of struggle on the cold and cruel earth-plane."

"Can't you describe this spirit world a little more definitely?"

"No, it is so different from this plane that I have no words in which to describe it. All I can say is that it is very bright and warm and beautiful."

Something in her face and voice quite won my good will. "Mrs. Smiley, you are the first psychic I have known with whom I can discuss these matters freely. I am an official investigator. To me there is no value in merely sitting in the dark listening to an uncontrolled medium operating from a cabinet. I want to test what happens. You believe in your powers, I can feel that. Do you believe in them strongly enough to permit me to put you under control during a séance?"

With candid, serene glance she replied: "I will submit to any test you wish to make. You may handcuff me or put me in a cage if you wish."

"Bravo! You have the blood of the martyrs in you. I wish I could ask you to come to Boston and sit for the directors of the Psychic Society, but I can't take the responsibility. Thus far we have met no one of your quality. I will try to arrange a sitting in Los Angeles before I go East; but I can't promise it, for I am giving several lectures there and have no evenings free."

II

That night as I rose to give the first of my addresses, I saw little Mrs. Smiley sitting demurely in one of the rear seats, a most inconspicuous figure with nothing in her face or dress to indicate, in the slightest degree, her possession of occult powers.

My talk was under the auspices of the Public Library, and Miss Tessie Kelso, the director of the library, presented me to my audience. At the close of my lecture she took me down upon the floor of the hall and there introduced me to a group of her friends.

Seeing Mrs. Smiley standing near, timidly waiting for a word with me, I called Miss Kelso's attention to her. "There is the little medium I told you about. She seems an honest one—and I am going to test her powers while I am here."

"You must let me share in your tests," Miss Kelso exclaimed.

Approaching Mrs. Smiley, I said, "Come and meet some of my friends."

Miss Kelso was pleased by the quiet dignity of the psychic and especially by her gentle and candid utterance, and turning to me she said: "Let's go to my apartment and have a sitting tonight. It's only nine o'clock."

"I am willing if Mrs. Smiley is," I replied, amused by her outspoken enthusiasm.

Mrs. Smiley was also amused by this impulsive demand. "I am perfectly willing to do so, but I must go and get my trumpet," she explained.

I am setting down these preliminary details in order that the reader may sense the casual way in which the whole affair was arranged, and also to explain the high character of the group which assembled a half-hour later in Miss Kelso's library and sitting room. No preparation was possible, no wires could have been laid.

Furthermore, Miss Kelso, a vigorous young woman with no experience in psychic phenomena, was frankly sceptical; and, so far as I know, the men and women who met with us that night were equally out of touch with the spiritualistic world. The men were practical business men. One of them was the editor of the leading paper in the city. Several of the women were social leaders, and all were vouched for by Miss Kelso. "They are my friends," she said.

After seating the guests about a long table in Miss Kelso's library I put Mrs. Smiley in an armchair at the head of the table. I then tied her wrists to the arms of the chair with silk twist, knotted so tightly that she could not bring her hands together or lift them in the air. I explained as I did so that I used silk thread for the reason that it was impossible to untie such a knot. "If I were called upon to tie a conjurer, I should not use a rope or his kind of cord; I would use a silk thread."

After looping the psychic's ankles with thread I tied the ends to the back of her chair while the sitters made humorous remarks on my severity. Mrs. Smiley defended me. "I want to be confined."

The room contained the usual furnishings of a young woman's sitting room: books, banjos, and the like. Directly behind the psychic and within reach of my hand stood an upright piano with its lid closed but not locked. The company, composed of three men and four women, were seated like guests about a dinner table, a heavy oak piece. On the end near me I placed the trumpet (a tin cone about two feet long) together with some paper and pencils. The horn stood on its larger end about three feet from the medium, who was on my left.

It was about ten o'clock when we took our seats and Miss Kelso turned out the lights. Miss Otis, who sat at the psychic's left, rested a hand on the pyschic's wrist whilst I was in touch with her right hand; but I will not say that I was touching her at all times. I trusted to the silk twist.

For over an hour we sat in the darkness while I told stories of my previous experiments in order to pass the time. Nothing happened, nothing moved, for nearly two hours, and I was just at the point of giving up the trial when a faint sound came from the piano, as if the strings were being timidly plucked. The sound came from *the inside, from the strings, not from the action of the keys.* This interior twanging kept time while we sang "Annie Laurie" and other familiar melodies. I do not know what the other sitters thought, but I was astounded.

We then removed our hands from the table but kept them clasped, making a circle broken only at the psychic's end of the table. Lifting my hand from the psychic's wrist I told Miss Otis to do the same. "I am willing to trust our faithful silk twist," I said. As we sat thus a drumming sound came from the table and later upon the trumpet. To show that this sound was governed by intelligence I whistled a tune to which the invisible hand kept perfect time. This sound changed to a sharp ticking. "It sounds as if made by finger nails," I remarked. Almost instantly the trumpet was smitten as if with a palm. The invisible agent wished, apparently, to prove that he had a complete hand.

While we waited, commenting on these inexplicable happenings, the trumpet was heard to rock on its base. Soon it rose in the air, and a few moments later dropped to the floor. From this position it rose and took its place upon the table as before. "This action was entirely out of reach of the psychic," I said to the other sitters.

This movement of the cone was followed by the sound of writing, apparently on the pad in the center of the table. "Whoever is doing that writing, speak up," I called out. "It is not Mrs. Smiley. I am controlling her hand."

When the trumpet rose again, I distinctly heard a whisper which seemed to come from its larger end. The lady opposite me said: "I hear a whisper. It says, 'I am with you.'"

Another clearer whisper followed. "I came with Mama," were the words. A name was then whispered to Mrs. Spencer, who recognized it as that of a relative.

While this was going on I put my ear as close to the psychic's lips as I could, listening intently. I heard no sound indicating movement on her part. Apparently she was in deep motionless trance. The whispering was now directed toward the sitters at the far end of the table and was not audible to me. So far as I could detect *the words did not originate at my end of the table.* They were plainly heard by those seated at the other end of the table. Several direct communications were thus delivered, and the names of the invisible speakers given.

At last the mouth of the trumpet was apparently directed toward me, and a peculiar, hollow, breathy, inarticulate whisper came from it. Attempts were made to utter a name, but I could not distinguish it.

"Won't you write it for me?" I asked.

"I will try," replied the invisible from the cone. A little later I heard quite clearly a man's voice from the cone: "I have written, but the writing is very miserable."

Various raps, rustling, and drummings followed. I was tapped once upon the knee. I commanded the cone to touch me upon my right shoulder. This was done. I was touched very softly on my right cheek by the *small end* of the trumpet.

This is highly evidential for not only was this the cheek farther from the psychic but the trumpet at my request had been reversed. The large end was over the table and several feet from the psychic's hands. The gentle precision of its touch was amazing. The cone then touched me on my right breast partly under my arm, a spot impossible for the psychic's hand to reach even had it been free.

At my request the trumpet was then raised high in the air and drummed upon while in that position, three feet above and away from the psychic—a performance requiring two hands.

I asked the sitters to observe that to do this the psychic would need to occupy a standing position and have the use of *both her hands*. Immediately thereafter the pencil and paper were lifted and thrown upon the floor and the table strongly pushed farther away from the psychic.

Seizing this opportunity for a still stronger test, I then said: "Put the pencils and paper back on the table."

This was done instantly, an amazing phenomenon. It was simply impossible for Mrs. Smiley to stoop and find these objects in the dark. If deception is charged it must be against one of the sitters—not against the psychic.

This test closed the sitting. On relighting the room we found the psychic exactly as I had fastened her. Indeed the silk was so deeply sunk into her wrists (which were badly swollen) that I was obliged to insert the points of the scissors with care. I called attention to this fact. "She could not have lifted her wrists an inch from the chair arm," I declared.

The persons present were all well known to Miss Kelso, and as they had all sat with clasped hands while the final tests were made, I was disposed to absolve them of any complicity. Aside from one or two who were greatly excited by the wonder of the experience, they were all alert and decidedly doubtful. Much laughter and joking characterized the evening. Some of them, however, confessed to a complete change of attitude. Notwithstanding the bonds of the psychic, one or two thought she might have moved her chair forward and obtained control of the trumpet. But all admitted the insoluble mystery of the sounds coming from the inside of the closed piano.

In discussing this astounding séance with the editor, I recalled the fact that aside from the darkness, the conditions were our own!

"Our control of the psychic I regard as complete. We must therefore not only inquire how the cone was moved, but how the voices were produced. If one of our sitters moved the cone, he must be a ventriloquist as well as a mind reader for the voices from the trumpet gave recognized names and messages. The name of my sister was whispered. Furthermore, for one of us to pick up that pad and those pencils from the floor without hesitation would necessitate the breaking of our chain of hands, and the use of abnormal vision."

As for myself, I was not only puzzled, I was shaken. It was the most convincing test I had ever made, and I spent many hours analyzing it.

Reporting to Flower, I wrote: "There can be no question of prearranged machinery. The sitting was unpremeditated and held in a private library which Mrs. Smiley had never entered. The circle was of the highest character. I confess that it has made a radical change in my attitude toward the phenomena on which spiritualists base their faith. If this happened, anything can happen. We are to have another sitting tomorrow night."

III

Our second sitting was in the same place, and the group was substantially the same as before. As in the first sitting, I again tied the psychic to the arms of her chair with even greater care, and as a further precaution I passed a tape line around her knees so that she could not slide down and touch the floor. I did this to meet the criticism of one of the men. Mrs. Smiley did not object to the extra bond; on the contrary she again said, "You may handcuff me if you wish."

Nevertheless, despite these added precautions, the trumpet was again active, and the voices which came from it were much clearer than before. The chief speaker, whose name was "Mitchel," addressed himself directly to me and had much to say concerning the work of our society. He spoke clearly, fluently, and forcibly, with grave precision, like an elderly, intelligent, but rather pedantic college professor. His words related wholly to methods of communication and the health of the psychic.

The physical disturbances, however, were rather less than before, and notwithstanding "Mitchel's" voice the entire sitting was less exciting to the sitters although they admitted that what did happen was of higher value by reason of my added control.

Some of the women professed a belief in the personal messages which they had received, and the words of "Mitchel" were clearly heard by all. His utterance was at times almost pure tone.

"Who is 'Mitchel'?" I demanded of the psychic.

She replied: "He was a friend of my father and a brother of O. M. Mitchel the astronomer. He has been one of my chief guides for many years. He is greatly interested in your society and tells me to coöperate with you in every way possible."

There was something so candid, so patient, so compliant about the little woman that the entire company was won to a genuine liking and respect for her. All agreed to meet again at my call.

IV

On the following day I went with Mrs. Smiley to have a daylight sitting with another "sensitive" who had expressed a desire to meet me. Her act was the one called "impersonation," and I found it rather moving. After sitting for a few moments in the ordinary light of her little parlor, the psychic rose and with her hand on her thigh limped painfully about the room as if seeking a book or paper, talking meanwhile on some literary topic. No name was given, but I at once recognized her action as a very clever reproduction of the walk and gestures of Walt Whitman. This had no great evidential value, for she may have read the account of my visit to him. I can not think she had read this, but it was *possible* that she had.

On the same day I went to the home of a woman in Pasadena, to see some paintings, done while in trance, by her Swedish housemaid. They were amazingly intricate drawings in black and white, each representing some philosophical or ethical subject, all circular in form and divided into light and dark sections. One which I vividly recall was filled with hundreds of faces and, most amazing of all, these faces were so drawn that the lines on the light forms served as outlines of the dark forms. It was as if the artist had produced each picture according to a fixed pattern to show that the impossible could be wrought by spirit aid. They were done, I was told, almost instantly. I did not see the girl, and I give her mistress' statement as she made it to me, merely as another of the incredible forms which mediumship is able to assume.

The third sitting with Mrs. Smiley took place as before in Miss Kelso's library and began at eight o'clock on the last day of December, 1892, with substantially the same group of interested sitters.

Enlarging the circle, I removed the table entirely out

of reach of the psychic. In the presence of the sitters and under the supervision of the men I once more lashed the psychic to her chair with great care; and with the aid of the women I passed a loop of tape around each of her ankles and nailed the ends of this tape to the floor behind her. I then drew chalk marks around the feet of her chair (without her knowledge) so that any slightest change in position could be measured.

"I wish to avoid all criticism of our method of control," I explained. "I have made it impossible for Mrs. Smiley to move a single inch."

I then placed pencils and paper and the trumpet on the table as before.

After the lights were turned off we sat for nearly *four hours,* part of the time singing, part of the time in unconstrained conversation. Mrs. Smiley was pathetically concerned by this failure of the phenomena and I, feeling sorry for her, was about to break the bonds when a faint tapping began, apparently on the top of the piano which stood as before at the back of the psychic and within easy reach of my hand.

In answer to my query, "Are we sitting right?" the invisible hand tapped once—an emphatic "No." And at command of this invisible I changed places with Mrs. Spalding, taking a seat on the psychic's left and a little back of her so that with my right hand I could easily reach the piano.

This is one of those small changes which appear to be important to the invisibles—or to the psychic—for immediately thereafter, a soft drumming came on the top of the piano. The drumming was about two feet back of the psychic and a little higher than her head.

"I can not see how she is able to produce this with her bound hands," I remarked. At my command these invisible fingers drummed in time to my whistling.

Suddenly this drumming ceased and the strings of the piano *twanged* as if to invite a test. The cover of the instrument was down, and reaching back I laid my hand on it and called out: "Ladies and gentlemen, the cover of the piano is closed and my right hand is upon it. The psychic has no physical connection with it. It is a clear case of telekinesis."

In order to show that this sound could not have been caused by the jar of passing street cars I then said to the invisible one, "Keep time to my whistling." This he did. I whistled "Yankee Doodle" and the twanging kept perfect time to every note. I then said, "Strike softly," and this it did. "Sound on the treble," I commanded, and this was done. "Now sound the bass strings," I said, and my command was obeyed.

Calling the attention of the circle to the fact that the sound did not come from the keys but from a twanging of the strings, I said: "If the piano cover were open— which it is not—those sounds could come only from a hand *picking at the strings.*

"It is of no value to say that the piano was wired, for we had this effect at our first sitting which was arranged at the close of my lecture. Furthermore—I *dictated what was done.* Besides you all know that Miss Kelso and I examined the piano. It will not do to say that a cat or mouse is on the strings, for they would hardly keep time to my whistling of 'Yankee Doodle.'"

At this point the force left the piano and fell upon the table.

" 'Mitchel,' move the table still farther out of the reach of the psychic," I commanded.

This the force did while we all sat clear of it, and while in this removed position a bell in the center of the table was rung at a moment when all hands were clasped. Drumming on the cone followed. It was possible to recognize the tunes intended. "Yankee Doodle" and other ballads were characterized. This led me to say to the invisible performer "You must have enjoyed topical songs while here on earth."

Instantly from the trumpet came a clear, strong whisper, *"I do now."*

From this time forward whispering voices were heard coming from the trumpet as it floated about the circle. Two of the voices were so strong in tone that I could distinguish them as individual utterances. One of the speakers was a brisk, jovial, not too intellectual young man who gave his name as "Wilbur," the other was the very precise, rather ponderous and oratorical "Dr. Mitchel" who had spoken to me on the previous night. His speech was cultivated but old-fashioned. The third voice, sweetly clear, was apparently that of a little girl who said her name was "Maudie."

Just at this moment the clamor of bells and horns announced midnight, and "Maudie" asked, "What is all the noise in the street?"

"It is the coming of the New Year," I replied.

"Oh, yes," she exclaimed. "I remember."

This was curious but not evidential for this voice seemed to come from the psychic and she may have momentarily forgotten that it was New Year's Eve. Sometimes "Maudie" used the trumpet but at other times she seemed to speak from the lips of her mother.

" 'Maudie' is my little daughter," Mrs. Smiley had told us. "She looks after me and helps me in every way possible."

In an interval between the speaking from the trumpet, I asked that the small end be placed against my temple on the side away from the psychic. This was done. At my request the sitter on my left, entirely out of reach of the psychic, was touched gently with equal precision. I asked for these demonstrations as added proof of her telekinetic powers.

Just before the little girl began to speak through the cone, Mrs. Smiley, who up to this time had been awake and perfectly normal, began to breathe heavily, and a few moments later became deathly still. She failed to reply to my questions and, so far as I could test it by putting my ear to her lips, her breathing stopped. The voice of the little spirit "Maudie" was a curiously sweet, silvery replica of Mrs. Smiley's voice, and she had the same manner of speech; and yet while not a sound came from the psychic's lips "Maudie" spoke. The voice appeared to be entirely disassociated from the psychic's organ of speech.

The childish voice said "Good-bye," and after turning on a dim light we all sat for a few minutes waiting for the sleeper to awake. At last she began to breathe again and in a faint voice asked for water.

I did not cut her bonds till the full light was turned on, and I was conscience-stricken as I watched her helplessly drinking from a glass held to her lips by Miss Kelso. I called the attention of all the group to the fact that the chair had not been moved a hair's breadth and that every fastening was unchanged!

"They are precisely as I tied them. The threads are not broken but deeply imbedded in the skin of the psychic's swollen wrists."

It was necessary to chafe her hands and arms to restore the circulation and obliterate the creases which the threads had made in her flesh. She seemed weak and a little dizzy but soon recovered her ability to walk.

Under the conviction of the moment I said to some of the sitters: "Mrs. Smiley did not lift her hands one half-inch from her chair. She was at all times out of normal reach of the table, the cone, and the piano. She could not reach the lid of the piano, far less pluck its strings, for it was closed and my hand was on the cover. In fact, no one in this room could have touched those strings. If we had obtained no other phenomenon, the twanging of those strings at my dictation remains of the greatest value. Some of us might have uttered the whispers, but no one could twang those strings.

"To suppose that some one of us was the trickster involves the collusion of two others: those who held his hands. No one could enter the room, for the slightest crack would let in the light from the hall. Whatever happened here tonight can not be referred to any fraudulent action of the psychic."

The more I reflected upon these sittings, the more amazing they became. Here was a psychic of pleasing character, intelligent, candid, self-sacrificing, just the person for the American Psychical Society to use. All the other mediums I had met up to this time had been suspicious, elusive, on guard, refusing to be put under test conditions, whereas Mrs. Smiley, convinced of the spirit agency of all phenomena which took place in her presence, was not only willing but eager to put herself in my control for any number of experiments—and without pay.

She frankly said to me, "I want to convert you."

To this I replied: "I must be honest with you. I do not believe in your 'guides,' but I believe in you. I am quite certain that you are not *consciously* fraudulent, but these phenomena may come from your subconscious self, from me or from all the sitters acting together."

She was visibly saddened by this candid statement but remained unshaken. "My guides will prove themselves to you yet. I would go to Boston if I thought I could bring that about."

"If there is a possibility of your coming East," I hastened to say, "don't fail to let me know. A series of sittings with you on the part of our directors would have enormous value to our Society."

At this point I should like to take the reader back over the course of these three sittings and call attention to our lack of tension, of nervous exaltation, and to emphasize the *naturalness* of every phenomenon. The playing of the closed piano did not seem the revolutionizing thing that it really was. It was done so quietly, so humorously. The performer not only knew the tune "Yankle Doodle" but rejoiced in it. He was obliging. He did exactly what I asked for instantly and cheerfully. He was no angel come from heaven or hell to do my bidding, he was one of the circle. All the other

sounds and movements were equally commonplace—
in a sense.

I may say, further, that what was true of this sitting,
was equally true of others. I was not out to expose
mediums but to study them. I was not creating in my
own mind or the minds of others clouds of necromancy.
I did not regard Mrs. Smiley as a marvel of fraudulent
skill, on whom I was to expend my supernal craft as a
detective; I considered her for what she was, a commonplace little woman who had a peculiar endowment.
What this endowment was I could not define and for
the moment made no attempt to explain. I merely
wish my readers to clear their minds of any emotionalism
and all thought of elaborate machinery of magic. What
happened seemed as normal (and as mysterious) as pop-
ping corn!

At this time, 1892, I had no knowledge of any other
instance of a closed piano being played by invisible
fingers plucking the strings, but later I came upon
precisely this phenomenon in Alfred Russel Wallace's
book. He gave a page to a description of it. He did not
remark upon the twanging of the strings, but to me an
added absurdity lay in the fact that the invisible fingers
found it easier to grasp the strings than to strike the
keys. There was no explanation of this performance.
As I *dictated* the action of the force at work no question of rat or cat or wires can arise.

Here again the motive (so far as a motive is brought
into it) was to astonish us—to puzzle us. It had no relationship to spiritual consolation or instruction. It
was the action of a Puckish intelligence. A poltergeist,
as the Germans call it.

CHAPTER FOUR

A PUZZLED PHYSICIST

I

ALL the way back to Boston, I pondered the significance of these amazing phenomena. I could not think
of that little woman as a trickster, for I had full control of her, and yet to grant the playing of that piano,
meant a negation of all that I had been taught of space
and matter. Had it happened in a prearranged room,
the room of a friend, the case would be sound, for no
one could have known that I would *dictate* the performance. No one could have predicted the tune I
would whistle or the order in which I would ask for
changes on the keyboard. The thing was impossible,
and yet it happened.

In my report to the directors of the society I supplemented the report by saying: "Here is a psychic made to
our hands. She is deeply religious but is willing to be
tested in any way we can devise. No other medium that
I have thus far met has this willingness to be pitilessly
investigated. She is willing that I shall apply any sort
of test or manacle."

As a result of this report, I was commissioned to secure Mrs. Smiley for a series of official scientific tests.

According to my dated records, I met her in Chicago several months later and secured her promise to visit Boston. My recollection is that I was authorized to say that the board would pay her expenses from Chicago. I am quite certain that she made no charge then or thereafter for her services. In this she showed the spirit of the true evangelist.

She came East early in November, and immediately after her arrival we announced a sitting in the editorial rooms of the *Arena* on Copley Square and all the directors were present. With the coöperation of Mr. Allen, our secretary, I put the psychic under such test conditions as she had never known.

She consented cheerfully. "All I ask," she said, "is that you give me at least six sittings before passing judgment on me."

The first two or three sittings were almost barren of results, and the committee, as usual in such cases, lost faith in the psychic. They laid her failure to our severe control. Rappings and slight movements of the table were authentic but feeble evidence of psychic power; nevertheless I refused to admit defeat even after seven negative meetings.

"My experiences in California were too important to be disregarded," I argued. "This room is unsuitable, and it may be that the psychic is too eager for results: moreover she is a Californian and our cold weather may have weakened her energies."

Notwithstanding my pleas, the chairman lost interest and turned the case over to me, and to Dolbear, who surprised me by saying, "Bring your wonder-worker up to my house and we'll give her one more trial." To this he added, "As a thoroughgoing physicist this is a grand concession." And I so considered it.

From the printed report (which I have before me) this sitting took place on November 10, 1893, and the circle included only Mr. and Mrs. Dolbear, Mrs. Smiley, and myself.

The psychic was tense and somewhat awed, but Dolbear, genial and kindly, welcomed her cordially and gentle little Mrs. Dolbear aided greatly in restoring her customary serenity.

Dolbear, eager and interested as a young student, had carefully prepared his study for the experiment. He had darkened it by hanging shawls at the windows, and had provided a wooden chair and a plain wooden table. His confidence in me and in my California report had led him to expect something out of the common, and although he left the actual control of the sitting to me, he supervised every detail with keen attention.

Placing the psychic in an old-fashioned chair with flat arm-rests, I set about tying her wrists with silk twist. Using a spool of such thread, I passed a loop of it around her right wrist six or eight feet from the end of the thread, and tied it in a square hard knot about the arm of her chair. Carrying the thread to her left wrist, I encircled it in the same manner. The spool-end of the unbroken thread I handed over to Dolbear.

I then tied a strong tape around each of her ankles, using the middle of an eighteen-foot tape. The ends of this tape I then brought through the rungs of her chair and nailed securely to the floor; she could not possibly reach these tacks directly behind her. Her chair was also tied with tape, and the two ends brought back and

nailed firmly to a bookshelf about eight inches from the
back of her chair. It could not be moved forward.
At Dolbear's suggestion I then pinned a spread newspaper over the psychic's knees, tacking the edge of it
to the floor.

"Like the geese of Rome," said the professor, "this
sheet will cackle a warning if you move."

The reader should distinguish between these tyings
and those which conjurers use on the stage. A silk twist
can not be untied by the fingers even in daylight and a
newspaper once pinned and tacked can not be moved
in dark or daylight without noise. Furthermore, the
reader should remember that this test was not made on
a stage or in a séance room but in the study of a
distinguished physicist and writer on scientific subjects.
The only door to this room was locked, and the key was
in Dolbear's keeping. The only other person present
was Mrs. Dolbear, a small, gentle, elderly woman to
whom a sitting of this sort was unfamiliar. She was
entirely passive in the trial.

Mrs. Smiley, with an amused gleam in her eyes, sat
quietly in her chair, expressing perfect confidence in me
and acquiescence in my precautions. "You may put me
in a wire cage if you want to," she said. "Other people
have done that with me."

On the table, which was square and fairly heavy,
we laid pencils and paper, and at her request we placed
upon it the long cone or megaphone which she always
carried and which she guarded. She always used it in
the belief that it had become "magnetized" by use. She
had put a stream of cold water through it before turning it over to us.

Mrs. Dolbear took a seat at the end of the table directly opposite Mrs. Smiley. Dolbear, who sat at her left, kept the spool-end whilst I, at her right, held the other end of this unbroken thread.

The conditions were wholly ours, the control was in our hands; and when all were in readiness the lights were turned out. At first the room appeared almost perfectly dark, but as my eyes widened, a streak of light showed faintly in the window back of Dolbear. I could faintly distinguish the head of the medium.

Joining hands with Mrs. Dolbear and touching Mrs. Smiley's wrists, we sat for ten or fifteen minutes quietly conversing.

The psychic's right hand, which I was controlling, became cold and moist and at last drew away from my touch as far as the thread would allow. She did not speak, but it was evident that for some reason she wished us to remove our hands. She seemed at the same moment to fall into trance.

With full trust in our bonds we took our hands from her wrists. To Dolbear I then said, "I have released her hand but I am holding my thread taut and I am resting the tip of my finger upon it. The slightest movement of her hand will be telegraphed to me."

He replied, "I have the same arrangement."

Raps now came upon the table, and the psychic speaking with the voice of a little girl (her daughter "Maud") said, " 'Mr. Mitchel' would like to have you tie the threads to the legs of the table."

Making no objection to this, we tied the ends of the thread which we had been holding, to the table which was fully two feet away from the utmost reach of the psychic's hands. We made no change in the knots about her wrists, and the newspaper was still on guard.

After another period of silence, the psychic complained of the thread about her right wrist. I loosened this a bit, but to offset it I tied another hard knot with doubled thread about this wrist. This second bond therefore added to her control rather than lessened it. The table at this time was more than two feet from her finger tips.

As an hour or more passed without result, Dolbear began to lose hope of anything happening. He believed that our ingenious device of tying her with thread had made all movement impossible. I urged him to continue a little longer.

At this point our prisoner began to moan and writhe as if in pain, and after each paroxysm, in a dead silence, the table moved itself away from the psychic toward Mrs. Dolbear, who was at last forced to move backward. Each time the table moved I listened for the crackle of the newspaper but heard no sound. As the paper was tacked to the floor in front of the psychic's feet, which were also encircled by tape nailed to the floor, she could not possibly shove the table with her feet.

With a note of amazement in his voice Dolbear called out, "The cone is rocking!"

Taps now came on the table, which was fully three feet from the psychic's manacled hands, and we heard the pencil rattling against the table as though fumbled by clumsy unseen fingers.

"Is it 'Wilbur'?" I asked.

The pencil tapped briskly three times. "Yes."

"Can you write for us?"

Three taps. "Yes."

At this point, to the astonishment of Dolbear as well as of myself, something fell upon the table. I felt for it and reported that it was a book.

"It must have been taken from the shelves back of the psychic," I said, "and it certainly was carried over our heads."

Other volumes followed rapidly—a bombardment of them—till something like two dozen were piled upon the table about the cone. Strange to say, the cone was not disturbed by the books which came whizzing over our heads. None of them struck the cone so far as I could judge from the sound.

"Note this, Dolbear," I said. "In order to bring those books, normally, the psychic must free her hands, twist about in her chair, reach back of herself, and pick them from the shelves."

He did not reply, so deeply was he puzzled by these unexpected, seemingly impossible phenomena. At my suggestion Mrs. Dolbear now made a test of the mysterious agent. She said, "There is a small candy box on the shelf above the books behind Mrs. Smiley; I wish you would bring it to me."

"That is a preposterous request," protested Dolbear, but a moment later the box was laid upon the table and shoved down against Mrs. Dolbear's hand, who identified it. Dolbear was silent.

Addressing the guide I then said, " 'Wilbur,' I want you to write your name in one of those books."

After a vigorous clicking of the cone, apparently with a pencil, the sound of writing was plainly heard on the pad a full yard from the psychic's fingers. For a few minutes all movements halted.

The light from the window back of Dolbear was much stronger now, and as another test of the invisible I said: " 'Wilbur,' I want you to show me your hand. Pick up a book and hold it between me and the window."

Instantly and to my amazement a book appeared in the air several feet above the table, plainly outlined against the streak of light. I called out, "Dolbear, I can see *two* hands holding a book. They are thumbing the leaves. Can't you hear them?"

Dolbear with his back to the window could not see the hands, but he said, "I hear the rustle of the leaves."

The thump of the book as it returned to the table was heard and reported by us both.

"Now show me your empty hand—your right hand," I demanded.

A shadowy hand appeared between me and the light and waved up and down thrice. "Dolbear," I called out, "I see a huge hand in the air above you. It is three times the size of the psychic's hand. The fingers are spread wide and are *pointing toward the psychic*. It is a man's hand; and it comes from the direction of Mrs. Dolbear and is fully three feet from the psychic's left hand. The wrist and elbow are over the table. Such a position is impossible for the medium's normal arm."

Dolbear coldly replied, "I see nothing from my side."

This aroused "Wilbur" to give further evidence of his presence. The cone with a ringing scrape now rose high in the air, and a man spoke to us as clearly as if he were a living being.

"I told you I'd astonish you," he said. "Don't get in a hurry—there's more coming."

For two mortal hours this invisible kept us wondering at his power and laughing at his "wise-cracking." He was philosophic as well as humorous. At intervals he played jokes upon us. At my request he touched my face on the side *away from* the psychic and six feet from her. As a still stronger test I asked that the small *end* of the cone touch me on my right nostril. This was done with such gentle precision that it seemed a caress.

I then said, "Cover my right ear with the big end of the cone. This will bring the small end of the horn over toward Mrs. Dolbear."

The horn *reversed itself* and covered my right ear with the larger end. This it did gently yet unerringly.

To do this fraudulently, the psychic would have required both hands and entire freedom from her chair. She could not handle the cone in her position. To my thinking she did not so much as touch it. The pressure upon my nostril in the dark was a miracle of exactness.

"Dolbear," I called across the table, "what can you say of this cone and its voice? And what about the skill of movement shown by the invisibles? Apparently darkness is no barrier to the action of these agents. That horn touched me just as I directed it to do, and with unerring swiftness. It came to my call like a sentient thing, with supernormal capabilities. Could any trickster perform under our control such miracles of delicacy and precision? What is the power which directs this instrument? Can you tell us, 'Wilbur'?"

A chuckle came from the horn. "*I'm* doing it."

"How can you *see* to do it?"

His reply was instant. "Day and night are all the same to me."

Dolbear interrupted. "Prove it. I am holding my right hand high in the air. Touch my knuckle."

I heard a light bang and "Wilbur" called out with a laugh in his voice, "What made you jump?"

Dolbear explained that the cone had banged his *left* hand!

In all that he said and did "Wilbur" gave me the impression of a rollicking Western or Southern man, yet he flitted like a shadow from point to point in the room. He was disposed to have fun with us. He was as real as any person in the dark could be. He responded to every question with readiness and humor. He continued to play jokes on us. He bumped Dolbear on the head and caressed Mrs. Dolbear gently on the temple. At my command he covered her right ear with the broad end of the trumpet; this brought the small end six feet from the psychic and at right angles to her.

He interested me as a personality. "Who are you?" I asked. "Is Wilbur your family name?"

"No, my middle name," he breezily replied. "My full name is Jefferson Wilbur Thompson."

"What did you do when on the earth plane?"

"I was a soldier."

"In the Civil War?"

"Yes."

"On which side?"

He hesitated a moment, chuckled softly, and said: "Now, now! That's a leading question."

"Oh, come, come! The War is over."

As if throwing aside restraint he briskly replied, "I was on the Southern side—a brigadier-general."

"Where were you killed?"

"I was invalided home to Jefferson City and passed out there."

"How did you happen to become a guide to this little woman?"

He hesitated again. "I was attracted to her," he replied, and gave no further explanation.

At this point the psychic's other guide, "Mitchel" took the megaphone and gave us a formal oration. He said, in substance: "We are deeply interested in your experiments, Mr. Garland, and we will afford you all the aid in our power. It is hard to meet your tests— hard, I mean, for our medium; but we will assist her to fill the requirements and save her from injury."

To this I replied gravely: "Thank you, 'Dr. Mitchell.' I don't see how any psychic could be more submissive. She has won the respect of all our members."

"Mitchel," was quite as real as "Wilbur" and as fully characterized, but less amusing. He was disposed to discuss basic principles with me and to argue the need of faith. "Wilbur" may be said to represent the jovial side of the medium, "Mitchel" her serious sub-self.

Now came a new force. The table was grasped and shaken violently from side to side as if by a powerful impatient man; and yet the newspaper on the psychic's knees uttered no sound and the threads tied to the chair legs remained unbroken! Such violent side-to-side motion requires two hands.

This astonishing demonstration was followed by the sound of hands beating a pillow on the couch directly behind Dolbear, and wholly out of reach of the psychic's left hand even if free.

Mrs. Dolbear then said, "Bring the pillow to me."

The pillow was lifted and beaten violently in the air, as if to indicate that *two* hands were in action. It was then tossed against the back of Dolbear's chair.

In all these phenomena the intent, apparently, was to prove that the psychic could not possibly have any normal hand in them. The invisibles coöperated with us with cheerful readiness.

So far as the senses of hearing and feeling go, Mrs. Smiley remained in deathly trance. I listened intently but heard no sound from her. While the movements were going on, she was absolutely silent; but *after* each demonstration, I could hear her troubled breathing.

Perfectly certain that she had not stirred, I said: "Dolbear, our victim has not moved an inch. She is right where we placed her."

Having demonstrated the telekinetic power of their "instrument," the invisibles now returned to the cone, and "Mitchel," the elderly pedantic speaker, again addressed himself to me, saying, very seriously, "Your aid is welcome, and we are sure that great results will flow from your experiments." He promised me the aid of all his allies and urged me to keep on "but be considerate of our instrument."

So clear was my concept of him that I answered him precisely as I would have spoken to an elderly college professor.

Mrs. Dolbear, who had herself fallen into trance, now became clairvoyant. She declared that she could see forms moving about the room, and a voice then spoke to her, giving a name which I could not hear but which she said she recognized. She addressed this person as a relative and conversed with him for some time.

Dolbear was also addressed by a voice but not very clearly, and at last a very faint whisper came from the cone to me giving the name of one of my dead sisters. The psychic knew nothing of my sisters.

The cone moved freely about over the pile of books, always without jar or confusion, and at last broke itself in two pieces and fell upon the floor. This ended the séance.

II

Asking Dolbear to turn the lights on slowly, I minutely examined Mrs. Smiley. She was sitting precisely as we had confined her. The newspaper was still on guard, the threads about her wrists were unchanged, but strange to say the threads which we had tied to the table legs *were taut*. The table had been pushed to the extreme limits of the threads, two feet beyond the utmost reach of her hands or feet.

I called Dolbear's attention to this. "If the psychic had freed her hands and pushed the table away first, she could not have loosened the threads to slip her hands back into the loops. If she slipped her wrists back into place she could not have shoved the table away to make the threads taut. All of which argues that the table was moved by some supernormal force."

Upon close examination I found her wrists much swollen. The silk threads were deep-sunk into her skin and could hardly be seen. To cut them required care. Her pulse was irregular and very faint. For a few minutes I could detect only a feeble sluggish throb at long intervals, followed by a rapid fluttering so feeble that I was unable to count the pulsations. Her hands were cold and clammy, and her arms inert as lead. In truth she resembled one returning from a deathlike swoon.

Following her murmured directions, I placed one hand against her forehead and the other at the base of her brain. This action seemed to help her. Her voice came back, her pulse steadied; but it was nearly half an hour before she could use her limbs.

"Did anything happen?" she asked.

"A whole lot happened," I replied.

She professed to know nothing of her groaning and very little of what had taken place. She rose at last and, leaning heavily on Mrs. Dolbear, left the room.

After the two women had passed into the hall I closed the door of the study and challenged Dolbear. "What are you going to do with these facts? Whence came those huge hands? Who transported the trumpet? Who brought the candy box?"

He slumped into the chair to which the psychic had been lashed and stared at the books on the table. "I don't know *what* I'm going to do with them," he replied in a tone of complete bewilderment.

At that moment he granted the psychic's honesty and acknowledged the reality of her amazing powers. How could he deny the evidence? Two dozen books lay piled on the table. Hypnotism could not account for them. And, more incredible than all, "Wilbur's" signature was in one of the books along with a message from "Mitchel" and other invisibles.

"If she could have freed her hands," Dolbear mumbled feebly, "she could have reached the books."

"But she did not! She could not possibly have gotten out of those loops of silk thread—and if she had done so, she could not have gotten back into them. What are we to say about those two huge hands? What about the one with the fingers pointing toward her face? Those fingers might have been yours; they were not Mrs. Dolbear's; and they were not mine. The psychic's hands remained exactly where we put them. They did not move."

He did not answer, and I went on. "What about the voices? What about the amazing force which shook the table from side to side three feet away from her? Why didn't the paper crackle while the table was being shaken? Not a sound came from the psychic even when the books were arriving. What more can you demand? You prepared this room before she had so much as crossed its threshold. Handcuffs or an electric wire would not have been more faithful than our thread and tape and tacks. Barring the darkness you and I have had things all our own way, and yet the woman met our tests."

For an hour we argued, measured distances, and discussed possibilities. At the end of it all we agreed that the psychic had triumphed over us and our control.

"It is not a question of one sitting," I finally said. "You must remember I have had ten or twelve sittings with this psychic. I had a still more marvellous demonstration in Los Angeles, when a closed piano played to my dictation."

Dolbear sat like a man who has been dealt a stunning blow. "It is all preposterous, impossible. There must be some natural way of explaining it. There is no place for the supernatural in my world."

"What about the supernormal? The possibilities of unknown biodynamic forces are infinite!"

"If she will permit me to hold her hands while the cone moves, I will surrender."

"Oh, no, you won't! You think you will, but you won't. You can't believe till a certain weight of evidence brings conviction. To quote another doubter: Your doubts are not due to any defect in any actual experiment but to the inexorable strength of prepossession which holds you back from acceptance of the phenomena we have witnessed. In your book on matter and motion you reduce all substances to assemblies of 'whorls of energy.' Is there no place there for the forces we have felt tonight?

"What can you say in explanation of those silk manacles deep-sunk in the woman's wrists? Did she simulate that? What about the candy box coming to your wife from a shelf? What about the hands beating the pillow in the air?"

I confess I took a malicious delight in cataloguing these preposterous facts. Dolbear remained silent, sprawled out in the chair which the psychic had occupied, his mind so involved with the problems presented that he hardly heard my parting word.

*　　*　　*

It was a deliciously clear and weirdly still midnight, and as I walked down the hill to the street car I looked up at the glowing stars and asked myself, "Can it be that the good old theory of the constitution of matter is about to be revised? What is a silk thread anyhow?"

That Dolbear was still seated in his study pondering the implications of what he had seen and heard, I could not doubt; but of his willingness to carry his conviction to his laboratory on the morrow I was not so certain. "He is shaken, astounded, almost convinced; but as he meets his fellow instructors he will not mention any of these baffling phenomena; or if he does he will jest about them. They will have taken on the fantastic character of a dream."

CHAPTER FIVE

THE IMPOSSIBLE HAPPENS

I

FLOWER was delighted with Mrs. Smiley's success in Dolbear's study and highly amused when I described the professor's bafflement.

"It is almost impossible for a physicist to accept a result of any experiment one factor of which is the human soul," said Flower. "He will admit that he knows nothing of an acid or a salt—except that it does so and so; but when he witnesses a series of spirit phenomena he is quick to deny the reality of what he sees. I hope the professor will follow this up, but I am not very hopeful of it."

Nevertheless he did.

He came into town several times to our sittings in Flower's office, but alas! for some reason, our psychic's power suddenly failed, and even Dr. Savage began to question the value of further experiment with her. Allen, Flower, and I, however, remained loyal to our promise, and I did my best to keep Dolbear on the committee.

"You must remember," I argued, "that the bleak climate of Boston has weakened our medium. She is plainly less robust than when she came to us. Certainly the control in your library was quite as rigid as in any of these later tests, and yet—the phenomena were marvellous. Furthermore, there is something in the air of a business office, like this of the *Arena*, which is antagonistic to subjective action. I wonder that we can get anything from our psychic in such circumstances. We are not dealing with acids and carbons but with an extremely subtle problem one side of which is a delicate feminine organism and the other a changing mixture of discordant personalities. In spite of our determined use of literal brass tacks and rolls of tape, there have been inexplicable movements of the table and other objects. I do not despair of valuable results."

At the end of my plea Dolbear was moved to say, "I would like to have one more sitting in my library to see if your psychic can duplicate the marvels of her séance there."

This was arranged a few days later with conditions of control about as before, but the phenomena were rather disappointing. No voices came from the cone, but the table moved under absolutely test conditions. Dolbear had taped Mrs. Smiley's feet and hands, placed luminous stars on her knuckles and nailed the hem of her dress to the floor, and yet in spite of these precautions the heavy table moved, sliding by short impulses, and in dead silence, away from the medium whose hands and feet could not stir. The newspaper which we had tacked over her knees remained silent, and the luminous paper stars did not even waver.

I was still expectant of more powerful action when Dolbear (thinking he saw the star move) jerked the thread which ran from her wrist to his thumb and fingers. The psychic at once began to twist and sigh, and the voice called "Maudie" said: "Mama has been hurt by Professor Dolbear's thread. The sitting must stop."

On lighting the room, we found the psychic exactly as we had bound her, every tack in place and the table entirely out of her reach; but she was suffering from a cramp in her left arm and side, and fully half an hour passed before she could stand and walk. Dolbear was apologetic, but nothing could be done. The sitting was spoiled.

He said, "I begin to wonder if the books *did* fly from my shelves on the night of our other famous sitting."

I laughed at him. "You *know* they did. You're only puzzled by a novel problem. As for myself, I can not suspect our gentle little Californian of conscious deceit. She has put herself at our disposal and is ready for any test. We can't stop here. We can't ignore what happened at previous tests just because other sittings are partial failures. We must go on to other tests."

He agreed to meet with me once more, and I arranged a circle at the home of my friend Dr. Tompkins, one of our associates in Jamaica Plain.

By this time I had become convinced that our medium was much more than a passive instrument. I believed that results were related in some subtle way to the sitters as well as to her own mental and physical state. I observed that when she was worried or when any of us were physically uncomfortable, nothing happened.

"The forces, whatever they are, come not only

through her but from her," I argued. "We are all parts of the machine. For example, if our psychic knows that some one must leave the séance in order to catch a train, her power weakens. We must keep her serene."

The next sitting was in Dr. Tompkins' home, in Jamaica Plain, and the Dolbears, despite my warning, announced in Mrs. Smiley's hearing that they must leave early. They were not only uneasy, they worried our psychic. Nothing happened while they were present, but after they were gone, leaving no one but Mrs. Tompkins and myself, "Maudie" spoke to me, saying: "Put Mama in a wooden chair and take the cone apart. Put the small end on the table."

This I did, and immediately "Wilbur" spoke to me through the trumpet. "Tie the psychic as before," he said.

"Oh, no," I said. "Let things go as they are. I am content with previous tests."

"No. Make *this* a test. Confine the medium as you usually do. Nail her to the chair."

Sensing something important in this, I knotted the tape about the psychic's wrists as before and, drawing both ends taut under the tip of my finger, took my seat at the small table. Again the voice of "Wilbur" was heard.

"Nail the psychic to the arms of her chair," he urged.

"I am satisfied," I replied.

With no one but my friend Mrs. Tompkins, a clear-eyed investigator with a doctor's training, I sat with the small end of the cone almost in the hollow of my left arm. I could detect no slightest movement in the tapes which I held, and yet the cone at once rose from the table and was drummed upon as if to show two hands in action as it moved about over my head. A few moments later it caressed my cheek.

"Wilbur's" voice, strong, vital, humorous, came from it, and for an hour we conversed as readily, as logically as if he were a human being; and at the precise instant that he was speaking, my faithful tapes remained taut over my finger. No slightest movement in her hands was communicated to me, but just *before* each flight of the horn she shivered convulsively. While the cone was in the air she was as still as the dead.

My impression was—my belief at the moment was —that she had nothing to do, *in any normal way*, with the voices or with the flight of the horn. If there is any virtue in tacks or woven cotton, she did not raise her arms so much as an inch from her chair. Then at my very elbow stood "Wilbur," invisible yet audible, as vocal as Mrs. Tompkins.

Then came "Mitchel," the elder guide, who greeted me with old-fashioned courtesy. "We approve every test you are putting upon our instrument," he declared. "Let me assure you that she will yet triumph over Professor Dolbear. Conditions have been unpropitious. The sitters have been too often changed, and the places of meeting have not been well chosen."

"You are quite right," I replied. "I realized all along that conditions were wrong, but could not bring the directors to my way of thinking. I shall do my best to secure better conditions hereafter."

"All must be harmonious and unhurried," he went on. "Do not be discouraged. Our instrument is adequate."

I admitted that I had been a bit discouraged. "However, this sitting has given me new interest, I shall be faithful to the end."

These two voices were as perfectly characterized as if they had come from two separate bodies. They were as distinctly individual as the voices of Dolbear and Flower. "Mitchel," grave, scholarly, considerate, was in direct contrast with "Wilbur," whose talk was vivid, rollicking, waggish. There was something serious under all his jesting, however.

In a momentary silence I said to Mrs. Tompkins: "I am closer to a solution of this problem at this moment than ever before in my life. Here in the crook of my elbow the incredible is happening. I feel that if I could turn on the light, 'Wilbur' and 'Mitchel' would stand revealed. My faith in the supernormal powers of our psychic is completely restored."

The reader will say, "Why not turn on the light?" I answer, "For the reason that if the psychic's etheric double was abroad in the air, as seemed probable, white light would be to her a serious physical shock. She had submitted to all my restrictions, and, having her under bonds, I was willing to accept the darkness—for the time."

Of my conversation with these invisibles, I retain only a general impression that it was highly intelligent and that it dealt mainly with the methods which should be used in future tests and warnings that we must not put too great a strain upon our medium. The talk of "spirit plane" and "spirit action" was, as usual, vague and of slight value to science or to literature. It all seemed an echo of the medium's thought or of my own. It was the physical or metaphysical problem which absorbed my interest.

At the conclusion of the sitting we found Mrs. Smiley in a deep trance, very white and weak, her hands hanging limply over the arms of her chair. She was cold, inert, and mentally confused. She knew very little of what had taken place and was cheered by my assurance that it had been a success.

II

The twelve succeeding sittings were almost barren of result, and my belief in Mrs. Smiley was sorely tried. In truth all the directors save only Flower, Allen, and myself lost interest and failed to attend our meetings.

Flower was positive that, as soon as our psychic recovered her health, her power would return. "I agree with you that it is our duty to give her every chance to make good."

Mrs. Smiley was in great distress of mind over the situation. "I guess I'm no good any more," she said pathetically. "I never sit now without a fear that my power may be gone forever. Your Eastern climate is so harsh. I long for my home in California. But don't give me up yet!" she pleaded.

"You have done your part," I assured her. "We do not forget what you have already done. We are going on."

Mrs. Flower now came to the rescue. "Why not meet in our house next time? We will sit in a warm quiet room, and we will have no one in the circle but ourselves and Mr. Garland."

She appointed an afternoon for the sitting, and as Allen, the secretary of the Society, found it possible to be present, he and I arranged the room, and confined the psychic. Our control was more rigid than ever.

I am aware that all this description of control is repetitious and boresome, but with our critics in mind it is necessary that I should repeat each time the exact process of nailing the psychic to her chair and the chair to the floor.

As an additional precaution Mrs. Flower suggested *stitching the tape to the psychic's sleeves.* "No one can assert that the psychic could unstitch herself."

"Capital!" I exclaimed.

When she had finished this stitching, I drove a long brass tack down through the psychic's tight sleeve, and also through the double and stitched tape. It was impossible to escape from these bonds. They were surer than a steel bracelet. There were no trick knots, no duplicate keys, no hinged handcuffs in this arrangement. She could not pull those tacks, draw those stitches—or if she did she could not replace them.

Not content with these precautions, however, Flower knotted a second tape about each of her wrists. "They will take off the strain," he said, "and prevent any unconscious movement from pulling the tacks."

To keep our psychic from sliding down in her chair, we pinned a long tape to her dress just below her knees and drawing the ends together, knotted them to the back rung of her chair. As a final precaution, against the use of her feet, we nailed the front hem of her skirt to the floor with three stout tacks.

With a chuckle in his voice Flower then said, "Now let the ghosts walk!"

Although a convinced spiritualist, he was an admirable investigator, as was Allen who likewise urged me to employ every precaution, every device, mainly, I think, in order to see me confounded by phenomena which all my relentless care would fail to prevent.

On the table we placed five or six sheets of paper and a pencil; then, taking the cone apart, I put the small end of it on the table and set the larger end on the floor beside Flower.

It was about three o'clock of a winter afternoon as we drew the curtains and took our seats. A fire was flickering fitfully in the open grate, but otherwise the room was fairly dark. It was a roomy chamber on the second floor of the mansion, which stood in an ample lot.

Here I must emphasize the fact that our circle on this night consisted of Mr. and Mrs. Flower, Secretary Allen, the psychic, and myself. No stranger was present, and the control was more rigid than at any previous sitting. Excepting the darkened room, conditions were perfect for a test of phenomena.

Flower controlled Mrs. Smiley's right hand, I her left.

Having been chief inquisitor of this little woman for nearly thirty test circles, I had developed (apparently) the ability to throw her into deep sleep almost immediately. A few moments of monotonous humming while my hand lay upon her wrist sufficed to bring on the first stages of her trance.

I had adopted the theory that it was in this first and lightest state of coma that she spoke unconsciously and wrote automatically, and that it was only in the second and profounder trance that she became possessed of certain telekinetic powers, and that in the third, death-like and almost breathless pulseless state her etheric self—let us say her spirit double—wrote on a pad, spoke from the trumpet and touched us with invisible hands. That this etheric self was thus at work was not a conviction, a belief; it was only a surmise, born of my reading and sustained by certain phenomena which I had many times obtained under control.

After we had been sitting for half an hour, I began to chant my potent monotonous spell. In a few moments she sank into what seemed like profound slumber. She gave no answers to my questions, and premonitory tremors (which I had before noted) developed in her hands. These were followed by a slight convulsive straining movement of her arms. The hand I held grew hot, and her fingers vibrated swiftly as if with intensive electrical energy. Ten minutes later all motion ceased. Her temperature abruptly *fell*. Her breathing became tranquil, slowing down from moment to moment, till at last it stopped. So far as I could detect she ceased to breathe!

At this moment the sweet childish voice of "Maudie" came apparently from the psychic's lips. " 'Mr. Mitchel' wants Mr. Garland to change places with Mr. Flower. Be very careful as you move about. Don't joggle Mama. It is very dangerous to her."

As we rose to comply the voice went on: " 'Mr. Mitchel' wants the threads fastened to Mama's wrists.

He wants you and Mr. Flower to hold them the way you did at Professor Dolbear's house."

Turning on a soft light, we tied a strong silk thread to each of the motionless woman's wrists and passed the ends under the chair arms. Flower then took one of these and I the other. I called Allen's attention to the fact that the table at the moment was seventeen inches from the utmost reach of the fingers of the psychic and that all our tacks were in place.

"Maudie" then said, "Put the pieces of the cone together and place the cone on the floor by the table."

Flower did this and drew a chalk mark around the legs of the table, numbering it "Position I."

Immediately on our return to our seats the table was moved away from the psychic an inch or two at a time till it rested against Mrs. Flower's knees.

"Do you feel any motion in your thread?" I asked Flower.

"Nothing but a faint quiver."

He went on to say: "I can not imagine how a thought can be transformed into muscular energy, even in the simplest everyday action; and here we have this table moved at least two feet from the psychic's knees while her skirt edge is nailed to the floor. So far as matter can testify, Mrs. Smiley is not concerned with these movements of the table."

At this moment the psychic began to stir. "Look out!" I called warningly. "Let every hand be accounted for. Some new demonstration is preparing."

In this hush, the cone was lifted as if by a feeble fumbling hand. "Keep test conditions," I urged. "Don't make a movement without announcing it."

I then addressed the invisible: " 'Wilbur,' see if you can handle the cone under these rigid conditions. Come now, lift it! Lift it!"

Twice the horn rose from the carpet only to fall back helplessly. Each time Flower replaced it, he marked its new position with chalk.

After each fall of the cone the psychic writhed and moaned as if in agony. Not till the hush of apparent death again came over her did the horn begin to move. So intense was the silence of these moments that we could hear the slightest breath and the slightest scraping of the cone on the carpet.

At last it rose in the air, soared over our heads and was lowered softly to the table. It did not fall with a bang. It came to rest gently as if under control not only of a hand but of a brain which could see and accurately measure distances.

It is of no value to accuse our circle of cheating. None of us moved, and the psychic could not possibly have lifted that cone to the table.

"So far as my hearing goes and according to the testimony of my thread, the psychic had nothing to do, normally, with that movement of the horn. She is as silent and as motionless as a corpse."

Flower corroborated this statement. "I feel nothing but a minute continuous tremor in my thread," he added.

"We are all in some way, in varying degree, concerned in these movements," I said. "There is no use in denying the facts presented; either the psychic is able to put forth an etheric limb and to direct its action, or an entire etheric body is abroad in the room, a sentient entity, capable of speaking, of seeing in the dark, and of raising that piece of tin."

Flower laughed. "It is easier for me to imagine that 'Wilbur' did it."

"I can't follow you there," I replied.

Notwithstanding my theorizing, my mind was clear and my senses unusually alert. I allowed nothing to escape me.

A curious interruption now took place. The psychic again began to twist about and moan, and "Maudie" asked, "Is Mr. Garland going to take a train at seven o'clock?"

This question convinced me that deep down in the mind of the psychic lay the disturbing memory of a remark I had made about catching a certain train. To remove her uneasiness I now replied, "No, I am going to stay, for I think 'Mitchel' has some special phenomena in store for us."

We had been sitting for nearly three hours when "Maudie" said: " 'Mr. Mitchel' thanks you and says you are now to go down to dinner. Leave Mama just as she is. He will take care of her."

This was a surprising request. I hesitated. "To leave this little woman nailed to her chair, hungry, thirsty, and stiff with three hours of immobility, is cruelty to a martyr."

Flower replied: " 'Mitchel' and 'Wilbur' know what they are doing. Let's follow directions."

At the dinner table I remarked: "If Mrs. Smiley is doing this for her own entertainment, she has a singular taste in amusement. If she is doing it to advance 'the cause,' she is a devoted martyr. The sceptic will say that she is now seeking to free herself from the bonds—but nothing can invalidate what has already taken place. The lifting of that cone from the carpet is a physical problem of enormous importance."

Our meal was a hurried one. In less than half an hour we were again in the séance chamber. Our first care was to examine our psychic's bonds. We found them precisely as we had left them and the psychic apparently in deep sleep. She could not have unstitched and restitched herself. Every stitch was unchanged.

Picking up the threads attached to her wrists, Flower and I resumed our places so that the four of us formed a crescent at the end of the table, directly opposite and about two yards from the psychic.

"This position," said Flower, "makes us one pole of a battery of which the psychic is the other."

Hardly were we in our places when *the psychic awoke and spoke in her natural voice.* I was disappointed, for I considered this the end of our sitting.

Convinced as I was that the most important phenomena happened only when she was in a deathlike state of trance, I was confounded by what followed. All my theories were upset. While the cone rose in the air, and while voices came through it, Mrs. Smiley was not only awake but took a lively and wholly natural part in all that went on!

She said, "I am numb, but I am not in pain; and my mind is clear."

To judge from her voice, she was making no effort to produce or change the action of the invisibles.

Once or twice Mrs. Flower said, "I hear the sound of lips whispering, but it is outside the cone."

At last the whispering came from the cone and she said, "I hear the name of my father." She spoke to this invisible who identified himself to her. Some of her questions he answered correctly, but some he failed to answer. This ended the phenomena.

At the close of the sitting, we were delighted to find the sheets of paper which we had placed on the table, filled with writing. These sheets lay with their bottom ends toward the psychic and wholly out of her reach. The critic must therefore shift his charges from the psychic to some one of us.

The messages had very little value to any of us, but the method of their production was inexplicable.

To Mrs. Smiley I said: "At our next test I want to control both your hands in my big fists at the precise moment when the cone is being lifted, or when the writing is going on."

"You may make any test you please," she quietly replied.

The critic will say that the darkness and the break in the continuity of the sitting invalidate it, but this I do not grant. Suppose the psychic had unstitched and restitched herself in our absence—we reëxamined every stitch and tack and found them all in place, and we took control of the threads just the same *after* the intermission as before. If matter exists at all, if thread and tacks have any integrity whatsoever, that woman had no hand in what took place before or after dinner. I can not affirm that she was wholly ignorant of Mrs. Flower's father's name and character, but I trusted in the watchful care of our tapes and tacks.

CHAPTER SIX

SPECTRAL DRUMBEATS

I

THE results of this sitting at Flower's house were so valuable that we arranged to meet in the same room at the same hour a few days later.

All the precautions and controls of the first meeting were exactly duplicated in the second, and in addition Mrs. Flower sewed *two* bands of tape around the psychic's sleeves and *four* tacks were driven down through both tape and sleeves deep into the arms of her chair.

It is important to state that, as Allen was not able to be with us, our circle was narrowed to Flower, Mrs. Flower, and myself.

"Whatever happens this afternoon," I said to Flower, "you or Mrs. Flower or I must be held responsible."

"Why leave out 'Dr. Mitchel' and 'Wilbur'?" retorted Flower.

Wonders began to happen immediately. The cone, at a distance of nearly four feet from the psychic's manacled hands, was lifted and tapped, keeping time to our singing. Later, *strange noises like the beating of a kettledrum were heard,* and the sound of hammering came apparently from *inside* the cone—all absolutely out of reach of the psychic's hands.

This spectral drumbeat was wholly unexpected and enormously impressive to me. Its value as evidence of supernormal force is very great. With no outsider to accuse of trickery, I listened to these sounds in amazement but with keen ears. There was nothing in the room, nothing within reach of Mrs. Smiley which might have given out that strange noise. It was wholly unlike the metallic clicking which had been coming from the cone. It was a dull, distant booming sound—and yet it was in the room.

True, we were dependent on our sense of hearing alone, but we all agreed that it was not an outside noise.

The reader may say, "You imagined it," and I can only retort: "We did not imagine the movement of the trumpet, for we found it in a different spot from that on which we placed it. I am certain we did not imagine the drumbeat, for we all heard it at the same time and remarked upon it." It had never happened before and I may add it never sounded again.

At last, the psychic impersonating "Maudie" spoke. "Go down to dinner. Leave Mama just as she is. We will take care of her."

We were in the midst of a most interesting series of phenomena at the moment—movements and sounds were being produced beyond the utmost reach of the psychic—and I was reluctant to leave the room. However, as it had worked well at our previous sitting, I made no objection.

During dinner we discussed the implications of the

sound of the drum. Flower argued that it definitely proved the honesty of the psychic. "She had nothing to do, in any normal way, with the beating of that drum. How could she produce it, with no drum in the house? What about the voices which came from the cone?"

"I can't see how she could have had any share in the voices, and yet I am not satisfied. I want to cover her lips with my hand while 'Wilbur' is speaking, and I want to control both her hands at the exact moment when the cone is in the air."

"All that you can have," he replied.

On our return to the upper chamber we found Mrs. Smiley as we had left her, still in deep trance. Nothing had been changed. Every tack, every stitch was in place. We took seats as before at the end of the table.

"Mitchel" now asked us (speaking through "Maudie") to move the table away and put the cone in its place. This we did, expecting some new demonstration, but nothing came of it. His experiment, whatever it was, did not come off. I did not lay this up against him, however, for such failures are often of value as evidences of intention.

We put the table back in its former place, stood the cone upright in its center, and laid several marked and numbered sheets of paper and a pencil beside it.

Almost immediately a measured clicking like the sound of a pencil on the cone began. "Is that you, 'Wilbur'?" I asked.

In answer the cone swung into the air and a vigorous throaty whisper came from it: "Yes."

"I want to ask a few questions."

"Proceed."

"Can the psychic be awake and speak normally while you are present and speaking?"

"Yes, we have planned that."

At this moment the psychic seemingly passed into a painful struggle for breath, and then, a few moments later, she spoke to us in her quiet gentle voice. "What time is it?"

"Half past eight. How do you feel?"

"Very numb and cold," she plaintively replied.

"I can believe that. You've been sitting there five hours."

"Is any one here?"

"Yes, 'Wilbur' is here—or was a few moments ago." I addressed the air. "Are you still here, 'Wilbur'?"

The cone again swung into the air and "Wilbur" replied still more clearly, "Yes—still here."

One strange fact must now be noted. All through this sitting as at previous sittings, neither of the invisibles spoke directly to the psychic. They spoke *of* her but never *to* her. They alluded to her as "our instrument," but they never asked "Mary, how do you feel? Can we do anything for you?" Even her daughter "Maudie" spoke of her as "Mama" but never said, "Mama, do you want a drink?" as a child would do.

Observing these facts I wondered if the spooks were not merely doubles of her psychic sub-self.

" 'Wilbur,' " I said, "I don't like all this long-distance experiment. I ask the privilege of going to Mrs. Smiley's side. I want to get closer to this mystery. I want to make absolutely sure that she does not use her hands."

"You shall have that privilege," he replied.

"Shall I go now?" I persisted.

He did not reply, but three feeble raps on the cone signified a doubtful consent.

Creeping slowly forward, guided by the thread which I held, I took a seat at her left hand. "I am close to the source of phenomena now," I said as I placed my hand on her wrist. "Proceed, 'Wilbur.' "

With tense expectation I leaned over and put my ear close to the psychic's lips, and as I listened to her faint breathing, the horn soared into the air and was drummed upon as if to show that two hands were at work and that my control of the psychic's wrist made no difference—*but no word came from the cone.* Marvellous as this demonstration was, I remained unsatisfied.

" 'Wilbur,' your silence is suspicious," I said aloud. "Can't you *prove* to me that your voice is independent of the psychic's organs of speech? Can't you give me a decisive test right now!"

He did not reply but, while my hand was still on the psychic's wrist (please remember that both her sleeves were nailed to the chair), the loose leaves of paper on the table four feet from her hands rustled as if they were being gathered together and written upon. At last they were whisked away to the left. I distinctly heard them fall upon a sofa near the door several yards away.

"There is no justice in charging this movement up to the psychic," I remarked. "Flower, you or Mrs. Flower may be accused of whisking those papers away, but Mrs. Smiley's left hand had nothing to do with it.

So far as her normal powers are concerned she is innocent of any share in it. During the flight of the papers she did not move a finger of her left hand. Flower, are you controlling your wife's hands?"

"I am. She had nothing to do with causing that noise. Apparently those sheets of paper have been placed on the couch in the corner. I can't see any loophole. You have demonstrated that the flight of those papers was supranormal."

"Yes," I replied, "we seem to have done just that."

Addressing the guides, Flower said, "May I also go forward?"

A decided "No" was tapped.

"Why do you not speak, 'Wilbur'? Do you want me to change places with Flower and control his wife's hands?"

Instead of a voice three sharp raps answered, "Yes."

"They seem as anxious for a conclusive test as you are," remarked Flower. " 'Wilbur,' do you mean that you want Mrs. Flower controlled by Garland?"

A rapid fusillade of raps replied, "Yes—yes—yes."

Flower now came forward to Mrs. Smiley's side while I returned to the table and took both of Mrs. Flower's hands in mine. "I want to set my big shoes on the tips of your slippers," I explained. "You will then be wholly eliminated from the test."

She consented, and I put my huge soles on her toes. She could not move hand or foot.

At this precise moment, while Flower was pressing the psychic's imprisoned right wrist and I was in control of Mrs. Flower's hands and feet, the cone rose and banged about most furiously, *describing wide circles high in the air*—motions which gave *at the moment* perfectly convincing proof that the psychic had no normal hand in the performance. As the same movement had taken place whilst I was in control of the psychic, each one of us was now completely absolved of any complicity in the action.

"Mrs. Smiley," I said, "I want Flower to return to his seat, and I would like permission to place my hand over your lips or to muffle you with a handkerchief in order to demonstrate that you have nothing to do, in any normal way, with the production of these voices. Will you permit this test?"

"Certainly," she answered with patient sweetness. "You may gag me in any way you please. I am sure you can secure the proof you want."

Acting upon this permission, I took a large silk kerchief from my pocket and tied it tightly around her head and over her mouth, knotting it at the back. In some excitement I then challenged the ghostly voice. "Now, 'Wilbur,' let's hear from you!"

A moment later he spoke seemingly *from the cone* but his voice sounded *muffled and blurred*. "You are not articulating well," I observed sarcastically.

Instantly his voice rang out sharply, more sharply than ever before. "I was fooling you!" he said with a chuckle. "I knew what you wanted and so I gave it to you."

I applauded. "There, that's better. Your voice has improved wonderfully."

"I've taken a lozenge," was his whimsical reply, and his tone expressed the delight which a joker takes in a successful trick.

Flower then said: "Let's consider this test for a moment, Garland. Let us suppose Mrs. Smiley has been able to loosen your gag. How did she handle the cone? Let us say she is a marvellous ventriloquist. How does she handle the pads in the center of the table, and how does she gather up our sheets of paper and whisk them away? It is not only a matter of voices but of action. All that has happened, every phase of the séance, must come into the discussion. Mrs. Smiley has met every test."

To this I replied: "I admit that everything points to an exercise of supernormal force. The movement of the cone appears, so far as anything in the dark *can* appear, to be caused by the action of etheric hands. I still think the phenomena are controlled by the psychic in some subconscious way."

"I don't see how you can escape the spirit hypothesis," replied Flower. "What about the voices of 'Wilbur' and 'Mitchel' and Mrs. Flower's father? What about the spectral drum?"

To this I could only say: "I don't know. A man can't *will* to believe. I must await further evidence. I want to examine that gag and I want to hold *both* of the psychic's hands. Will you permit that, 'Wilbur'?"

There was no reply to this, and Flower offered an explanation. "We had that test at a previous sitting."

Again I addressed the invisible. " 'Wilbur,' it is absolutely essential that you should prove to me that your voice does not come from the vocal cords of the psychic." I turned to Mrs. Smiley. "You see the importance of this, don't you, Mrs. Smiley?"

"Indeed I do," she earnestly answered, her voice sounding very faint and muffled through her kerchief. "I am anxious for the test."

"Very well then. Now I want you to hum a tune, and while you are singing I want 'Wilbur' to speak. Will you do that, 'Wilbur'?"

The cone was drummed upon in sign of vigorous assent.

While Mrs. Smiley sang or rather hummed, we listened for "Wilbur's" voice, but no word came. A moment later she called faintly, "The kerchief is slipping down, Mr. Garland."

Going to her side I untied the kerchief. She said plaintively, "I am sorry we didn't get the voices as you wanted them. I am sure we can if we try again."

A vigorous drumming on the cone seconded her plea, but no spirit spoke.

However, it was getting very late and I said: "I think we will postpone further experiment tonight. You have endured enough. How do you feel?"

"Almost paralyzed. I can't move, and I am partly deaf; but that often happens. My feet are quite dead. I can not feel the floor. It is as if I had no feet at all."

"But your mind and speech appear to be perfectly normal."

"Yes, I am wide awake mentally."

Soon after I returned to my seat, the cone was lifted high in the air silently and broken apart, an action requiring *two* hands, and then, with the small end jangling inside the larger one, it was carried in a circle over the table and dropped to the floor. It fell with a bang which seemed to indicate disgust.

"That means good-bye," said Mrs. Smiley.

Upon lighting the gas we found our poor little victim sitting exactly as we had placed her and bound her. The table edge was exactly twenty-four inches from her finger tips and the place where the cone lay was thirty-six inches from one hand and forty inches from the other. But most inexplicable of all the phenomena, and a tangible record of supranormal force, was the transfer of our seven sheets of paper from the table to the couch.

They lay on the cushion sixteen measured feet from Mrs. Smiley's left hand; and not only had they been written upon, they had been brought together *and a black pin had been thrust through them!* The pin had pierced the *writing.* To do this, vigorous and skilled use of two hands was necessary. Only two deft and powerful hands could hold those sheets and thrust that pin through them.

On examination we found that "Wilbur" had scrawled his name on one sheet, and on another sheet Mrs. Flower's father's name was signed to a tender message, along with several other signatures unknown to any of us. The pencil was on the carpet, forty inches from Mrs. Smiley's hand. The leaves of paper at the moment when they were grasped and lifted were more than forty inches from the psychic's finger tips.

"How this was done I can not conceive," I said to Flower; "but I am absolutely certain that *the psychic did not remove them from the table by means of her ordinary hands, for they were controlled by mine.*"

II

Barring the failure to disassociate her voice from that of "Wilbur," our psychic had met every demand we had made upon her.

"Her powers are truly magical," I reported to the Society. "I can not say that I saw the pencil move, but I assert that the psychic did not touch it. She did not write the names upon the papers. I can not swear that Flower was controlling his wife's hands, while the cone was floating and while I held the psychic's imprisoned hands; but I believe that he was."

In short, excluding the sense of sight—an all-important sense test, I admit—these happenings were at the moment convincing. They fitted in with many similar phenomena which I had secured in the presence of other psychics, but I was not yet satisfied. We needed a fifth person in the circle in order that Flower and I might control both of the psychic's hands at the precise moment that Mrs. Flower's hands were also se-cured: "So long as a single hand is left free, the doubter will question our results."

III

Two of the sittings which followed were partial failures—so much so that I made no record of them. Possibly conditions were not strict enough. At any rate the final and most conclusive sitting came a week later. It was held in the same room under the same conditions as those recorded above, but with the addition of a friend of Mrs. Flower—a young man who claimed some psychic power. We will call him Frank.

Again I took entire charge of the psychic, and made certain that her bonds were even more carefully stitched and nailed than before.

I began the séance as usual by a low humming chant which put Mrs. Smiley to sleep, and very soon "Maudie" spoke, saying, " 'Mr. Mitchel' wishes the thread again fastened to Mama's hands in the way Mr. Garland desires"—a command which gave further evidence of the hearty and intelligent coöperation of the invisibles.

In addition to the tape stitched to her sleeves and nailed to her chair, I now fastened a strong thread to each wrist as I had done so many times before, passing the ends under the chair arm in such wise that any slightest movement of the psychic's arms would be plainly and instantly registered. I then returned to my seat.

Conditions seemed favorable, but no marked phenomena took place. The cone was lifted, it is true; but this we now accepted as a commonplace preliminary to something more startling.

At six o'clock the voice of "Maudie" came, directing us to go down to supper. " 'Mr. Mitchel' says he will be able to give you what you ask for after you return."

I had no notion what "Mr. Mitchel" had in mind but my most dominant desire was to prove that his voice was not dependent on the psychic's vocal cords. At dinner we discussed this. "If Mrs. Smiley will let me put my hand over her mouth while 'Wilbur' is speaking," I said, "I shall be satisfied."

Flower's eyes gleamed with humor. "Do you mean that you will then believe in spirits?" he demanded.

"Oh, no, I won't go so far as to promise that," I hastened to protest; "but I confess that it would help me to *infer* their existence. Let's fix our minds on two things: first, to secure writing, or at least movement —with every hand controlled; and second, to get the voices—while Mrs. Smiley's mouth is covered by your hand or mine."

"Very well," Flower agreed. "We'll try; but it is often the unexpected which happens in performances of this kind."

We were away from the psychic but twenty minutes, so eager were we for further demonstration. We found everything quite as when we left. She was asleep, the fastenings undisturbed.

Flower and I at once regained our threads and resumed our places at the sides of the table while Frank and Mrs. Flower sat side by side at the end opposite Mrs. Smiley. I must again remind the reader that the psychic's ankles were encircled with tape which was nailed to the floor behind her chair, and that two bands of tape which had been sewed to her cuffs were tacked solidly to the chair. In addition to all these precautions three strong upholstery tacks had been driven down through the hem of her dress into the floor, and finally Flower and I were holding the threads which encircled her wrists.

In spite of all these bonds, the cone was immediately lifted and "Mitchel" spoke through it, in a deep, clear, well delivered, and decidedly masculine tonal whisper. In stately periods, he promised the complete coöperation of the spirit world in the great work to which I was devoting myself. He directed his exhortation to me and not to Flower, and for the benefit of those who think the spirits are always trivial or foolish, I wish to say that "Mitchel's" remarks were dignified and thoughtful. He was old-fashioned in his phrasing but never vague or wandering in his thought. I observed, however, that he never went outside the circle of Mrs. Smiley's intellectual interests or transcended her thinking.

For fully a quarter of an hour he discussed with me the value of my investigation, assuring me—as they all do—that he and his band were working as hard from their side as we were from ours. "We are as intent upon establishing channels of communication between the two worlds as you are, and I respectfully urge you to proceed in your grand work."

At last he said, "Good-bye for the present," and deposited the cone on the table. "Maudie" then spoke from the psychic's lips.

"If Mr. Garland and Mr. Flower will go quietly up to Mama's side holding all the time tightly to the threads, 'Mr. Mitchel' will do what Mr. Garland so much desires. Please be very careful not to touch Mama until I tell you. Keep as far apart as you can as you go up to her. When you reach her side, you may put one hand on her head and one on her wrist. 'Mr. Mitchel' says to please have Frank take Mrs. Flower's hands so that every hand in the circle is accounted for."

I was now eager and very alert. At last, after many requests and many trials, I was about to secure a clear, complete, and satisfying demonstration. Surely no trickster would permit such vigorous control as that towards which we were now invited. My admiration went out to our heroic little psychic who was enduring much discomfort for my sake. "She believes in her guides," I said. "If she succeeds in this test, all honor to her."

Slowly we crept to her side, being careful to touch nothing until directed by the voice of "Maud."

At last the childish voice said: "Mr. Garland may put his right hand on the top of Mama's head and his left hand on her wrist. Mr. Flower may place his left hand above Mr. Garland's right hand and his right hand on Mama's right wrist. 'Mr. Mitchel' says he will then try to have the voices come."

I did as bid, then said aloud, "My right hand is on the psychic's head, my left is on her left wrist."

Flower repeated, "My left hand is resting on Garland's right hand, which is on the psychic's head, and my own right hand is controlling the right wrist of the psychic. Now, 'Wilbur,' go ahead."

Our challenge was almost instantly accepted. Despite this double-safeguarding, the cone, which had been resting on the table a full yard away, rose with a sharp metallic sound and remained in the air for fully half a minute, during which I called out sharply: "We are absolutely controlling the psychic; her hands are motionless. Mrs. Flower, are you holding both of Frank's hands?"

"Yes, I have both his hands in mine," she answered.

As the cone was gently returned to the carpet, Flower was moved to say: "Garland, that is a supreme test. The psychic was absolutely not concerned in any known physical way with that movement. Save for a curious throbbing wave-like motion in her scalp, she did not stir. If she lifted the horn it was by the exercise of a force unrecognized by science."

To this I was forced to agree, and I here definitely declare that the psychic was not concerned in any way with this flight of the cone. If she produced the voices, they too must have been examples of supernormal ventriloquism, for they came through the megaphone—of that I am as certain as any one can be of an auditory impression.

A few minutes later we returned to our seats and "Wilbur," "Mitchel," and several other voices conversed with us. Flower, now that I had admitted telekinesis, wanted me to go further. "Is the psychic now speaking to us," he asked, "or are these voices independent of her?"

"An investigator is never satisfied," I answered. "I must have the voices through the cone at the exact moment when I am covering the psychic's mouth."

To this "Mitchel" replied, "We are doing all that we can now, but we will soon be able to meet every demand you make upon us."

"I am anxious for conviction," I said. "I want to secure the voice of the psychic and your voice at the same time, 'Dr. Mitchel.' Can you do that for me?"

He seemed to hesitate and at last said, "We will try." I perceived in his tone a certain doubt and indecision.

Again we were permitted to hold the psychic's wrists and head while as before the cone was lifted and drummed upon as if by two hands indicating its position high in the air, but no voices came!

Hidden forces appeared to be struggling for escape

beneath our hands. The woman's brain seemed a powerful dynamo. I could not rid myself of a feeling that there was an actual externalization of the psychic's nerve force, and with this conviction I could well understand why the command had so often been given not to touch her unbidden. If her astral body were abroad a strong light turned suddenly upon it might prove a dangerous shock.

Now came a singularly engrossing game of hide and seek. Convinced that Mrs. Smiley was innocent of any trick in the movement of the cone, I tried every expedient to satisfy myself that "Wilbur's" voice was independent of her own, but I did not quite *succeed*. Mrs. Smiley spoke *almost* at the same time but never *precisely* at the same moment with "Wilbur."

She was now fully awake and answered all my questions calmly and readily, lending herself eagerly to my experiment. All in vain! At no time did I succeed in getting "Wilbur's" voice at exactly the same moment as her own though the whisper, following swiftly on her speech, interjected remarks as if echoing her questions. There was always a perceptible interval between her voice and his whisper.

This was to me a very significant fact and strengthened me in my impression that the entire series of happenings while inexplicable was, after all, the work of the medium. Miracles were taking place, but they were all within a short radius of her body and somehow related to it.

When the gas was lighted, we found the cone had been placed on the table a distance of forty inches from the utmost reach of the psychic's hands, her feet were twenty-three inches from the nearest leg of the table. We carefully examined the tapes which encircled her wrists and were sewed to her sleeves. They were tied and the doubled ends precisely as described so many times. To remove the tacks we were forced to use a hammer. To talk of a possible release of her arms during the phenomena of the cone is absurd. Had she freed her arms she could not have renailed herself to her chair.

* * *

As I was about to leave the house that night, Mrs. Smiley said: "I do not feel able to sit any more for the present, Mr. Garland. I feel myself growing weaker, and the weather depresses me. 'Mr. Mitchel' tells me I would better stop for the present. I feel that my power belongs to the world, and I want especially to convince you of the truth of spiritualism; but the strain is too great."

"I grant that," I responded, "and I can not blame you for demanding a rest. No one could have endured our tests more uncomplainingly. You have been a model subject, and we are deeply in your debt. I am sorry Dolbear was not with us tonight; he would at least have been convinced of your supernormal power. Have no fear of my report. I have found you honest and very patient. I thank you most sincerely for what you have done."

IV

Having shared more than thirty of these exacting sittings with Mrs. Smiley, each one more rigid than the others, I had gained a sincere respect for her courage and her patience. Believing her mediumship to be a dangerous tax on her physical organism, I admired her devotion to her faith, for to her it *was* a faith—a religion. She was poor, not strong physically, and yet she had stayed on in our harsh climate, subjecting herself to a dangerous strain night after night with no promise of pay, seeking to convince me and others like me of the reality of her voices.

In addition to my formal reports, I submitted the following notations:

1. So far as the senses of touch and hearing go, Mrs. Smiley's arms and feet had nothing to do (in any normal way) with the movements of the cone, the table, or the pencils.

2. Her "guides" lent themselves intelligently to every test, and labored to make each experiment a success. They seemed at all times eager to have me exercise the most rigid control but warned me not to go too far while the psychic was entranced or when her etheric body was at work.

3. That all the phenomena were accompanied by marked physiological changes in the psychic. Her convulsive movements, her groans and sighs, her writhing as she passed from one state of consciousness to another were, at times, so moving that Mrs. Flower and others of the sitters demanded her release. Her temperature fell, her hands became cold and clammy, and at a certain stage her breath and pulse became so faint as to be almost imperceptible. All these symptoms, in my judgment, were not under the control of her will and argued a close connection with the phenomena.

4. My impressions of her performances as a whole were favorable to her mediumship. The movements of the horn took place just as I have described them, but I am not ready to admit that "Wilbur" and "Mitchel" are spirits. I grant the existence of all the phenomena but differ from Flower and Allen in my interpretation of them. In so far as I have gone, "Wilbur" and "Mitchel" impress me as distinct personalities, but they may be dream people.

5. As to voices, I have no theory, far less an explanation. They may be ventriloquistic.

6. That the psychic when sitting is under great strain would appear from the fact that she was sadly convulsed by Dolbear when he jerked the thread attached to her wrist, and that once when I, with the full consent of the guides, passed between her hands and the table, brushing the fingers of one hand, she was again convulsed and unable to proceed.

It appears that some part of her substance exteriorizes itself during these trances. Furthermore her entire body and brain seems aroused to abnormal action. Flower's description of her brain as a dynamo fitted my concept. As I rested my hand on her head, it seemed semi-liquid. It did not throb, it appeared to wave under my palm. This may have been merely an action of the scalp but in any case a highly wrought condition of the brain was indicated.

The temperature of her hands in every sitting fell markedly (a mere touch revealed this), and her pulse and breathing varied abnormally. I did not register her temperature with a thermometer, however, nor did I take her pulse with an instrument.

These physiological changes led me to treat the psychic with care. I found that by proceeding gently and quietly along desired lines, I was able to tighten control on her limbs. If my control was not absolute, the fault was mine, not hers. She made no objection to any of my restraining devices.

7. On the mental side I observed that when she was disturbed by a sense of *our* discomfort, or when she knew a sitter was worried about losing a train, nothing happened. Whenever she was overeager for results or when one of her sitters became impatient for any cause the phenomena diminished in power. Without doubt it was because of the serenity she felt in Dolbear's study, that her powers were strongest. Similarly in Flower's home, even though the control was doubly rigid, she was entirely at ease.

She did not appear to will the phenomena but to passively await the action of the invisibles. That her health was affected by the climate was evident. Some of the failures were due to the severe winter weather.

As the time came for her to return to her home, five members of the board united in a letter thanking her for her "uncomplaining coöperation" in their severe tests.

"We feel that the conditions which we found it necessary to impose fell upon you with peculiar hardship considering the state of your health, but no word of complaint from you was heard nor have you raised any objection to control. However meager the results may seem to you, they are to us exceedingly interesting and we hope at some future time to have your most valued aid again."

To this she replied December 11, thanking us for our "forebearance and patience. I am sure no psychic could ask more. While the conditions were rigid there has been nothing but a spirit of gentleness and patience manifested, no matter how wearying and disappointing the sittings have been. I understand perfectly the necessity of rigid conditions and am sorry not to have been in the best of physical health for the sittings."

In closing this series of experiments, I wish the reader to see them as they were, carefully prepared and calmly studied always in the spirit of modern science. The invisibles worked harmoniously with us, often with humor. We jested with them as well as among ourselves. With the exception of a darkened room, the conditions were all we desired them to be.

CHAPTER SEVEN

I COMMAND SPIRITS

Soon after the conclusion of this series of experiments with Mrs. Smiley, I gave up my apartment in Boston and returned to the Middle West. With Chicago as my literary headquarters I spent a large part of my summers with my father and mother, in West Salem, Wisconsin, or in the Rocky Mountains. This abandonment of Boston as a place of residence took me out of the active management of the Psychical Society, but I continued my researches and from time to time sent in a report of my experiments.

The World's Fair, which was just closing, had brought to the city not only a throng of artists and literary men but a swarm of religious teachers of all sorts. Among them were many mediums who were paying their way at the fair. From time to time I went in search of these who had been recommended to me by those of my friends who, despite the noise and confusion of the city, had maintained their interest in the spirit world.

For the most part I heard these magicians chanting their spells in mean dwellings on the South Side or over in the still humbler streets of the West Side. At each guarded door, I was called upon to transfer a dollar from my pocket to the palm of the doorkeeper, but I did not allow this to prejudice me. Mediums must eat and be clothed. I can not blame them for dramatizing and selling their powers, whatever they are. An honest medium has a perfect right to charge for her time and energy.

I made no formal report of these experiences for the reason that by contrast with what I had already sent in they seemed trivial or dubious. One curious fact I did report to Flower.

"Not one of all these mediums, good or bad, had the slightest clairvoyant clue to my name or my purpose. I sat obscurely and quietly in the back row of chairs and whenever they had occasion to address me they called out—'the gentleman in the third seat of the last row.' Never once did any sitter or psychic clairvoyantly discover that I was connected with the psychical society."

Some years after the fair I chanced to be lunching with John M. Judah in the University Club of Indianapolis, and in the course of our conversation, my host remarked: "By the way you should know Henry Wallace, a brother of General Lew Wallace. He is deeply interested in psychical matters and might be able to recommend a medium."

This suggestion led me to ask for an introduction to Mr. Wallace, and at the close of our luncheon Judah took me around to his office, presented me, and retired.

Mr. Wallace was willing to talk of his experiences and in reply to my question "Do you know of a good medium in the city?" instantly replied: "Yes. I know of one who is a wonder. She lives within ten minutes' ride of this office. You should see her. She is not only a slate-writer but also a trumpet medium of extraordinary power."

"I should like to try her this afternoon. I am always ready for further experiment on the physical side."

"Very well. Now this is my suggestion. I'll drive you to the street just this side of her cottage and drop you there. I've had many sittings with her, and it won't do to let her see you with me. She must not know your name or how you came to knock at her door."

His plan appealed to me, and as he was prepared to carry it into immediate execution, we went down to his "buggy" (this was before the days of motor cars) and set forth.

As we drove along he continued his instructions. "Don't take 'No' for an answer. Just say, 'I've come for a sitting.' She is a queer old body, illiterate and notional. She will eye you sharply; but she needs your dollar, and if you insist will surely let you in."

Halting at a row of wooden houses, he pointed to one in the middle of the block—a small drab two-story cottage. "She lives there."

As I knocked on the designated shabby portal, I heard inner doors opening and shutting, and at last the face of a faded, middle-aged woman came into view. She was gaunt, dark-complexioned, and sad, plainly of the Southern mountaineer type as Wallace had described her to be.

She studied me through the half-opened door while I explained that I had come a long way for a sitting and that this was my only hour. "I am a stranger here, and I am leaving for Chicago on the night train."

She held the door to a narrow opening, listening with grim impassivity, her big dark eyes appraising me. That she considered me a possible enemy was evident, but I explained that I had heard of her wonderful work and that I couldn't think of leaving without a sitting with her. She appeared to be listening to some inner voice rather than to mine, and at last she hoarsely and grudgingly said, "Come in."

Nothing in the hall into which she led me suggested that she was a female Houdini, earning large sums of money by trickery. Her dress indicated that she was her own housekeeper, and her hands were those of a toiler to whom a silver dollar was a large piece of money. She was wearing a long apron and had the distraught air of a cook who, having been called away from the making of a pie, resents it. She was tall, bent, hollow-eyed, and sallow, a type of womanhood I had often seen in the South, a reticent, infinitely patient, and enduring family drudge.

Her eyes were her best feature, and as she gained confidence in me her face took on a certain nobility. Her brow smoothed out, and she answered my questions regarding her psychic powers with the air of one who is perfectly certain of her ability to meet any tests. To think of her work-worn, stiffened hands playing tricks with a slate was ludicrous.

Leading me into her parlor with its cheap golden-oak furniture upholstered in yellow plush, she gave me a seat at a small center table which stood in the light of the bay-window. This stand was covered with a chenille lambrequin—I believe that is the proper name—which came down on all sides nearly to the floor. So far as I could discover we were alone in the house. I heard no sounds other than those we made. It seemed foolish to expect anything marvellous in such pitiful surroundings. The little room was flooded with direct afternoon sunlight.

I had brought with me a pair of folding cloth-edged school slates, and these I laid on the table, making no demand for any specific message; I merely said, "Let's see what will happen."

The medium put a tiny piece of pencil between the slates and thrust them under the table in the usual way. She said, "Hold one end of them."

I made no objection to this at the moment but determined to have my own way later.

Almost immediately a volley of snapping sounds arose from the slates, sounds which resembled the creaking of a cane-seated rocking chair. These noises were followed by three loud taps indicating a completed message; and when she withdrew the slates and opened them, I found the inner sides filled with messages, *all addressed to Henry Wallace.*

This interested me keenly—much more than any message addressed to me. It was evident that while she could get nothing of me, could not even derive my name or business, she could sense, and did sense, in me something associated with Wallace. It was as if I had brought in my clothing the scent of his pipe or, to be more mystical, something of his "aura."

Another possible explanation is that his many sittings with her had left in the room a psychic influence which still dominated her. Her "guides" were equally helpless. This fact in itself is valuable.

At my request we tried again, holding the slates under the table as before with our right hands while our left hands remained in full sight on the table top.

As the writing began again, she called my attention to a twitching of the muscles of her left hand and arm, a series of minute movements which kept time, so to say, with the pecking sounds on the slates beneath the table. This synchronism profoundly interested me. It made certain that some occult relationship between her normal arm and the writing going on below was in operation.

The sound of writing was still heard as she slowly withdrew the slates. *After they were laid on the table the ticking noise could still be heard.*

Reaching over she took the upper slate by the corner with her thumb and finger—and slowly lifted it while the phantom fingers continued to write at a furious rate. The pencil point seemed to be hopping up and down, pecking out its lines. This noise coming from the slates reminded me of the sizzling of fat in a frying pan when the cook lifts the cover to turn the meat.

Putting my head down flat on the table, I tried to catch a glimpse of the pencil at work but failed. As she opened the slates wider, the noise ceased.

The messages were again disappointing. They had no relation to me, none whatever. The "spirits" had not yet discovered me.

This was an excellent test of power, for the reason that the psychic had opened the slates to the sunlight! There was no machinery, no hocus-pocus, no chance for mistake. It happened as I relate it, wholly under my eyes and with no third person present, but there was no clairvoyant power at work.

At this point I decided to take control. I said to her: "I am myself a psychic. It is not necessary to place the slates under the table. Lay them down on the top. I want to put my hand on them." She did this. I then said, "Now put your right hand above mine."

She did as I commanded with wondering submissiveness, and with my left hand I flung the end of the long table cover over our two hands and the slates, thus shutting away the light.

Her meek compliance in this test surprised me. She accepted my suggestion as a command from an older and more powerful practitioner. She showed no hesitation, no doubt of the outcome, and I confess to a sense of new-found power as I felt the writing beginning *under my hand*. My success amazed me, but I gave no sign of it.

The psychic again called my attention to the multitudinous twitchings in her left hand and wrist. Her fingers were drawn and tense—curved like the claws of an eagle—and the muscles in her thin forearm moved convulsively. Her hands, I may add, were knotted and calloused by toil, having nothing of the smooth deftness of a conjurer. To credit her with prestidigitation or with hypnotic power would have been absurd. She was in my control.

While the writing was thus going on, phantom fingers darted out below the fringe of the table cover and touched me on the knees with lightning swiftness, motions impossible for the medium's work-worn hands, which were fully accounted for on the top of the table.

Speaking to the invisibles, I said: "Show me your arm. Shake me by the hand."

Wallace told me that he had often had this done for him, but I could not induce the spirit hands to do more than touch me. The critic may say, "They were the medium's toes," but I am quite certain that they were hands for I saw them. During this time the psychic did not speak a word. She gazed at me expectantly. I had become the wonder-worker.

Let me repeat. This test took place in a sunlit room while I was in full control of the conditions. I assert that a miracle as inexplicable as any in an oriental story now took place, for on opening the slates I found them filled with messages!

To have writing appear on closed slates under my own hand is as mysterious in its way as the East Indian conjurer's momentary development of a mango tree. In this case the wizardry came from a gaunt middle-aged housewife, at my command. That some of the messages came from her, I have no doubt, for they were badly spelled and badly written; but others were beyond her knowledge or skill in penmanship.

My unexpected success so wrought upon me that I decided upon a supreme test.

"As a matter of fact," I said with quiet assurance, "it is not necessary for either of us to *touch* the slates. We need not even cover them. Put them down on the table top and lean back in your chair. You and I are a powerful battery. We can do anything."

Without the slightest hesitation she did my bidding. Settling back in her chair she fixed her eyes on the slates, which were lying in full sight in the center of the table.

We had but a moment to wait. The sound of writing began at once and went on with greater power and speed than when our palms were on the slates. The medium's hands were in her lap fully two feet from the table's edge and in clear daylight. I was bent above the slates, listening.

On opening the slates I again found them filled with writing. No demonstration of supranormal writing could have been more absolutely convincing, but none of the messages were related to me.

One was a letter addressed to Wallace and signed "Joseph Jefferson"! Another script bore the signature "Lew Wallace." Several of the previous messages had been poorly written and phonetically spelled, quite as the psychic herself would write them and spell them; *but these two final messages were dashingly written and boldly signed*. "In short, the method was convincingly supranormal, and the messages impossible to the unlettered psychic." Such was my report written and signed that afternoon.

Those two signatures of Jefferson and Wallace must be minutely reckoned with. They remain wholly inexplicable, for if we grant that the psychic and I had the power of reproducing on a slate, wholly without contact, the signatures of two famous Americans, how is it that she had no knowledge of me? She knew that I came for a test but nothing more. Why should she confuse me with Henry Wallace, a man not in the least like me?

That she had no hint of my name or my work was evident. Whatever her powers, she was not a mind reader. She did not associate me with the American

Psychical Society. Furthermore "Jefferson" and "Lew Wallace" themselves were not clairvoyant. They did not address themselves to me.

If the doubter says, "You were deceived—nothing is so deceptive as our senses," I again reply: "Very true, but they are all we have. I controlled all the conditions. I dictated all the methods. I shared the entire process. What more could I ask?"

The psychic, now wholly convinced that I was a powerful fellow practitioner, suggested that we go to her dark room and try for voices. "We'll work the trumpet," she said.

Her séance chamber, which was on the second floor of the stairs, had but one door. It was hardly more than a large closet and was lighted with a single gas jet. It contained nothing but two wooden chairs and a small stand. The floor was bare and its one high window was filled with a light-proof shade. The door had an inner sliding bolt which I myself shot into its staple after the psychic had lighted the gas and taken her seat.

On the floor beside the chair in which she seated me, stood three tin trumpets. They were all of equal size and about two feet tall. At her suggestion I placed a chair directly in front of hers and turned out the lights. As I took my seat my knees were touching hers. At first the darkness was complete, but in a few minutes I was aware that under the badly fitting door a band of sunlight glowed increasingly. This fact is important, and I ask the reader to bear it in mind.

After singing with the psychic one or two hymns, I sat at ease and in watchful silence.

Suddenly the cones which stood near my right elbow

began to jostle one another. Leaning toward the psychic, I said, "Give me your hands."

Without a moment's hesitation she held out both her hands, and I took them firmly in mine. I then said, "I want to put my toes on yours."

She granted this test as readily as the other; and while I thus controlled her feet and her hands one of the cones rose from the floor and began to circle the room. I could see it plainly as it floated above my head, for it reflected the light from the threshold. Its lower side shone like a golden rod.

For several minutes it roamed the room, up near the ceiling, like a huge dragon fly. At last it came down and rested on my shoulder. After a moment of pause it moved slowly round before my face. With both my hands still grasping those of the psychic, I bent my head and touched the cone with my forehead. Instantly it fell, as if my touch had in some way short-circuited its power.

A little later, when the psychic struck a light, another cone fell from its position in the air. It had also been in motion although I had not been able to see it. It may be that all three had been afloat at one and the same moment.

Again, while I held the psychic's hands and put my toes on hers, one of the cones swept into the air and circled about our heads. It moved horizontally as if floating on a liquid. It touched me again and again, always with the gentlest precision. The light from beneath the door now made it seem like a shaft of fire-lit copper.

Voices appeared to come from these cones, but as they

were all colored by the vernacular of the psychic I did not value what they said to me. I could not relate them to any other personality. Not one of them had any message for me. Not one of the invisibles spoke my name.

Nevertheless the physical side of this performance was highly satisfactory. The cones soared at moments when the psychic was under my rigid control, but I observed a very curious fact—*the voices did not come while I held her hands.* In stating this I am far from saying that she could not have produced the voices while I controlled her hands. As a performance it was one of the most marvellous of all my experience, up to that date.

In characterizing this psychic as a hard-working housewife and in describing her shabby little home, I hope to aid the reader in visualizing the commonplace surroundings in which this wonder-working woman wrought. For two dollars she had presented more inexplicable phenomena than any conjurer could offer with his guarded stage, his black curtains, his wires, his mirrors, and his black-robed attendants. It may be that I helped to produce these phenomena. Certainly I dictated the method of their working out. My only sensation of sharing the process was a shudder which ran over me at certain moments of the séance. This may have been purely physical.

As I was going away I heartily clasped the psychic's hand. "You and I together could rival the work of any mediums in the world. By doing things in my way we brought new forces into action. Didn't we?"

For the first time she smiled, a faint smile, and said

rather wistfully: "We certainly did. I hope you'll come and try again. I like to work with you."

"That I shall do," I replied. "I shall come again soon, and we'll perform new marvels."

I never did, and I fear that she is now herself an "invisible." If she is, I await a message from her. I can not recall her name, but if she comes she will be able to identify herself.

The value of this experience can not be overstated. It demonstrated once again that mediums do not know the scope of their own powers. They fall into grooves of action. They are reluctant to try new ways of procedure, and their inhibitions limit their activities. Most of the mediums I had examined would not permit me to divert the action of their "guides," nor to override their advice; but in this case I had the fullest freedom of arrangement and control. I was apparently a part of the show.

My experience that day strengthened me in the belief that these "parasitic personalities" are built up by the psychic and her circle, and that they can be influenced, taught to act in new ways by a stronger will than that of their medium.

Wallace was waiting for me, eager to learn the outcome of my sitting. "Well! How was it? Did it work?"

"Perfectly, amazingly. It was a marvellous experience, but it did not at any time demonstrate clairvoyance."

"Did she find out who you were?"

"No. That is the most puzzling part of the whole séance. All messages were absolutely supernormal in the method of their production, but they had no reference to me. They were all addressed to you. The medium gained no hint of my name or of my official purpose. She showed no clairvoyant or telepathic ability —not the slightest."

Wallace stared at me in amazement. "The messages referred to me?"

"Yes, and to be quite fair, two of them were signed 'Lew Wallace' and 'Joseph Jefferson,' in a dashing individual script, quite impossible to the medium. Others were badly written and wrongly spelled—as I imagine she would write and spell."

Wallace slowly replied, "I have always found her honest."

"So did I, and I believe in her. She is a plain hardworking housewife. She came out of her kitchen to work these miracles for me, and when I left, I've no doubt she put on her apron and went back to her stove —but what shall we say of her failure to discover my name? Shall we say that she and her guides had no divining power? Furthermore, Jefferson had some knowledge of me, and if death has added to his clairvoyant powers why should he address me as if I were you? Is it possible that he could not see me or feel me in any way? General Wallace was equally unperceiving."

We came to no agreement concerning these inconsistencies, but I went away enriched by a most valuable discovery. I had discovered that I too could command spirits of the vasty deep and they would obey. Apparently my will—up to a certain point—had been dominant,

There is an element of absurdity in the slate-writing, I am free to confess, but we should not let that interfere with a sense of its essential mystery. Women of this type follow precedent in their experiments. Having seen others write upon closed slates, they adopt the same method of procedure. They are eager for results, for messages—and they are not curious about processes. They keep to the well trodden path.

The theory of the folded slates is that they furnish a dark cabinet in which the forces work more easily. "The slates are put under the table to shield the spirits from observation while at work," believers explain, but the doubter says "for purposes of fraud." In my case I had broken up both these traditional practices. I had obtained the writing on the slates without contact and on the top of the table.

Furthermore, we must reckon with the fact that the messages thus produced could not have been written by the psychic. She could not have imitated those signatures with her hand free, and I doubt if she could have spelled the words. I had probably seen Jefferson's signature many times, but I could not have imitated it. I leave the puzzle with my readers.

CHAPTER EIGHT

THEORIES AND METHODS

I

INTEREST in psychical experiment seems to go in waves or cycles, and the years lying between 1895 and 1903 were unproductive (in America) of any notable developments. The Boston Psychical Society slowly disintegrated; our journal died, and the *Arena*, the friend of all reformers and new-thought organizations, passed out of Flower's hands. I still kept in touch with him and with Dolbear, but I met them only at long intervals. Then, too, my literary work subordinated all matters occult.

For more than two years, 1895 to 1897, I was busied with writing a life of General Grant. In 1898, I took the long overland trail through the Northwest wilderness into the upper Yukon Valley. In 1900 I began a series of novels dealing with the red men and their neighbors —writing which kept me on the move and in the open. Consideration of psychic problems was curtailed.

Nevertheless, when opportunity offered, I kept tryst with certain of my invisible friends and monitors. I recall sharing some of Prof. Quackenbush's experiments in hypnosis, and somewhere about 1903 Mrs. Smiley, who was visiting in Cleveland, gave me several additional sittings, sittings in which only one other person was present. The first date chanced to be on a very warm night, and the room in which we sat was small and uncomfortably close. To Mrs. Smiley (who was ten years older and considerably less powerful) I said, "I shall not count it against you if we fail of voices tonight."

After putting her under control as I had so often done, I heard almost immediately the voice of "Mitchel" who greeted me as if we had parted but the day before. Speaking from the trumpet, he said:

"I am glad to greet you again, Mr. Garland. I have read your reports of our tests, and I commend you for holding an even hand over the evidence. To change my figure of speech, we prefer that you should lean a little backward when pronouncing judgments. Your words will then carry more weight with the scientific world."

"Wilbur" then took the horn and joked with me precisely as he had done ten years before. He had not changed in age or character—apparently. His most serious sentence was a hope that I would continue my work: "Stick to it. We are depending on you."

Nothing essentially new developed during the two following sittings; they only confirmed what I had previously recorded, but Mrs. Smiley promised to stop in Chicago on her way West and sit for me in my own home.

In anticipation of a lively séance I invited Mr. and Mrs. Robert Millikan to join our circle. Alas! It was another smotheringly hot night and Mrs. Smiley, tensely eager to impress Professor Millikan, failed entirely. She went away heart-sick over her failure and my disappointment. I never again had an opportunity to meet with her.

Although various public mediums in Chicago were commended to me, I did not follow up the suggestions. I had been so fortunate in my work with non-commercial self-sacrificing psychics that sitting through the conventional—not to say traditional—dark circle of miscellaneous sitters seemed a waste of time. I kept up my reading, however, and now and again tried out an experiment with a friend.

Some of these experiments, while of no evidential value, not only made me aware of the latent mediumistic power which many of my friends possessed but convinced me that my own ability to develop this power and make use of it was increasing rather than diminishing. Impromptu sittings yielded curious and in some cases alarming results. It appeared that any group of people sitting regularly with me for a week or two would almost certainly develop from their circle a medium and a guide.

If America during these years was laggard in the scientific study of psychic phenomena, France, Italy, and England were not, for they were all sending to us year by year reports, essays, and books which recorded scores of colorful experiments, in scholarly and precise wording. In 1905 a journal called *The Annals of Psychical Science* with an international board of directors established a London office and began the publication in English of reports of the work which was being carried on in several European laboratories.

The directors of the enterprise were Dr. Darieux and Professor Charles Richet. The editor was Caesar de

Vesme and the advisory committee headed by Sir William Crookes included Camille Flammarion, astronomer, Caesar Lombroso, distinguished alienist, Enrico Morselli, professor of psychology, Dr. Joseph Maxwell, a French Deputy, and other men of high repute as physicists and psychologists.

It appeared from these reports that certain universities of France and Italy were taking up the study of mediumship as they would examine any other problems in biology whereas no American university professor would publicly admit that the phenomena existed.

One of my most intimate friends at this time was Henry Blake Fuller, the Chicago novelist, who was not only a man of wide reading along lines of philosophical discussion but an enthusiast on all phases of Italian life and history. He often translated for me articles dealing with experiments in Milan or Rome. French reports I was able to read for myself, and I was delighted to find my own deductions confirmed by detailed reports in the *Annals of Psychical Science*.

As I read I discovered to my joy, that one scientific investigator commended me to another. Crookes led to Zöllner, Zöllner to Maxwell, Maxwell to Morselli— all of whom treated mediumship as a human attribute, something to be calmly studied and precisely reported. "Science is a method, not a dogma," they said.

With their laboratory experimentation a new nomenclature came into use. In place of "etheric" limbs and "astral" bodies I began to read of "ectoplasmic hands" and "ectoplasmic phantasms." In fact these professors carefully avoided the use of the word "medium," substituting "psychic" or "sensitive," by which they intended to indicate an individual who had developed supernormal perception or supernormal energies.

According to these thinkers there was no such thing as a *supernatural* agency or event. "Every phenomenon, no matter how puzzling, is a part of nature and subject to natural law," they declared. "Phenomena may be for the moment inexplicable but never above or beyond nature. Agencies can be supernormal but not supernatural."

More and more of these investigators adopted the hypothesis that the psychic and his sitters, working together, were the main cause—some said the sole cause—of physical as well as mental phenomena. Words like "metaphysical" were supplemented by "metapsychical" to indicate that they were dealing with unknown psychical laws, just as the metaphysical phenomena were inexplicable by known physical laws.

In the conduct of these scientific séances all prayers, hymns, and inspirational addresses were excluded. The phraseology as well as the methods of the séances tended to become those of the laboratory. Theories waited on experiment.

In all this, Fuller and I rejoiced. "In no other way can we get at the fundamental facts involved," he argued. "I doubt if they can ever make these experiments yield unvarying results, as in chemistry; but they can come near to predicting phenomena."

From the earliest attempts at scientific observations and experiment in 1855, writers on these subjects had agreed that a subtle form of matter impalpable and intangible emanated from the medium and in lesser degree from each person in a séance. This substance was called by early writers "odic force," "psychode," "etheric fluid," and various other names. Later observers testified that it was this semiluminous and exceedingly subtle exudation which caused objects to be moved, and that from it all phantasmal bodies were built up.

"Ectoplasm" was the later name for this mysterious element. This word was formed from the prefix "ecto-," meaning "outside," and "plasm," which biologists use to describe the vital content of body cells.

"This substance [writes one observer] takes on several colors, gray, white and blue. It is excessively mobile. It often resembles smoke but easily becomes viscous. It is sensitive and its sensibility is confounded with that of the psychic. A bright light upon it gives pain to the psychic.

"It has an immediate irresistible tendency to simulate a body of some sort and remains but an instant in its original misty vaporous shape. With the rapidity of thought it forms itself into heads, hands and faces.

"It has no means of defending itself. It is like a timid animal—it retreats for protection back into the body of the psychic. It can move upward as well as downward. It produces organs complete in themselves, ephemeral though they are. Sometimes it exudes from the body of the psychic as a vapor and settles on her dress like hoar frost thus forming an apron of white, out of which a head or face may appear.

"Everything goes to show that this substance is the material of the medium partly externalized. It exists. It has been photographed. The feet which it forms have left their print on wax and supernumerary hands built of it have been moulded in paraffin. It is the primary substance into which the grub melts in his dark-cabinet, and from which he emerges a gorgeous butterfly."

This thinker concludes with these words: "*This elementary substance can be modeled by the mind of the psychic or by the thought of the sitter as a sculptor models wax.*"

According to reports in the *Annals of Psychical Science*, experimenters with improved cameras had caught and reproduced these ectoplasmic forms as they issued from the body of the psychic, and had thus recorded their growth and dissolution.

As a result of these experiments, analysis shifted from the medium as a supposed telephone between the dead and the living and centered upon a study of his body and his brain as dynamos teeming with unknown and immeasurable rays of biochemical energy. From the worship of a medium as the basis of a new religion, these relentless European students of biological fact began to test his capacities in a laboratory.

These interpretations ran harmoniously with my own experiments and observations, at the time, and so far from diminishing my interest in psychic phenomena, this new theory made each "sensitive" of still more absorbing interest. It also caused me to resent the sneers and evasions of our own university professors and specialists.

"Why should not American colleges enter this 'field of unexplored biology' as they are doing in France, Italy, and Germany?" I said to Fuller. "It is not a religious problem with Richet or Lombroso: it is a question of fact. Are these supernormal powers, claimed by individual psychics, demonstrable? That should be the question with American men of science."

"Our scientific experts are afraid of criticism," he replied. "They can't afford to lose the good will of their employers."

II

In America our best known investigator at this time was William James, but he, like Oliver Lodge, was exceedingly cautious in affirmative statement. Richard Hodgson, the American secretary of the English Society, was not connected so far as I knew with any academic laboratories and was collecting evidence rather than producing it.

One or two "commissions" had been appointed to put an end to mediumship, and from time to time their chairman called upon the psychics to come forward and be "exposed." But as no one had volunteered the commissioners soon used up their funds, retired into oblivion. They were not patient truth-seekers, they were bent upon discrediting spiritualism.

Reading the *Annals of Psychical Science* emphasized the fact that "spirit" phenomena are of like character all over the world, and that patient practitioners had been able to name the conditions which should govern all experimental séances. Some of these I had discovered for myself.

1. Use a small room.
2. Sit regularly, in a circle.
3. See that all the sitters are comfortable.
4. Use a plain wooden table and plain chairs. Double-top tables give best results.

5. A bare floor is best.

6. Have only six or eight people in the circle, men and women in equal numbers, and do not change the personnel.

7. Begin with a dark room or dim light. Green or yellow or red light is less antagonistic to the psychic force than white light.

8. Don't argue. Anything which irritates or disturbs the medium or any member of the circle will prevent results. Sing or converse quietly.

9. Have only one spokesman. Many questions at once confuse the situation. Consult the "guides" as to conditions.

10. Don't get impatient. Count on sitting two hours, and have at least ten sittings before rendering judgment concerning the powers of the medium.

As my readers will recall, I had already applied most of these rules, and some of them I had successfully contravened. My best séances had been with only three or four sitters—as in Dolbear's study and Flower's chamber. In some instances I had humored the psychic, in others I had insisted on doing things in my own way.

Very early in my experimentation I had discovered that comfort and serenity were necessary in order that the psychic should be at her best. A sitter's sceptical attitude of mind has little effect on the phenomena provided he keeps his doubts to himself and does not irritate or distract the psychic. Each circle is in fact a kind of chemical compound. Any new personality adds another element which may increase the force or diminish it.

When approached for advice by those about to form a circle I usually replied in these words—or near it:

"Phenomena seem to be the result of a mixture of chemistry and personalities. Faith is not essential to successful experiment, but patience and good temper are. Whatever the cause of the phenomena, their production seems to be a severe physical strain. Treat your medium with kindly care. Having control of all the conditions, eliminate all chance of trickery by gradually covering every loophole in your investigation. Make each succeeding sitting an affirmation or verification of the others.

"Mediums are highly suggestible. They work best when the circle is harmonious. Some of them succeed only when their routine is rigidly followed, others can be induced to experiment. Nearly all of these gifted individuals consider their power a sacred gift, something to be used for consolation or for conviction of others. Some use it to make a living but do so at the advice of their guides. You will gain best results by gaining the confidence of these wonder-workers. Only in very exceptional cases will mediums lend their power to aid in the advance of psychic science. In fact I do not expect it of them."

Although constantly beset by those who wished me to aid in these developing circles, I declined to do so. It was too tedious and too uncertain of results. Then, too, the difficulty of meeting regularly and with the same persons in the circle was a barrier. Although I sometimes took charge of such sittings for the entertainment of guests I did so reluctantly. I could not afford to spend long hours getting faint raps on a chair or slight movements of a table.

III

For nearly ten years I continued my search for another co-laborer like Mrs. Smiley and Mrs. Simpson, one who would lend herself whole-heartedly to a series of experiments, and so bring me a little nearer to an understanding of the mystery of mediumship.

Accepting the biodynamic theory which leading investigators in the years following 1900 used as a working hypothesis, I resumed my experiments. Respecting the belief of the mediums that their "guides" were persons, I consented to advise with "Coulter" and "Wilbur"—or whatever the guide's name happened to be; but I drew the line at "Red Thunder" or "White Bird." I knew too much about the speech and character of the red man to parley with these traditional figures. I regarded them as survivals of a primitive method of experiment.

"Trance controls may be dream creations," I argued, "and all mediumship only impersonation, in the one case through the body, in the other by ectoplasmic forms, but nothing is gained by arguing the point with any psychic."

Most of the mediums I met were enslaved to these "dream personalities," implicitly obeying their commands. Some said, "We are forbidden by our guides to make money. They fix our hours and define the methods of our sittings."

Considering their guides supremely wise, they sought their advice on all perplexities.

"The personality of the spirit manifesting must be discovered by exploration of the psychic," European investigators declared. "The problem is biologic and the study of error is also essential to an understanding of these metapsychical phenomena. In this exploration we must expect to come upon absurd acts."

The Old World advance into this field of unknown biology was not paralleled in America. Our researchers then gave no thought to Richet, Maxwell, and Boirac, or if they did they regarded them as dupes or dreamers. Even my friend Dolbear, who had confessed to me his complete inability to explain the phenomena which he had witnessed in his own study, felt obliged to hedge in the presence of his associates.

America had no scientific men of the stature and boldness of Crookes, Lodge, and Wallace. No American of high renown came forward to study this most vital problem although Tesla and Edison both privately hinted that there was "something real in psychic phenomena."

Edison once said to a friend of mine, "All along my way I've come upon hints of these mysterious forces—and sometime I am going to stop commercial inventing and follow out these leadings." This he never found leisure to do.

The truth is, our professors were not only afraid of "losing face"—as the Chinese say—they were afraid of losing faith in what they had gained. Orthodox biology has no place for a study of metaphysical phenomena. Professors who are quick to accept new facts in chemistry rage against the words "metapsychical" and "metaphysical." In the presence of a psychic they cease to be men of science and become bitter antagonists of a theory of which they know nothing.

My only hope was that of finding a few young men who could not be intimidated by a board of regents or overawed by their fellow instructors. I sympathized with the scornful psychologist who said, "I refuse to be bored by a lot of old women singing hymns in the dark to make a table dance," but I resented sweeping denials of the existence of such phenomena.

Granting that these inexplicable phenomena sprang from forces originating in the psychic and her sitters, I realized that time must be allowed for development.

Challenging some of my most distinguished scientific friends, I said: "If you will join me in a series of ten séances, making no audible comment in the presence of the other sitters, I will amaze you, as Dolbear was amazed. It can't be done with one sitting—perhaps not in five; but in the end you will be forced to grant the reality of the phenomena upon which I am willing you should put your own interpretation."

No one volunteered. They were all willing to sit patiently through a hundred barren experiments in physics but refused to give a moment's open-minded thought to my report of the writing on a closed slate under control.

They did not call me a liar when I told them of my tests, but they considered me a dupe. "You were hypnotized. Such things can't happen. They are opposed to all physical laws."

"To all *known* physical laws. These phenomena are as conformable to law as any other happenings, only we don't know what the laws are."

CHAPTER NINE

CHANGING CONCEPTS

I

DURING the first ten or twelve years of my experimentation, I made use of my material only in brief reports or in letters to Flower and others of my friends. I wished to be known as a fictionist and historian, not as an advocate of psychic research. After all, my pursuit of "spooks" was only a subsidiary interest, something to pursue in my leisure hours. I had no desire to become branded as a propagandist for any cause. My best advisers said, "Your report will be all the more valuable if it remains the statement of a literary man's convictions."

There was force in this suggestion, and so I kept the subject out of my list of lectures and out of my magazine articles for nearly ten years; but I had in mind to write, sometime, a novel with mediumship as its main theme.

It was not till 1903, however, that the weight of my garnered notes and impressions led me to begin their use in such a story. In 1904, I submitted to Harpers, my publishers, a manuscript which I had written under the title "The Tyranny of the Dark." Somewhat to

136

my surprise it was accepted for immediate use as a serial in *Harper's Weekly.*

It was the story of a girl whose parents, having discovered her mediumistic powers, set her aside as "an instrument of communication between the living and the dead," denying her the companionship and the recreations natural to childhood. She was forced to sit long hours in the dark, surrounded by solemn elderly people who had little regard for her pain and disgust.

Her mother said: "God has made you a special servant. You are different from other girls—you have a sacred gift."

To this the girl made piteous reply: "I don't want to be *different* from other girls. I want to be *like* them."

The title of this novel was suggested to me by the confession of one of my aunts (my mother's younger sister), who said to me one day, "For two years these spirit forces made my life a hell."

I could never get her to tell me the story of her slavery, but her tone implied that it had been a veritable "tyranny of the Dark." I imagined it to have been similar to that which Mrs. Smiley had described to me. In fact I had discovered in all the mediums I had studied this bondage to a cause. Either they believed it to be their duty to sacrifice themselves, or they had fallen into the way of making it a source of revenue—pitifully small in most cases. They all lived in an atmosphere of suspicion. Wherever they went they were asked to "demonstrate," and their "work" was the only theme of conversation. They soon lost the normal balance of body and mind. They were no longer free agents. In some cases insanity resulted.

The abstract theme of my novel, therefore, had the warrant of my aunt's report as well as that of the three most powerful and most intelligent of the mediums with whom I had experimented. The phenomena detailed were taken directly from my notes or from my diary.

The theme interested me. As a writer I argued that this was as legitimate material for a novel as the lives and deeds of the Cheyennes or the Sioux—of whom I had been writing. Furthermore I had the example of Howells and Henry James, who had turned aside —if you wish to call it so—to deal with this hidden world. While granting the beauty of the books which these two illustrious fictionists had written, I felt that they were both poor in exact facts. I knew that Howells had based his "Undiscovered Country" (a lovely story) on a few visits to dark-room and very dubious séances, at a time when no opportunity for exact observation had been given. Without hope of approaching the subtlety, the humor and grace of his book, I felt that I could contribute something to American fiction which he and James had left unsaid.

To my editors I wrote: "I regard this theme as a legitimate and interesting literary problem. 'The Tyranny of the Dark' is based on accurate observation. It is wholly different in tone and treatment from any other novel dealing with the subject. Every test which I therein describe, I have myself employed. I hope, however, that its scientific accuracy will not interfere with its acceptance as a work of fiction. It is a novel and not a biography or a treatise. Its characters are wholly imaginary."

This story published as a serial was well received by the public and brought me many letters from women who had been similarly "devoted." One of these was from the daughter of a nationally known spiritualist. I quote it in confirmation of my theme—and in support of the title of my novel as well as of its ending. She wrote:

". . . Early in the '50's my father took up the subject of spiritualism with all his heart and as a result was persecuted, ridiculed and lampooned. He was too much in earnest to be disturbed. About that time I, a motherless schoolgirl, undertook to keep house for him. I soon found, much to my chagrin, that I was what was called a 'medium.' I fought it for a year—my father being unaware of it. Then it became known to him, and I decided to give part of my life to it. I courted the severest investigation by outsiders.

"For ten years I was avoided and shunned as 'dangerous,' and in the end my health gave out, and for another ten years I had not the least indication of any sort of manifestations. At last I went to the mountains of North Carolina. There I lived outdoors and rode horseback, and suddenly the psychic power returned. Ever since I've been called upon from all quarters for advice as to how to treat the subject and my aim has been to instill common-sense and reason. . . ."

Here was the precise problem which I had made the chief basis of my novel.

In 1905, Harper and Brothers brought the novel out in book form and sent out many copies to writers and critics who had expressed a special interest in it. This brought in many other letters, a few of them critical, some demanding why I had not committed myself to the spirit hypothesis. These letters have value as showing a change in the attitude of academic experts.

II

One of the most amusing of the letters was from my old friend and fellow investigator Amos E. Dolbear of Tufts College:

"I was delighted the other day to receive from you a copy of your book 'The Tyranny of the Dark.' (Bless me what a name for a book!) Down I sat in my spare hours for a day or two and read it thru—in the same room where we had those *tyrannous* happenings twelve years ago! I got so absorbed in your story that every little noise gave me a start. 'Wilbur' was expected and I would have welcomed him heartily.

"That 'delicate finger' high on the window. That horn touching my forehead and the voice saying, 'I ain't dead,' and the alarm clock suddenly stopping, and the candy box being brought to the table!—Every happening is a mystery until it is explained by a deeper mystery. . . ."

I ask the reader's attention to that last sentence.

The scientist who is a large figure in my story was suggested by my good friend Dr. T. M. Prudden, bacteriologist in New York, who had been my companion on the trail in Arizona and whose "bug-farm" I had visited. From him came a letter equally jocose:

"I have enjoyed 'The Tyranny of the Dark' mightily;

all the more because you were good enough to inscribe a copy for me. . . . Of course you story-telling folk wouldn't scruple to make a promising scientific man drop his career like a hot potato just as soon as an alluring bit of femininity appears upon his horizon. Think what that chap might have done for science if you had been willing to let him alone with his ideas! But there would have been no story, so you may be absolved."

He had no criticism to offer on my scientific statements, however.

The value of the book as a novel was of more concern to me, and when Israel Zangwill called it "the most engrossing book you have written" I was wholly reassured. He went on to say: "You hold the balance so impartially that you achieve all the thrill of a detective novel. I have met all the circle to which you refer —Crookes, Lodge and others—at the house of my father-in-law, Professor Ayrton, who also read your book with keen interest."

With these judgments from two experts—one a distinguished critic and fellow novelist and the other a distinguished man of science—I was fortified against attack.

While at work on this manuscript I had written William James asking if he had any new material for me.

In his reply he had said: "I have myself had no direct contact with mediums for many years, and am still in a state of *bafflement* as to all these phenomena. It seems as if they were intended deliberately by the Almighty never to be either proved or disproved definitely.

"I wish I had had *your* experience. There are waves

of public interest—it may be that there is just now an ebb—but there will sometime again be a flood, and things will hitch a little forward. Practically I am quite out of it. Haven't the time or energy!"

His letter confirmed me on my theory of psychic waves or cycles.

I had sent a personal copy to William Stead, editor of the English *Review of Reviews*. His acknowledgment indicates the thoroughgoing spiritualist who recognizes no ebbs in spirit progress:

"I have just finished making a review of your most interesting and suggestive book on 'The Tyranny of the Dark.' I hope you will bring out a sequel when your own ideas are a little clearer on the subject.

"As you have left it, the story is an ethical outrage. The destruction of such a human telescope into the Great Beyond as Viola is painted, merely to provide a very self-sufficient dogmatic prig of a young biologist with a wife, is an offense against ethics, against science and against the sense of proportion. [The ethical outrage to me is that of making this girl a 'telescope.']

"I quite agree that it would have been criminal to allow her to remain in Colorado with Clark and Pratt. But that is a very different thing to destroying her mediumship which you have been bent upon doing. There is no difficulty if you complete your task by making him realize when married the crime he has committed and restoring Viola to her proper mission, seeing to it that she always keeps possession of the key of her own piano. [Some would say her proper mission was motherhood.]

"The trouble about Viola was that she, being a great

natural psychic, instead of being carefully trained and
taught that the first law of safety is to be the keeper of
her own house so that the spirits can only enter with her
permission and remain only so long as she pleases, was
handed over to the absolute control of the unseen. *No
one can be trusted with such ruthless power, certainly
not the disembodied dead.* But this was an abuse which
earlier could have been remedied. The girl was healthy.
Clark had gone—her mother was quite intelligent
enough to see that there must be moderation in communication. [After all we are living on this plane.]

"I enclose you a very sensible discourse on the subject
of the dangers of obsession. I notice you do not touch
upon the phenomenon of the Double. It is the most interesting of all, and to my mind of absolutely indisput-
able reality. Pray pardon the unceremonious freedom
of this letter. I like your book and I think it will do
good."

In my response I admitted that my story offered no
solution. "It is an advance on the mediumship novels of
Howells and James only in that it states a belief in the
facts of mediumship." I did not say, as I was tempted
to, that his use of the words "human telescope" was
abhorrent to me, voicing as it did the selfish desires of
the bereaved who are willing to violate a young life
for their consolement.

After this critical estimate of Stead I welcomed a
letter of praise from a fellow novelist, Eden Phillpotts,
who thanked me for the book and said: "You bring great
store of knowledge to the task. I would only offer one
criticism and that with deference—since to criticise a
kindly gift may seem discourteous. But I think your

biologists would not have animadverted against the honored name of Ernest Haeckel. He is no dogmatist and where he permits himself to assent, you shall find fifty years of amazingly close and patient study behind the assertion. Can it be that your scientists did not know 'The Evolution of Man'?

"I do not quite grasp what becomes of the 'spirits' when the end of your book is reached. Is the hero's will stronger than theirs? If they were real ghosts, as of course you imply, why did they abandon their notable determination to regenerate the world through the heroine? [No one knows why this power comes and goes.]"

This letter was a surprise. I did not know that Phillpotts was in any degree interested in psychic matters.

Sir Oliver Lodge's reply was cautious. In a letter to my publishers dated May 24, 1905, he says:

"I am rather struck with the book you sent me. 'The Tyranny of the Dark' indicates more knowledge and sympathy with several sides of the question of psychophysical phenomena than is customary in authors of fiction. On the whole it should be instructive to the average reader, since it represents, in many respects fairly, the spiritualistic attitude, and also represents fairly some aspects of the scientific attitude.

"It is too much to expect that either representation can be quite life-like or satisfactory to the persons concerned; but still on the whole it represents a genuine amount of information and a somewhat remarkable knack of sympathetically depicting opposite sides to a question and holding the balance fairly even between them."

W. H. Mallock, another English author, wrote that
he had been contemplating a novel dealing with some
of the well known abnormal conditions of the brain—
"not precisely those introduced by yourself," he explained, "but others more amenable to ordinary scientific interpretation . . . I must congratulate you on
the skill with which in more than one passage you sum
up the scientific view of the extreme complexity of
the human brain with all its latent and stored-up an-
cestral contents."

I have quoted these correspondents not for their
comment on the value of my story but to present a
picture of the attitude of literary and scientific men
thirty years ago—not merely toward psychic research
but toward the physical universe.

At the suggestion of my publishers, I composed an
open letter designed to meet some of the criticisms
which came in:

"Those who complain of me for only 'hitting the high
places' are forgetting that my story is, after all, a romance, intended to be diverting rather than informing.
It is a study of life precisely as my 'Hesper' is a study
of life. I have not 'departed from my method.' I have
merely delineated certain characters who, while differing little, externally, from their neighbors, move in a
world of mystery, associating with those whom we call
'the dead' on gentle and respectful terms. Such characters are as legitimate in fiction as any other individuals
holding to a differing rule of living. As a writer I found
these confiding folk of the utmost interest, and in certain conversations I have tried to present their theories
without exaggeration.

"However, to come back to my original explanation, 'The Tyranny of the Dark' is a story whose first aim is to interest by delineating a phase of modern life—and secondly to picture the essential martyrdom involved in mediumship. As to the scope and direction of the chapters, the quality of this or that scene, I can only say that my 'guide'—old 'Subliminal Consciousness'—ran that way!

"Without claiming anything epoch-making in this volume, I think I may say that it has definitely advanced the serious study of mediumship. It has won for me the good-will of the psychics, especially those who are willing to suffer for 'the good of the cause.'

"The 'death blow to spiritualism' will not be dealt by those who ridicule the testimony of Lodge and Lombroso. It will come—if it comes—from the inside, by a new interpretation of ancient facts. Arrogation of superior intelligence—smartness—is the main characteristic of assaults on the reports of Crookes and Richet. 'If I had only been there!' is the thought expressed or implied in most of the books by these critics, some of whom get their living by doing 'stunts' for pay. Personally I prefer to consider the word of the scientific man who is sacrificing his time, his health and his reputation in the effort to solve a persistent mystery, than the snap judgment of a professional conjurer or even that of an objector on the side-lines.

"I take no account of the academic sceptics, the men who say, 'Nothing mysterious ever happens in my presence,' and who are so cocksure of their own penetration and judgment that they decline to investigate for themselves, delighting to sit in judgment on those who carefully and painstakingly pursue the problem. If these fault-finders condescend to take part in an experiment, they do so with a sneer, expecting to be instantly convinced of fraud on the part of the psychic. The 'credulous weakness' of distinguished scientists who have been patiently experimenting for years in their laboratories earnestly trying to solve the mystery, is lightly assumed.

"The office of these professional doubters seems to be that of writing books, to satisfy those who say, 'I told you so'; and yet whenever a serious sceptic goes into prolonged investigation to accept facts, he ends as Lombroso did, in a conviction that the phenomena exist, whatever reserves he may hold concerning their interpretation.

"Mediumship appears to be a negative state, a giving up of control. Psychics only partially govern their manifestations. When they claim to do so, they are not mediums but wonder-workers. This being granted, it is evident that no expert can rush in upon a true medium and club the secret out of him. Investigation is not so simple as that."

Referring back to another sort of thinker—one who affects to despise the physical side of mediumship, as though there could be a physical effect without a psychical cause, I added: "These spiritists speak of 'matter' and 'material phenomena' with scorn, as if they were somehow less honorable, less to be trusted than spirit; and curiously enough, they join forces with the critics who ridicule Crookes and Zöllner, forgetting that all matter is at bottom as mysterious as spirit and that the man who concerns himself with the physical side of mediumship is (or may be) just as devout a worshipper of reality as the spiritist. The investigator should be a judge, not an advocate.

"So far as I am able I shall present the evidence in a spirit of fairness, and especially do I wish to promulgate the philosophy which acknowledges nothing 'supernatural.' Facts are known or unknown, they can't be above or beyond nature. They may be supranormal, that is to say unusual, and new to our senses. If a ghost really walks, why be alarmed about it? If an astral hand touches you, why shrink and cry out? It is a natural phenomenon, startling only because it is new and not understood."

I concluded my statement by quoting another letter from William James: "One who takes part in a good sitting has, usually, a livelier sense both of the reality and of the importance of the communication than one who merely reads the record. Active relations with a thing are required to bring the reality home to us. It is a lack of participation, long and careful, which invalidates criticism of psychical researchers of today."

These and many other letters combined with the reviews brought to my publishers as to me a measure of satisfaction. The book notwithstanding its controversial matter had won a great many readers and had added something to the store of psychic research material. At the moment, I vowed never to write another page on this controversial (and engrossing) subject.

CHAPTER TEN

EDITOR COSGRAVE AND DANIEL PETERS

I

THE publication of "The Tyranny of the Dark" relieved the pressure of the psychic material in my head, and I returned to my work as novelist of the mountain West. Nevertheless I occasionally met with those interested in the occult and continued my reading of magazines devoted to the subject.

One of my New York friends with whom I lunched, now and again, at the club, was John O'Hara Cosgrave, the editor of *Everybody's Magazine,* which was one of the most widely read periodicals of the day. Notwithstanding his expert editorship of a popular periodical, Cosgrave was deeply interested in certain phases of Oriental thought. He was essentially a mystic but found interest in my scientific approach to spiritualism.

One night, in the autumn of 1907, I was a guest at a literary dinner in his home, and during dinner some one spoke of my book "The Tyranny of the Dark" and wished to know how much of scientific observation it contained. My reply led to a general discussion of the hidden world about us and for more than an hour I described my experiments with Mrs. Smiley,

Mrs. Hartley, and other professional mediums—and all the while Cosgrave listened gravely, saying little but very plainly absorbed by the turn which the talk had taken.

At the close of the dinner he said to me, in his low pleasant Irish voice: "What other subject could arouse and hold the interest of a group of varied personalities as this has done tonight? While you were talking I was asking myself, 'Would not an article by this man Garland interest my readers as it has interested my guests?' Presented as you have presented it tonight, I believe it would be a successful feature. Will you consider writing one or two articles for me?"

"I shall be glad to do so, but I should like to put my experiments and observations into the form of an after-dinner discussion, something like that we have just ended."

"That's an idea! I am certain that such an informal expression of the subject would interest. Why not write out a sample article and let me see it?"

Stimulated by his enthusiasm, I immediately set to work on a manuscript which pictured a group of people somewhat similar to his dinner party, in which scoffers, believers, scientific observers, and critics heckled me on the statements which I had put into "The Tyranny of the Dark."

This article which I turned in a few days later was read and approved not only by Cosgrave but by his assistant editors Gilman Hall and George Barr Baker, and I was commissioned to go on with at least two more —a commission which up to this time no American magazine of general literature had dared to grant.

It was in truth a perilous adventure, for it not only set me to work reading my files and digging up my notebooks, it led me to make new experiments in order to bring my articles up to date. I said to Cosgrave: "I am going to set aside all my other literary work and concentrate on this serial. I shall resume my search for new phenomena at once."

He took a personal interest in my plans and not only furnished me the latest authoritative books on the subject but promised to let me know the name of any reliable medium he might discover. The entire editorial staff became for the time psychical students. It was a most interesting and delightful excursion into new territory for them.

II

One day in Cosgrave's office on Union Square he said to me: "A friend of mine, Dr. Turner, has become interested in a young law clerk who is an amazing medium. The doctor wants us to dine with him and afterward witness a performance of this psychic's stunts. His name is Daniel Peters, and Dr. Turner would like our aid in testing his powers."

In this way it happened that a few days later I found myself in Dr. Turner's house, a handsome residence on one of the cross streets which used to have high social significance. The dinner party included three practicing physicians and their wives, and a musician named Potter—a lively, critical group.

During the dinner the question of male mediums came up and I admitted that I had met but few in my experience thus far. Cosgrave asked for an explanation of this. In reply I said substantially this:

"It is true that there are very few men who are willing to give the time and temper to developing this power. Men are more active in habit of mind and body, and far less disposed to make mediumship a means to maintain communication with their dead. In most cases mediums claim to have gone through a long and tedious training in the effort to acquire clairvoyance, clairaudience, independent voices, and independent writing. Materialization is a later and still more exhausting phase. Men who have anything to do decline to go through this training. In all my experience so far I have had but three men who were able and willing to demonstrate any phase of psychic power.

"My theory is that we all have this power in some degree, but its liberation appears to be outside the will. Women are readier to assume this passive attitude. They are more patient during long hours of sitting in the dark. It is easier for them to sit regularly. They have less demand upon their time. They are more emotional, more inclined to make a religion of their revelations. The proportion of men to women in the business of mediumship is not more than one to fifty —so far as my experience goes. It may be that it is one to a thousand. In truth, half the women I talk with on this subject have had what they call 'strange experiences.'

"It is for this reason that I approach with especial interest our sitting with the young man Dr. Turner has provided. I hope he will lend his powers to a scientific investigation."

At a quarter to eight the psychic was announced, and at the request of our host I went out to meet and detain him in the library while a room was being prepared for the séance.

Peters was a small pale young man with extraordinarily brilliant eyes. He was thin and bloodless, weighing (as he confessed) only a little over one hundred pounds, a mere wisp of a man.

"I am lately out of law school," he explained, "and I am one of the many legal assistants in the offices of a big corporation down on Wall Street. My superiors do not know that I am a medium, and I ask you not to use my name in print. They might fire me if they knew what I am doing."

He was plainly very tense, and as he walked to and fro he talked, talked incessantly. His manner was decidedly belligerent and his tone dogmatic. He knew! That he needed careful handling was evident, and I requested his story.

He said: "I have been aware of my power for about four years. My grandfather and a friend named 'Evans' are the ones who most frequently come to me. I have no 'guides'—I don't believe in guides," he added rather contemptuously. "I am not a professional medium. I am a lawyer. Dr. Turner has promised me a fee, but I usually make no charge, although an evening's sitting among strangers takes a lot out of me. I'm not much good next day."

I did not search his pockets, but I looked him over carefully and saw no place in which apparatus of any bulk could be hidden. He was wearing a lightweight short coat, dark trousers, and a knitted waistcoat. I particularly noticed the waistcoat for its odd pattern. Nothing of any weight was in his pockets—of that I made sure—and he carried nothing in his hands as we moved toward the dining room.

The place for the sitting was not especially suitable. It was a reception hall midway between the doctor's office and the dining room, and not only was too large but had more the character of a passageway than a room.

Peters sensed this incongruity at once and expressed his discontent with it but accepted the situation. He arranged our chairs around a small table which had been placed in the center of the hall, and named Dr. Turner as the sitter on his left and placed Mrs. Turner in the chair on his right. This put me out of close contact with him. Cosgrave was not pleased with this but made no objection. I regarded it all as preliminary. On the table were pencils and a pad of writing paper.

After we had all taken our seats, the psychic, who was in full control of the circle, curtly ordered us to clasp hands. He then linked his little fingers with the little fingers of Dr. and Mrs. Turner, and drew their hands down upon his knees. The lights were then turned out, and the room became almost perfectly dark; but in a few moments pale patches of light appeared around the windows.

For half an hour we listened while the doctors asked Peters shrewd questions concerning his muscular reactions and his mental state during a sitting. His replies were intelligent, keenly so, and some of his remarks were worthy of notice. "I seem to leave my body," he said. "When I *think* toward a person, I am there, all around him—inside of him, at times."

In expansion of this idea I then asked, "Are you conscious of your inert body—the body you have left behind?"

"No," he replied, "I look back at it and I am conscious of being in a different place, but *I am not conscious of being in two places at once.*"

In explanation I added: "I asked that question because several mediums have told me that they sometimes see themselves entering a room or lying on a couch but that they are never conscious of being both the man observing and the man entering. Consciousness is always in one place, as you say, never in two places at the same time. . . . Do séances like this affect your health unfavorably?"

"No, they weary me, but no more than a prolonged period of study would do. I am very fond of chess, and I find that I do not play as well the day after a sitting. The only signs of strain at the time are the tremors which come into my arms and legs."

At this point the first sign of psychic power was given, a steady tapping on Mrs. Turner's chair. A few moments later this tapping passed to the table.

"That is the signal of my friend 'Evans,' " Peters announced.

From this point on I began to direct the sitting, addressing "Evans" as a distinct personality. "Will you write for us?" I asked.

He answered by tapping out a vigorous "Yes."

Dr. Turner reported a violent and continuous tremor in the psychic's left arm.

"His right is also trembling," said Mrs. Turner.

Shortly after this the pencils and pad on the table top could be heard moving. A few moments later the sound of sheets being torn from the pad indicated that two hands were at work. One of these sheets was flourished in the air close to my face, more than two yards from the psychic, while Dr. and Mrs. Turner reported firm control of his hands; and a moment later Dr. Turner called out: "A hand is clutching my arm. Fingers are now tapping on my shirt front. There are *two* hands at work around my neck! They are taking off my tie."

"Be sure of your control," I warned.

"It is unchanged," Turner replied. "My little finger is linked with his."

Mrs. Turner now exclaimed: "The hands are now putting the collar around *my* neck—I plainly feel two hands. They are putting the doctor's tie around the collar."

"That cuts out the theory of hypnotism. Please leave the collar and tie where they are."

Shortly after this the man seated next to Turner spoke. "I feel a strong pressure on my arm as if some one were leaning on it."

Turner again spoke. "Hands have unbuttoned my shirt-front. They are stuffing pencils through the opening!"

Others reported hands patting them, but I felt nothing. I pretended to complain of this. "Is there no one here for me?"

"There *is* some one here for you," the psychic replied.

"Write your name," I urged, and immediately thereafter I heard the sound of writing. A sheet of paper was then torn off the pad and thrown across the table into my lap. A moment later something hard struck the table in front of me with a crackle. "What is that?" I asked.

"Those are my cuffs," said Peters. "They often remove my cuffs. They are the old-fashioned starched removable kind."

This suggested one of Zöllner's experiments, and in a spirit of banter I said to the invisible one: " 'Evans,' remove Dr. Turner's vest. If you can do that while the psychic's hands are held, it will parallel some of Alfred Russel Wallace's tests."

Turner reported that the hands which had been at work around him had left him, and Peters immediately called out, "They are working on me! They are taking *my* vest off. Please see that every hand is clasped."

With this warning we tightened our chain of hands, and in less than a minute something soft fell across my knee. I announced this. "I think it is the psychic's vest, but don't break the chain of hands! If this garment which I feel on my knee *is* Peters' vest, we have a phenomenon quite as marvellous as any of Zöllner's."

Dr. Turner then said: "His left little finger is still linked with mine. It has not been free for an instant."

Mrs. Turner added: "There has been no movement in his right arm. His hand trembled but it did not move from mine."

(If the reader thinks it an easy trick to take off his coat while his hands are being held, and while he is sitting between two alert people, let him try it. It is a complicated process even when one is free to use both arms. It is practically impossible to remove one's coat with one hand held. A man's torso writhes violently, his arms flail about, his hands grasp the collar of his coat. One arm must go behind him, he can not shrug himself out of his sleeves. Such movements could not take place without detection. In this case Peters would have been forced to free both hands three times: once to remove his coat, a second time to remove his vest and a third time to put his coat on. The theory of the doubter is that the trickster gradually brings the hands of his control together and induces them to hold each other's fingers while his own hands are freed for other purposes. Assuming that he did this, the clasped hands of the Turners would still be a barrier across his knees and they would instantly feel the motions of his body while writhing out of his coat. Furthermore linking of their own little fingers would naturally cause them to lean still closer to the shoulders of the psychic. We are to suppose also that Dr. Turner could not tell the difference between the little finger of the psychic and the little finger of his wife.)

As all this happened in the dark we now desired something else which could not be laid to hypnotic influence. I said, "I wish the invisible hands would lift the table out of the circle and deposit it on the floor; that would be evidence that we are not hypnotized."

The psychic consented. "They will do this; but every hand must be held firmly, and no one must move. Already, now. Silence! Don't stir!"

With all hands clasped we sat in deep silence waiting. Turner announced an increase in the convulsive tremor of the psychic's limbs. "But his hands are rigidly held."

We could all hear the sound of the psychic's deep breathing as he concentrated all his will power in this supreme effort. Just as he had predicted the removal of Dr. Turner's tie and promised me the removal of his own vest, so now he *commanded* the table to rise.

We heard it rock. He called out, "It is rising. Silence!" And as we listened we heard it drop softly to the floor outside the circle of our clasped hands.

Mrs. Turner said: "It went right over my shoulder. I had to lean away to avoid it. It is standing just back of me."

That this amazing stunt, similar to those which have so often been photographed by European investigators, came at Peters' command was evident. I granted its supernormal character, but Peters *willed* its movement. He could not free his hands and rise from his place to lift it, but his commands, his warnings to keep silence, his deep breathing, and the convulsive tremor in his hands—conditions which the Turners from time to time reported—indicated that in some unexplained way he was the wilful engine in this movement.

That we were not hypnotized was proven by the solid fact that the table was veritably outside the circle when the lights were lit, and that Dr. Turner's collar was about Mrs. Turner's neck.

We returned the table to its former position and again turned out the lights. The psychic then said, "If any one in the circle will *think* of a signature, I will put it on the pad in the center of the table."

He did not say "the spirits will put it on the pad,"

he said, "*I* will put it on the pad." Obviously he regarded this as another action wholly under his control.

Dr. Turner spoke. "I am thinking of a signature."

"Is it outlined in your mind?"

"Yes, I see it clearly."

Almost immediately the sound of writing on the paper in the center of the table could be heard.

Peters then asked, "Is it written?"

As I listened I heard the sheet being torn off. "They are folding it," I said. Raps indicated the completion of the task.

On turning up the lights Dr. Turner found a name written on the pad. "It is my brother's signature," he said. "Exactly as he was accustomed to write it."

The psychic said that he could produce in this way the signature of any one. He did not say that he could distinguish the signature of a dead man but left us to infer that he could. "The only thing necessary is to have a clear picture of it in a living brain."

A surprise was awaiting me. On the sheet of paper which had been ripped off the pad and thrown over the table to me I found the name "Taft" written in the peculiar up-and-down script of my wife's father, Professor Taft. I had not been thinking of him. I had not attempted to visualize his signature, and no one in the circle knew his writing or that he was related to me. There was something inexplicable in this fact.

As for the vest which had been thrown into my lap, it was plainly the one Peters had been wearing when we sat down, and he was now without a vest. If we are to suppose that he took it off before his hands were controlled, it must be said that at the moment it was thrown to me, his hands were in the grip of Dr. and Mrs. Turner. Furthermore I suggested the feat.

We all examined the vest closely. It was not a trick garment. It had no seams up the back or sides. It was a plain, soft, knitted vest. His cuffs, which had been taken off before the vest, were on my side of the table also.

Assume that here was a trick, how shall we explain the lifting of the table out over our heads? He could not have raised this table even with both hands free—but his hands were *not* free.

At the very moment of the table's flight, Dr. Turner and Mrs. Turner both said: "We gripped the psychic with especial determination to prevent movement. His knees trembled, but his hands did not move."

Nevertheless, I had the feeling that all these baffling phenomena somehow came from Peters' organism, reinforced by a force to which all of the sitters contributed.

Peters now rose, saying, "Conditions are so favorable, I shall try to produce some materializations."

Taking his chair in his hand he withdrew into the hall which led to the closed door of the dining room; and at his request we all took seats in a half-circle facing the portières behind which he had disappeared. The room was then darkened as before.

Almost immediately two or three lights like the twisting flames of candles (singular, glowing yet not radiant), violet in color, developed high up along the top of the portières and drifted slowly across, rising toward the ceiling, where they vanished. These were followed by a broad glowing mass of what looked like a white-hot axe blade. It was irregular in shape and about six inches wide. This reminded me of Crookes' report of a similar glowing substance which he declared he had held in his hands.

As this disappeared, a wild whoop startled us. It was as if a roguish boy had opened a door, shouted a word, and slammed the door after him.

This ended the sitting.

III

After the psychic had left the house we fell to a discussion of the puzzling aspects of this performance— for that is what it seemed to be. To me it was less of a novelty than to most of the others, but it presented some entirely new phases. The reader will recall that I had dictated words to be written under glass and on closed slates, and that I had many times witnessed the levitation of objects, some of them in the light; but never had I shared in a sitting wherein a man's vest was removed while both his hands were rigidly controlled.

"I am certain that two hands were operating when my collar and tie were being removed," Turner declared.

"To me," I replied, "the reproduction of the handwriting of my wife's father, Professor Taft, is the most puzzling of all. Taft was a professor of geology— he hated the word 'mystery.' He was intolerant of all spiritualistic discussion. Why should his name be written and tossed to me? I was not thinking of him. He and I were not especially sympathetic. Why should his name come rather than that of my own father?"

The Turners, deeply impressed with the events of

the evening, said to me in parting: "We shall ask this man to come again; and when we do, we want you to meet him at the door, search him, and afterwards take charge of the sitting. We shall have fewer people, and you can use your own methods of control. Make it as decisive as possible."

With this understanding Cosgrave and I went away together. "It was an extraordinary performance," said Cosgrave.

"It was indeed," I replied; "but I shall see that Peters' hands are controlled by something inorganic next time. There is virtue in tape and dental floss."

CHAPTER ELEVEN

MORE ABOUT PETERS

PETERS interested me. I gave a great deal of thought to his performance, which from any point of view was astonishing, and when Dr. Turner invited me to another séance and requested me to take full charge of proceedings, I was quick to accept; and so it happened that I again met our young psychic in the reception room of the Turner home, prepared to search him before he entered the sitting room.

He was less belligerent than at our previous sitting. He was indeed friendly in tone and submitted to my search of his clothing with serenity. He had nothing in his pockets but his handkerchief, a few coins, and his watch—and as I ran my hands over his body I was painfully impressed by his emaciation. He was almost a skeleton. He bore himself with dignity, however, and his replies indicated a very genuine pride in his singular endowment.

As he preceded me into the séance room I made certain that he carried nothing in his hands, and I made certain that nothing bulky was in his pockets. After placing him in an armchair on the same side of the same table as before, I said, "Dr. Turner wishes me to be in control tonight, and I would like to employ dental floss as a manacle."

"Employ anything you like," he retorted.

Taking out my spool of floss, I tied his right wrist to the arm of the chair and also to the left wrist of the young woman who had been given a seat at his right. I did the same with his left wrist which I was to control. His hands had some play in these bonds, but as they were tied to the chair and to me and to my assistant, I felt sure that he could not move objects at a distance. In addition I hooked the little finger of my right hand with the little finger of his left hand.

Almost immediately after the lights were turned out he was seized with a convulsive shiver which shook his whole body; but his hand did not move. Soon a faint, bluish, smokelike cloud developed in front of his chest just below his chin, filling the space between the arms of his chair. Out of this cloud a hand darted, swift as light, and clasped my left wrist firmly but for an instant only. It was a right hand. A moment later this hand came again and ruffled the sleeve of my coat as if to uncover my cuff as a place on which to write a message.

I ask the reader to observe that to do this *normally* the psychic would have been forced not only to break the link of his little finger with that of the alert young woman on his right, but to escape the bond of dental floss and reach entirely across my body to my left wrist. To do this without breaking the thread was impossible. There was not two inches play in the thread and no strain was reported by the girl whose wrist was tied to his.

As if to confound me, this spectral hand then darted out to the center of the table and took up the pad. I could see it at this moment plainly outlined. It possessed, apparently, only three digits. His left hand in my control trembled but did not otherwise move.

At this point he said, "I am thirsty."

We had placed on the table a glass of water but before I could decide to loose my hold and feel for the glass, the spectral hand darted out, seized the goblet, lifted it and brought it to the psychic's lips. I could see the fingers clasping it, and the arm, which was like a dim ray of light, seemed to go out from his bosom. The hand held the glass while the psychic drank. By bending his head he was able to touch his lips to the glass, which was gently tipped for him.

All this was not imagination on my part, for the glass moved and the psychic drank a part of the contents. Furthermore, writing afterward appeared a full yard from the psychic's hands and remained in evidence. It was not imaginary.

Sometimes the phantasmal arm appeared black, sometimes white; but always it appeared to be *a right hand,* although Miss Brown constantly reported no movement in the hand she held and the dental floss remained faithful to its task.

As the glass rose to the psychic's lips, I plainly perceived the arm. It appeared to be clothed in gray vapor and the hand showed only three fingers; but when it grasped my wrist, it was full-fashioned and vigorous. I felt it as distinctly as if it had been a normal hand—and yet the young woman who controlled his hand and to whose wrist he was linked, testified that he had not moved.

As dental floss is very fine, very strong and can not

be untied even in the light, I regarded it as superior to
handcuffs, rope, or cord, as means of control. The
psychic could move his wrists only an inch at most, and
to reach and clasp my left wrist without breaking that
filament meant a sweep of nearly a yard. If there is
any virtue in a silk thread, his hand did not move. True
I may have imagined the handclasp, but the water in the
glass was diminished—that was not imagined.

The sitting was less startling than before, but the
control was rigid and the phenomena wholly inexplicable. The writing on the pad in the middle of the table,
the lifting of the glass of water, and the clasp of that
spectral hand upon my wrist were the outstanding phenomena and are so noted in my diary. Other events
which were repetitions, I did not record.

According to an entry in my diary a month later, I
made a third test of this amazing young man. I quote:

"Determined to increase my control, I drew the
sleeves of his coat tight around his wrists and *nailed them
to his chair-arm* with long upholstery tacks. In addition
to this I used again the dental floss, and yet, while Dr.
Turner himself held one hand and I the other, spectral
arms developed before the psychic's breast, writing
appeared on a pad in the middle of the table and as a
climax, the psychic's undershirt was removed and
tossed across the table!

"Not much happened, but what did happen was
under rigid test conditions."

This brief but authentic note (made immediately
after my return to my hotel) covers a most astounding
performance—one which requires extended comment.

Again for the third time I had met Peters in the hall

and searched him to see that he carried nothing bulky to the séance room. Determined to make it absolutely impossible for him to lift his arms one inch from the chair, I had brought the cuffs of his coat tight about his wrists and had driven down through the double fabric two long upholstery nails. In addition I had again used the dental floss, and as a further control Dr. Turner and I had linked our fingers with his— and yet, according to my report written immediately afterward, his undershirt had been tossed across the table!

Assume that he had this garment concealed in a pocket. How could he draw it out and toss it across the table? He could not draw those tacks and reset them! To untie that thread and retie it with my control of his hands was normally impossible.

On the other hand, consider what is involved in the alternative. He must not only pull those tacks, free his fingers from our control, but rise in his seat, remove his coat, his vest, his white shirt, and then *draw his undershirt off over his head.*

Having done all this, he must replace his shirt, button it, put on his collar and tie, resume his coat, renail his sleeves to his chair, reinsert his wrists in the floss, and restore his fingers to our grip—all in a few seconds' time!

"How was it done?" you ask.

I don't know. I can only report the facts. Some would say it was due to the power which the East Indian jugglers use in their performances. That it was directed by Peters himself, I am quite certain. I can not conceive that it was done with any religious or philosophic intent. We were asking for astounding physical phenomena, and "Evans" gave them to us.

I submit that on its lowest terms this performance is amazing. I repeat the problem: A frail little man comes into a strange house, is searched by an investigator of much experience; his sleeves are nailed to the arms of his chair, and his hands are held in close grip by two determined men. And yet, despite all these precautions, these preventive measures, this man duplicates signatures which he has never seen, develops a powerful supernumerary hand which darts about like a serpent's tongue, and finally causes his undershirt to be tossed across the table.

I can not say that he was wearing this undershirt when I bound his hands; but that he was without an undershirt at the close of the sitting I can testify, for I went with him to the library and saw him strip to his bare torso and put the garment on over his head.

While he was resuming his clothes he said to me: "I sit every Sunday evening for my own family. Come down and see what happens. No one else but my wife and mother will be present."

This I promised to do.

(At the moment I thought this performance unique, but later I found in an essay by Alfred Russel Wallace the description of a precisely similar "trick." During a test séance with Davenport and Fay, two famous mediums of the seventies, a coat was taken from one of the bound men and put upon another man also bound. Furthermore the coat was photographed in flight. As in my test the motive in their case was, apparently, to puzzle the investigators by doing the impossible, just as with Zöllner the psychic astounded his investigator by linking solid rubber rings and steel handcuffs. Such feats of magic have only an indirect bearing on the spirit hypotheses, but they may be taken as an evidence of the fourth dimension.)

In accepting Peters' invitation to join his Sunday evening family circle, I had no anticipation of anything more than the usual dark sitting in which devoted believers hold intercourse with their dead. I did hope, however, for a candid talk with Peters during which I might learn more of his singular power.

He met me at the station, and as we walked up the leafy street of a commonplace little village, we discussed his mediumship quite frankly.

He admitted that it was a physical strain. "I find my office work difficult the day after a sitting. That is why I seldom sit for strangers. My Monday forenoons are always draggy, but my wife regards these Sunday circles as a kind of religious ceremony and I hate to disappoint her and her family."

His home was a small apartment in the second story of a detached frame house, and as the night was warm, the windows were all open. The group consisted of Mrs. Peters, her daughter (a girl of twelve), her mother, and a young Pole—a personal friend of the psychic.

The front bedroom, an alcove which led from this room, had a window but no door. Peters insisted on my searching this room. This I did, but found nothing to suspect. The window was open and looked down upon the sidewalk some ten feet below.

Two oil lamps, one at the piano and the other on a

small table, furnished the light. After the Pole, the old woman, and I had taken seats in a row against the wall, Mrs. Peters went to the piano. The little girl reclined on a bench by the open window. She was in full view all the time.

Placing a chair in the alcove, Peters drew the portières of the alcove, shutting himself behind them. Mrs. Peters then blew out one of the lamps and turned the other low. I could see her dimly as she began softly to play the piano, but as it was all in the nature of a family ceremony and not in any sense a test séance, I made no objection to the absence of control. I was merely a visitor and expected nothing important.

After a few moments' silence, I observed a cloud of glowing vapor slowly forming on the floor just in front of the portières. It resembled, as it rose, a cone of fire-lit steam, like that which rolls from a locomotive smoke-stack on a winter morning. It expanded as it slowly rose, and at last out of it the dim figure of a man emerged. He spoke in a foreign tongue, and I observed that his voice resembled that of the psychic. The Pole who sat beside me on the couch called out, "It is my brother!"

Then to Mrs. Peters he said, "Play the Polish National Hymn."

She complied, and as the hymn swelled out the Pole began to sing—if a husky tuneless moan can be called singing. It was evident that he had no sense of pitch, and when the phantom joined in the chant I noted that his voice *exhibited precisely the same lack of tune.* He, too, was unmusical. It was as if the "spirit" were a duplication of the Pole, and I said to myself, "The Pole is singing with his double." The spiritualist would say, "He was singing with his reincarnate brother," and perhaps he was.

This form then faded out, and another, supposedly a materialization of "Evans," the psychic's guide, took his place. This dimly seen figure appeared enveloped in a cloud of vapor, but his voice was distinct.

At his invitation I went forward to shake hands with him. He seemed taller than the psychic, but his manner of speech was distinctly similar to that of Peters. I could not see his face.

The hand he offered me was draped in an exceedingly fine, faintly shining material, cobwebby in texture, which appeared to melt away between my fingers and his. The hand was narrow and pointed. I felt its bones for a moment. When I released it the figure vanished like a bubble. It made no sound when it appeared and none as it disappeared. One instant it was there, the next instant it was not.

The psychic then called from the alcove, "More light!"

Mrs. Peters then turned up the wick of the oil lamp till I could see all the persons and all the furniture in the room; and when a few minutes later the psychic reappeared in front of the portières, I could see him plainly, even to the color of his necktie. In fact the light in the room was quite as strong as the usual lighting of a cottage. I could follow every movement he made, and I located Mrs. Peters and the little girl. The Pole and the old lady were seated beside me.

Peters appeared distraught. His face was white, and his hair rumpled. Taking a position about six feet from the center of the portières, he called sharply, "Come out!" His voice was commanding in tone, like that of an officer addressing a subordinate.

Suddenly, silently, and apparently without displacing the folds of the curtain, the form of a man appeared outside the portières and stood at attention like a soldier. He wore a turban of gray-white material, and his body was draped in the same filmy stuff. His shoulders were broad and well shaped, and his head and face clearly defined. His nose and chin were firm and manly, but I could not discern his eyes. His knees did not show, and although his drapery did not touch the floor he had no perceptible feet. He gave the impression of a form suspended—unfinished—in the air and yet with bulk.

Whether the psychic commanded him to greet me or not, I can not now recall, but the phantom (as if to show that he was alive) bowed to me three times gracefully, slowly, and solemnly, while the psychic with both his hands outstretched and with bent, trembling legs, crept slowly toward the figure. At the same time the phantom moved toward the psychic as if drawn by some magnetic force. They met in the center and appeared to coalesce like two drops of mercury. The figure vanished seemingly into the body of the psychic who reeled backward through the curtains and fell like a log on the floor.

The portières resumed their position, but one of his feet projecting from beneath the drapery gave evidence for some minutes of his prostration.

None of the family seemed disturbed. The wife at the piano played softly one of her husband's favorite tunes, and a few minutes later he reappeared outside the curtains, looking pale, weary, and bewildered but quite normal in speech and manner.

This experience standing alone has little value; but coming after my many experiments with ectoplasmic hands and arms, I considered it worth recording along with his testimony.

He said: "I held the form just as long as I could in order that you might study it. I held it till my legs felt hollow. I could feel the force go out from my forehead and from my solar plexus, and then I collapsed."

Mrs. Peters did not consider it an especially notable exhibition. "We often have much more powerful manifestations. One night a huge figure almost naked, a tremendous athlete, came out through the portières holding Daniel like a baby on his uplifted palms. Sometimes the voices which come shake the walls."

As I sat listening to these incredible tales I could hear the katydids snoring outside in the trees. The little girl was still sitting in bored silence at the open window. That they all believed in their phantasmal visitors and considered them celestial in origin, was evident. The doubter will say, "It was all a skillful arrangement of sheets and wires"; and I can not prove it otherwise, although at the moment I believed in the honesty of the psychic. After all, it was in harmony with the reports of Crookes and Richet.

Peters walked down to the station with me, subdued and rather silent. I said to him: "I believe in you, but that phantasmal visitor was not wholly convincing. I can not make report of this evening's work as I shall do with your sittings at Turner's. I would like your co-operation in a series of thoroughly scientific electrical and mechanical tests. Would you consider such a series?"

After a moment's thought, he gravely replied, "Yes, I'll go into such a series of experiments provided you will take out a ten-thousand-dollar policy on my life in favor of my wife."

"That is only fair," I agreed. "I will take the matter up with Cosgrave tomorrow."

On the following day I reported this talk to Cosgrave and his editors. "I believe in this man, but we must consider the dangers in such a trial. He is very frail; he might at any moment expire under test. Can't you imagine the newspaper headline: 'Psychic Expires Under Garland's Hands'? I'm not inclined to take the risk."

Cosgrave concurred with me, and I wrote to Peters saying, "We have decided not to make the experiment."

Thus ended my experiences with this singular and amazing person. I never saw him again.

A year or two later, when in the city, I tried to get in touch with him but failed. I could not find him in the telephone list nor in the city directory. Letters sent to his old address came back to me. Whether he had returned to his Southern home, or had died under trance, I never knew.

CHAPTER TWELVE

THE HIDDEN UNIVERSE

ONE of the commonest observations made to me, and one usually spoken with a sigh is this: "Nothing mysterious ever happens where I am."

To most men and women the earth is a good, dependable, but rather commonplace old ball. They find the soil firm under their feet. Clouds gather over their heads, and rains fall. Men walk behind their plows or wield hammers in their shops while their women go about their household duties with no sense of the hidden forces at work around them. Reporters and editors busied with news are liable to the same misconception even in the midst of an incessant clamor of accidents and crimes. Whatever is habitual is true but dull.

Murder, robbery, divorce are all in the day's work.— "Mankind is like that," they say. But stories of haunted houses, poltergeists, and phantasms of the living are different matters altogether. "They simply don't happen."

I will not say that the editors of *Everybody's Magazine* doubted the existence of the hidden world, but I am quite certain that they were amazed by the mass of letters and detailed reports of inexplicable happenings

176

which fell upon their desks as a result of my serial "The Shadow World."

Many of these manuscripts were addressed to me, but as it was impossible for me to read even a tenth part of them I asked that they be turned over to subordinates for classification.

"The most important fact about these letters," said Cosgrave, "is their agreement on all essential points. They show that a perception of the occult world is more general than any of us had suspected. The most illogical of these happenings are reported from opposite ends of the earth. One story confirms another. It is an astounding revelation of hidden forces. I'd like you to give thought to the best way in which to make use of this material."

In a conference with Baker and Hall, I suggested that it would be amusing to offer a prize for the best authenticated report of a metaphysical or metapsychical happening, and Cosgrave named me as the final judge to whom the best of the stories should be referred.

The announcement of this competition was followed by another astounding wave of correspondence. Bulky manuscripts began to arrive, each one accompanied by sheaves of affidavits from local authorities, all vouching for the story or certifying to the reliability of the writer.

"How can we authenticate the authenticators?" I asked when the stories were turned over to me.

With true editorial craft Cosgrave replied: "It is not necessary that we enter a court of law to prove that affidavits are fraudulent. After all, our job is to hold the interest of our readers in this subject for a few months longer."

I have on my desk the original copy of the call for these tales, and some of the manuscripts just as they went to the printer; and as I read them now, in the light of my later experience, I do not find them impossible of credence.

One of my reports is headed, "The Poltergeist," and reads as follows:

"At the bottom of every tradition there is a kernel of truth. The almost universal belief in ghosts, from the earliest times to the present, would seem to indicate that there is a real basis for such a belief. As Richet says, 'Tradition on the whole has not been deceived. The occult world exists. At the risk of being looked upon by my contemporaries as a fool, I believe that *phantoms* exist, and that they are the basis of the belief in ghosts.' "

Commenting on this, I went on to say: "I have never seen a ghost, but if there is any value in human testimony, there are times and places when phantoms in human shapes have veritably manifested themselves, with startling vividness. Men and women of all ages and all countries attest this. The mass of evidence in support of ghosts is enormous.

"These uneasy spirits wandering dim halls dragging clanking chains, uttering groans of agony, these invisible beings with echoing footsteps at midnight—all seem to be connected with murder, robbery or some other act of violence. Some of the phantoms are evil doers, some are the victims—but always they are connected with injustice."

One of the ghost stories sent in to us was so circumstantial in detail and so natural, even in its mysteries, that I put it high on the list of eligibles for the prize. It was written by a Chicago newspaper woman whom I had met and whose reputation for accurate reporting was excellent. Her story told of a haunted house in which she had lived for several years, and after recording the usual details of doors mysteriously opening and shutting, bells ringing, and the like, she wrote:

"The ghost in this case was the former owner and occupant of the place, who always appeared in a seedy Prince Albert frock coat while in the sitting room but when seen in the basement or kitchen dressed like a workingman. He came and went so often that we accepted him as an occupant. We merely said, 'There's old Lane again,' and turned to our reading."

The particular event which interested me was reported to Mrs. Ford by her housekeeper, a middle-aged woman who slept in an upper story of the house. Her first duty of a morning was to go down to the basement, shut the furnace door, and open its drafts. "One very cold morning as she lay dreading the task—so she stated —'I thought of our ghost. I said, "Old Lane, if you were any use in the world you'd shut that furnace door for me." No sooner had I spoke when *bang* went the furnace door, and in a few minutes I could feel the warm air coming up.'

"Did you ever before hear of a ghost doing a *useful* deed like that?" asked the writer of the article.

I never did, and it was this kindly practical action on the part of the ghost (with several others equally natural) which gave Mrs. Ford's story its most unusual character.

"We often saw him on the stairs," she went on to relate, "or in the kitchen always wearing a velvet skullcap, a brown corduroy jacket and shabby trousers, the costume (as we afterward learned) which he had habitually worn in the house, but when we saw him in the drawing room he wore a black suit with frock coat." In short, as a ghost, he was governed by a sense of propriety as when in the flesh. A most remarkable ghost.

Mrs. Ford's explanation involved the mediumistic powers of her housekeeper. "We came to feel that Mr. Lane was a beneficent presence always ready for a kindly response to any demand within his power. He seemed to prefer the basement and kitchen which he seemed always inspecting."

This story interested and amused us all, but the manuscript which won first prize was the vivid account of a series of rather horrifying events in a circle of psychic experimenters in Nashville, Tennessee. The reporter in this case was Itta K. Reno, well known in the city, who stated that their sittings were wholly private with no professional medium present. Her report, accompanied by voluntary affidavits from several distinguished citizens, reached a most startling climax. She stated that after a large number of sittings a beast of unknown sort made itself heard and felt beneath the table around which she and her friends were sitting.

I have not the manuscript at hand and can only write of it from memory, but one of the chief events remains in my mind.

Mrs. Reno went on to say that a well-known lawyer in the town not only scoffed at their reports but truculently said: "Let me come into your circle. I defy any phantasmal beast to manifest in my presence."

He went, and in the midst of the séance (a dark séance) some one called out: "There is a huge cat under the table, I feel its paw on my knee."

Another said: "It is not a cat—it is a dog. I felt it brush against my legs."

With a snort of derision, the lawyer sceptic replied, "I'm going to prove that there's neither cat nor dog under the table."

Getting down on the floor he began to feel about with his hand. Suddenly, with a yell, he scrambled to his feet, caught up his hat, and rushed from the house. On the following day he explained his panic. "A huge hairy beast hurled itself against me—a brute of enormous power. It followed me all the way home."

(Some months later, while lunching with Judge John M. Dickinson of Nashville, I mentioned Mrs. Reno and told this story. He said: "I knew that group, and I know the lawyer who fought the phantom. He confessed that he had been chased to his home by the beast.")

Up to this date I had received no well authenticated stories of the materializations of animals; but one came in from New Orleans. A woman asserted that she had held in her lap, during a séance, the materialized form of a favorite cat. Later reports from Paris described the photographing of strange animal forms during certain test circles of experts. A great bird was photographed with outstanding wings, sitting on the head of a psychic.

These stories of animal phantasms gave me a great deal of thought. "If a cat or dog can be materialized in a séance," I said to Cosgrave, "then any bird or animal can be materialized. Such thought-forms invalidate the theory of immortality. If a favorite cat can be thus re-created, then a pet canary, a horse, or any creature definitely thought upon and wished for, may be brought into the circle."

Our third prize went to a story in which an officer of a steamship related his experience with a phantasmal messenger. This story, which I must also quote from memory, was substantially as follows:

While on his way to Japan, and when his ship was about three hundred miles from Seattle this captain late at night had occasion to go to his office for a paper of some sort. "As I entered the door I was amazed to find a man seated at my desk. He was writing and seemed not aware of me. I saw him plainly. He was a powerful figure in uniform, evidently first mate of a ship.

"As I stepped toward him he vanished; and I thought of him as a vivid hallucination till I reached my desk and found there words plainly written: 'We are in distress. Steer northeast—one hundred miles. Hurry—we are sinking.'

"This vision so wrought upon me that I turned from our course and steered northeast as requested. After sailing for several hours we came in sight of a vessel in distress, and on boarding her I was met by the man of my vision—his exact double."

My recollection is that the officer of the disabled vessel assured the captain that he had no consciousness of being a phantasmal messenger, but that he had gone to sleep while greatly troubled about the fate of his ship. While mentally seeking for help he was wholly unaware of being in the other man's stateroom. In this case the ghost was the phantasm of a living man.

There are many other stories which seem to prove that phantasms of the living are possible. I have never witnessed such a phenomenon, but cases are reported where the psychic seems able to leave his body and visit distant chambers, describing what he sees there. But when an officer of a vessel visits another one hundred miles away and writes a warning, remaining unconscious of the act, we have an entirely different problem. The most unusual character of this manuscript gave it high place.

These authenticated tales proved that hundreds of thousands of the readers of my serial believed in an occult world, and were prepared to testify to personal experiences which revealed it. However, to these people, to most people, the birth of a chick, the change of a tadpole into a frog were commonplace everyday events. Only when a hammer moved by itself or a cannon ball fell from the ceiling, did they begin to marvel at the mysteries which make up life.

Many of the wonder tales which came in related the absurd antics of poltergeists. One long report from Virginia (authenticated by the village priest, the local doctor, and the justice of the peace) was so mad, so illogical in its sequences that no one could imagine them. Showers of nails and rusty bolts dropped upon two young girls in their beds. A cannon ball fell from the ceiling upon the stairs and remained there! Tools and horseshoes, taken from a distant blacksmith shop, hung themselves on nails in the kitchen, and many other equally absurd tricks were played.

Another story equally fantastic came from a Colorado ranch, where in the flash of an eye a dinner cloth, fully covered with dishes and food was swept from the table out into the yard. The cloth was found later, wound deep in a churn filled with buttermilk. Stones fell from the ceiling, and dishes flew about like a flock of scared hens.

In the *Annals of Psychical Science* many such tales were recounted, and Lombroso the alienist was sent out to investigate. He saw the pranks played, but could give no explanation of them. As I read his report I began to wonder whether ancient stories of witches, kobolds, leprechauns, and fairies may not have sprung from some such mediumistic pranks as these manuscripts reported.

With the awarding of those prizes, the editors of *Everybody's* closed the pages of the magazine to any further psychic discussion. This was a wise decision, but I for one secretly regretted the close of an intensely interesting review of the Hidden World. It had been a revelation of the universe of wonder which lies beneath the humdrum sod of ordinary life as "The Land of the Shee" underlies the bogs and fields of Ireland.

CHAPTER THIRTEEN

SIGNS OF PSYCHIC PROGRESS

As soon as these articles of mine had finished their course in *Everybody's Magazine,* I offered them to Harper and Brothers for publication in book form. They were accepted and put on the market in 1908 under the title "The Shadow World."

Their text was substantially the same as that which ran in the magazine. Each chapter was an after-dinner conversation dealing with the various phases of spiritistic phenomena, but in my foreword I assured the readers that the book was a faithful record of my experiences.

"For literary purposes I have substituted fictitious names for the men and women concerned but I have not allowed these necessary expedients to interfere with the precise truth of the reports. My aim throughout has been to deal directly and simply with the facts involved."

Nearly three years had elapsed since the publication of my novel "The Tyranny of the Dark," and a wish to again sound out the opinions of the academic scholars and experts led my publishers to mail advance copies to a list of biologists, physicists, and other scientific experts and instructors with a request for a frank statement of opinion. In this way we hoped to discover whether the interest shown in 1904 had increased or diminished.

The response was immediate and on the whole favorable, and in the belief that a chapter dealing with these replies may have historical value, I here pause in my personal story and include some of the more significant of the letters.

My old friend Flower, editor of the *Arena*, in whose home several of the most important séances described in these pages had been held, was one of the first to reply. He enclosed a review which he had written. Of this I quote a paragraph or two in confirmation of my own report:

"As one of the group of investigators who witnessed much of what Mr. Garland has described as taking place in the presence of Mrs. Smiley, I can testify to the accuracy of his descriptions of what happened. I knew that Mr. Garland was making extended notes, and this doubtless accounts for his clear and detailed narration of the extraordinary phenomena in the presence of the psychic, who, it will be remembered, came to us at her own expense, gave the sittings without a cent of pay, and urged us to make the test conditions as conclusive and satisfactory as we desired.

"In Mr. Garland's work we have the graphic description of a series of séances held in the homes of well-known citizens under far more conclusive test conditions than usually obtained in what are known as 'dark' séances.

"The character of the persons constituting the group, the precautions taken to render it impossible for the psychic to rise from her chair or use her hands in any

way, and the almost incredible phenomena that occurred, Mr. Garland has here given, interspersed with
discussions by prominent members of the group (in
which the opinions of various eminent psychical investigators of the Old World and the New are quoted), the
whole forming the most popular presentation of certain
psychic phenomena, together with views and explanations advanced by world-famous savants, that has yet
been published."

This review is especially valuable to me for the reason
that it endorses my own account of sittings in the
Flower home.

A most significant letter came from my colleague
Amos E. Dolbear, still professor of physics at Tufts
College, who quaintly said: "Glad enough to see some
evidence of your continued existence. That neither
'Wilbur' nor others have carried you off. Though it
would please me to learn that he or 'Mitchel' were doing
something today—some of that work was good enough
for a story and I am glad you think it worth while. I
can't remember that anything said had any significance
to Mrs. Dolbear or myself. I didn't make out how some
of the things were done. For instance, how the books,
24 of 'em, got off the shelves without Mrs. Smiley's hands
being free, *she was tied good*."

In another letter he admitted that there was an un-
solved mystery in the bringing of the candy box from a
shelf behind him to Mrs. Dolbear at her request. In all
his cogitation he found no answer to the puzzle.

William James delighted me with his frank endorsement:

"I have just read every word of the book, and find the

execution very good indeed. I must say that I envy you your privileges in the way of finding such good mediums in private life. Some people seem to strike it fat in that regard, others lean. I, alas! am one of the lean ones.

"The condition of opinion as regards 'physical phenomena' is really a scandal. Morselli's book, one would think, might settle it—I have read only the account in the *Annals of Psychical Science.* . . . I feel morally convinced—that is I would *bet* heavily—that the future will corroborate all this 'teleplasty' etc. as a field of real experience surrounding the acknowledged order of nature, and of tremendous cosmic import, whatever the import may be.

"I am also positively persuaded that mentally we dip our roots into a pool where minds communicate by gleams and flashes, but I have no plausible hypothesis as to the *organization* of the pool, whether it contains spirits or not, and if so, of how many sorts."

It was, however, in the judgments of the scientific men and heads of college departments in physics and biology, that I found a most decided change of feeling toward the entire shadowy universe which my book presented. I turned with especial interest to the letters which bore a university note-head. Most of the writers were surprisingly tolerant. Not one of them made vehement protest.

One which came to me in the first group may be taken as representative of many others. That the writer should have read the book at all was indication of a changing attitude.

Writing from the department of physics in a great university, this correspondent said:

"Concerning phenomena such as you describe, I feel sure that we can no longer consider them *all* fraudulent —there are too many careful observations by honorable men—we must accept some of them as facts. That these facts are due to the action of the returning dead, I can not believe, and I welcome any biological or physical theory which may serve as a working hypothesis."

Other communications of like significance followed. Another university instructor found himself able to confess that he had given careful thought to it.

"The results of your investigations concerning spiritistic phenomena are certainly remarkable, but after some personal experience which I have had in studying hypnotism and mind reading, *I am quite prepared to accept your results as genuine facts of science.* [The italics are mine.]

"After thinking over your explanation of the phenomena, it seems to me very probable that you have given the correct interpretation. You have done an excellent piece of scientific work, and I am convinced that it belongs to the realm of biology."

Another biologist in a Western university wrote:

"My own attitude could easily be stated, with great accuracy, by certain passages from your book; so what's the use! You probably understand my point of view better than I do myself, since you have formulated it, while I have not.

"I have no first-hand knowledge of the subject but I am sure that it is time to give it a more serious and sustained consideration than has hitherto been the case. Moreover the conclusions of men such as those mentioned by you are entitled to a careful study.

"Finally, your view that we have here a corner of the field of 'unexplored human biology' is, I think, the correct view. I should be strongly inclined to stick to this on general principles. Your arguments, however, to show that there is a 'natural' connection of some sort between the 'spirits' and the participants in the séance are very suggestive. They are, I doubt not, along the right lines. In some way or other the phenomena are determined by our own minds. But this is as far as I can go."

The predicament in which many specialists found themselves at that time is delicately and humorously outlined in the following letter from my friend Jewett, whose work is along the line of "applied psychology" —whatever that may mean. He, too, is connected with a state university.

"I am well aware that if one made ever so little a start towards the type of data which you regard as proper and adequate, one would stop only when there was nothing more or less plausible than anything else. So I am most careful about that first step."

I did not go so far as to call this man's attitude that of a shirker, but he was taking the easiest way out. By evading the subject he was avoiding controversy and possibly the opposition of his superiors in office.

Edison put the investigation aside for commercial reasons. "I am an inventor," he said, "not a scientific investigator." A professor of psychology, however, can not say that psychic phenomena are not in his field.

One of the most interesting of these academic confessions was written by a man who had been assistant in the department of physics at Harvard University but who had later taken up the practice of medicine and as a physician was able to speak his mind. He forecast some of the uses of photography in the examination of certain phenomena. "If someone with means could be interested to fit up a proper laboratory I believe that the next decade could be made an epoch in physics as well as psychics."

Many similar judgments came to me at this time, all clearly indicating a change in academic science which was much more general than our university heads cared to admit. One writer made a direct suggestion of procedure: "It would seem to me that yourself or someone familiar with the methods of such investigation, should give general directions in some well-known place for conducting such trials."

Here was the end toward which all my work had been directed, and which was the underlying purpose of my book. "These phenomena should be studied by skilled men of science in their own laboratories—just as any other biological fact is studied."

Religious teachers were less ready to accept the biologic theory. Thomas R. Slicer, a distinguished pulpiteer, asked this very pertinent question:

"My query with respect to the spiritistic hypothesis has always been this: Supposing it were possible to communicate with a so-called 'other world,' how can such messages be proved to be *from* that 'world' when their reception is conditioned upon the terms of *this* world? I can only become aware of anything in terms of my own consciousness, so that as soon as I am aware of a communication from any source it is no longer from another world but from this. [This is a very important admission.]"

From I. K. Funk, head of Funk & Wagnalls Company, came a gentle rebuke:

"Your 'Shadow World' is an able and fair presentation of a very difficult subject; but personally it seems to me that we are demanding the impossible when we ask for a demonstration by a spirit of his identity and at the same time hold telepathy to be a possible explanation. We do not, I fear, give the ghost 'a ghost of a chance.' "

My friend William Stead in London, editor of *Review of Reviews,* uttered a stronger protest:

"I do not in the least object to your concentrating upon physical phenomena. It appeals to you and I have no doubt it will appeal to a very great number of people. I know these things can happen and having once satisfied myself on that head I do not wish to verify my ready reckoner again. I want to use it for doing sums with."

Among these letters were several confessions from those who had discovered strange powers in themselves. They asked for guidance in the development and use of these forces, and to these I gave careful consideration. From one such medium I received this highly suggestive statement:

"In some twenty years of experiment I have only twice been able to catch a glimpse of my own astral self. I have sometimes had the feeling that my arms and hands were being duplicated outside my physical body. Some six or seven times there has appeared at my side an exact duplicate of my physical self from six inches to a foot away, and this second body followed exactly whatever movements I might make. I have resolved each time that I would speak to this apparition *but in its presence I have never been able to utter a word.*

"This experience happens without any act of will on my part and is always entirely unforeseen. It has always happened in the evening and on the street near my home.

"*I have had the piano play without contact* once when I was ten feet from the instrument and at another time when I was in an adjoining room. I did not feel that I myself was playing the piano nor that my hands were elongated. The sounds in the piano seemed due to *forces outside of myself.*"

I wrote to this man proposing some test sittings and he replied agreeably:

"While I should be willing to undertake the photographic test you ask for, I wish distinctly to say that it has never been possible for me to guarantee the nature or extent of any manifestation at any particular time. Whatever happens seems to arise from a combination of circumstances beyond human control."

No more appropriate close to this series of letters can be made than to include a letter from one of the psychics whose phenomena I had most carefully tested and recorded.

Mrs. Hartley wrote to thank me for the book and for the fair account I had given of her sittings. "It is indeed a faithful record of all that you received from the other world through me. I shall be pleased to recommend the book to my friends."

CHAPTER FOURTEEN

THE INVISIBLE COMPOSER

ONE afternoon in 1907, at the home of a friend in Chicago, I met a woman of striking appearance who was introduced to me as "the most marvellous psychic in all America." Having been called upon many times to test out similar claims, I greeted this wonder-worker genially but without enthusiasm.

Her name was not Hartley, but I shall call her that. She was a handsome woman, sturdy of frame, with a broad brow and fine dark eyes, but the quality which interested me most was the gravity of her expression. She was not exactly forbidding, but she made no effort to ingratiate herself. She faced me with unsmiling glance and frowning brow but surprised me by saying: "I have read your 'Tyranny of the Dark,' and I want to tell you that I found it so like my own case that I was amazed. You couldn't have kept closer to the story of my life as a girl if you had taken it down in short-hand."

Thanking her for the compliment intended, I replied, "The novelist is necessarily something of a psychic." I further won her confidence by telling her that my mother and one of my aunts had suffered, for a short time, a similar martyrdom in their girlhood.

"I am deeply interested in what our mutual friend, Mrs. McDevitt, has told me of your phase, and I would like to have you coöperate with me in a series of experiments. It may be that my powers would supplement yours."

To this she responded with blunt candor: "I am in Chicago on a visit, and I will not sit for any one while here. Furthermore, I am not a public medium. I sit only for my friends—or for such people as are sent to me by friends."

She softened her refusal, however, by saying, "If you are ever in my home city, let me know, and I will ask my guides to give you a sitting."

That she was alertly on her guard was evident, and as I won her confidence she gave a reason for it. "I am a widow with a twelve-year-old son, and I can not afford to become a newspaper sensation. I must be careful. You understand that, don't you?" she ended with an appealing note in her voice.

"I understand perfectly, and you can trust me. I am not one of these 'experts' who know it all before they begin. I have had many years' experience, and I grant some of the phenomena; but I am always in search of new phases of mediumship."

"I have read your books and I am prepared to trust you," she replied, and we parted with a definite agreement to try out her powers at her own home.

The impression which she made on me was so favorable to my purpose that I wrote at once to a good friend who lived near her in the same city: "Do you know a Mrs. Hartley who is reputed to be a powerful medium?"

In reply my friend wrote: "Yes, I've known Mrs. Hartley since she was a schoolgirl. She is well regarded here and all of my friends who have had sittings with her, report the most amazing phenomena. Why not visit us for a week and test out her powers?"

Notwithstanding this invitation and the most alluring reports of Mrs. Hartley's "phase" I did not find time to carry out this plan till 1908. My "Shadow World" was being written. In my record of this visit I find these words: "Nov. 10. As a guest of John and Mary Judah I received last night a detailed report of Mrs. Hartley. She is the daughter of a skilled mechanic and lives in a small cottage not far from the Judahs. She is respected as a woman, but her social world is not that to which my hosts belong. Mrs. Judah urges me to see her. 'Her sittings are all in the light. She does not go into trances—so I am told. My friends say that she is intelligent and perfectly sincere.' I shall see her tomorrow."

John Judah, who was something of a theosophist as well as a successful business man, was inclined to smile at my interest in Mrs. Hartley's "independent voices."

"Such phenomena are rudimentary, on the lower levels of thought," he said. But Mrs. Judah was entirely sympathetic with my purpose. "I will go with you and arrange a sitting."

Mary Jameson Judah, the daughter of Dr. Jameson, one of the pioneer physicians of the region, was Booth Tarkington's aunt. She was distinctly of the "first families," and a most intelligent woman. I greatly valued her friendship and welcomed her aid.

We found Mrs. Hartley's home to be a small frame cottage in one of the humbler sections of the city. The house was neatly kept, and while its furnishings were not beautiful, they were in no sense mean or sordid. The psychic met us composedly and promised a sitting on the following morning at eleven. "Bring your slates," she said, "and write on a sheet of paper the names of those with whom you wish to communicate."

Her manner was almost repellent. Her brow was dark, and her glance watchful. Had it not been for her words at our former meeting, I would have called her suspicious. She did not smile during our call.

On the way home Mrs. Judah said: "Mrs. Hartley has many 'notions,' one of which is a belief in the influence of flowers. She insists on having them near her. She imagines they help her produce the writing. I'll provide you with a bouquet for her desk."

Early the following morning with a few choice roses and a pair of new folding slates in my hands, I set out for the psychic's house. On the way I dropped into the University Club and on a sheet of its paper wrote these words: "Edward, write a few bars from one of your unpublished manuscripts to establish your identity, and for M's sake."

"Edward" was intended for my friend Edward Mac-Dowell, the composer, who had died a few months before. I had been much with him toward the end of his life, and my mind was filled with vivid memories of him. He had been for many years one of my most valued friends, and I thought this an excellent opportunity to test whether his personality could be brought into the séance in any way.

That this was an important test, will be granted, for while Mrs. Hartley may have read of my friendship with MacDowell, and of the fact that I had been with him

during his sickness, there was no possibility of her knowing any of his unpublished compositions. She was not
one to know even his published work.

She greeted me as before, smilelessly, and at once led
me to her study, a bright little second-story room on the
morning side of the house. It was simply furnished
with bookshelves, a desk and two or three chairs. A
battered old walnut table, which seemed entirely out of
key with the other furnishings, stood in the middle of
the floor.

She explained: "For many years I have used that table
for my sittings. I began my work with it, and the forces
insist on my continuing to use it. They have been very
rough with it lately and have banged it around till it is
almost falling apart. They won't let a carpenter touch
it, however. They say it must not have any nails or
screws in it."

"May I examine it?" I asked.

After a moment's hesitation she replied, "Yes."

Following an examination of it I assured her that I
could repair it for her. "I can tie it together and glue
it, if your guides will permit such repair."

Again she seemed to listen to an inward voice. "I wish
you would," she replied with friendlier tone.

As she watched me working she became almost genial,
and when I had restored the piece to a fairly stable
condition, she thanked me. I understood her reluctance
to its being handled by an outsider, and humored her
belief that metal of any kind would change its character.
(What do we know about matter, anyhow?)

When the stand was steady on its feet I called her
attention to the new slates which I had brought. "I

have already written a note and placed it between these slates. I should like to put them under my foot just as I brought them into your house and see what will happen."

She was not as yielding as I had expected her to be. She coldly said, "My guides say that you will get nothing unless I have passed my hands over the inner surfaces of the slates."

This was disappointing, but, considering this a preliminary séance, merely one of a series, I made no objection. Opening the slates, I took out my note, and handed the slates to her.

After wiping them with a cloth she held them between her palms for a moment. She then examined the small slate-pencil point which I had brought to place between them. "It is too hard," she said. "I will use one of my own that is softer."

I made no objection to this, and she then said: "I am going down to the kitchen—I have something cooking —and while I am gone, I want you to write the name 'Dr. Coulter' and the names of any of your friends whom you wish to call up."

Thereupon, handing me several small sheets of paper, she left the room.

Taking a single sheet of this paper, I wrote on it with a pencil these names: *Dr. Coulter, Jessie, Edward Mac-Dowell,* and *David*—being careful not to use a pad or any support which might retain an impression. This sheet I folded small and held in my hand.

On her return she opened the folded slates and told me to drop the note between them. She did not touch the folded sheet and could not see the writing—of that

I was certain—and as we took our seats on opposite sides of the decrepit table, she put the slates beneath it and asked me to grasp one corner of them. This I did.

While waiting I began to ask questions. She replied: "I have never been in a trance, and I never 'work' in the dark. I am not a trumpet or trance medium, and I dislike materializations. I prefer the higher manifestations like direct voices and independent writing."

Her methods interested me exceedingly, for almost all the mediums I had studied worked only in the dark and were subject to trance. Slate writing (as the reader will recall) was familiar to me, but I waited eagerly for the daylight voices which her friends had reported were her most distinctive production.

While I sat thus, with my arm extended beneath the table, a dull ache came into my elbow—something distinct from fatigue—a pain which ran to my shoulder, and at the same time a chill, a shiver, started in the small of my back, crept upward into my hair, and ended in a shudder, which I accepted as a sign that things were about to happen. I had felt this many times before but never so powerfully.

The psychic, becoming impatient, called to her invisible guide, "Come! I need you, dear." And after a few moments of further waiting she imperiously repeated: "Come! I want you. Come—anybody!"

The response to this *command* was a violent surge of the slates, a movement so powerful that I could not control it. Back and forth they slammed, shaking the table and almost lifting it from the floor. I put forth all the force in my big right hand, and the corner of the slates creaked under the strain. At times they shot toward me as if seeking my protection, then paused and shook from side to side.

She warned them, "Be careful—you'll break the table again!" She had commanded the forces to come—she now *entreated* them to be careful.

At last the slates quieted down and I could hear the sound of writing on them. I could *feel* the writing going on while the psychic's right hand was grasping the corner of the slate and her left hand was in full view.

At last she took them out and opened them. Both inner sides of the slates were covered with writing. On one was a courteous message from her guide, and on the other, these very significant words: "I would that you could see me as I am now, still occupied and happy to be busy. E. A. McDowell."

Under this message and a little to the left, four short lines appeared with three musical notes sketchily drawn between. The name was spelled "McDowell" instead of "MacDowell," but his initials, *which I had not given*, were correct.

At this point Mrs. Hartley said, this time with a smile: "I must go down to the kitchen again. You see I am my own cook."

While she was gone I wrote on a second sheet of paper, "Edward, give me a bar from your 'Sonata Tragica'— make it a test."

This I folded into a small square and I was holding it in my hand when Mrs. Hartley returned and took her seat opposite me.

She said, "Fold the paper once more and place it between your neck and your collar—at the back."

In compliance with my rule to respect all the whims

of a medium till I gain her good will, I slipped the folded sheet between my collar and the back of my neck—and again took the corner of the slates in my hand beneath the table. She had not touched the paper, and there was no possibility of substitution.

Again came the sound of writing and on opening the slates I found these still more significant words: "I was not a disappointment to myself but I was at a point where nerve force failed me. Edward."

This message was accompanied by several marks which seemed to be in answer to my request for an excerpt from the sonata but it was without the musical "signature." I asked aloud as if addressing the invisible, "Can't you indicate the key of the composition?"

He answered by taps, "Yes."

We tried for this but did not succeed; we did get, however, another bar on which the signature, a small C, was written. On second trial the bar was more definite.

It is worth while to consider this in detail. My request for a bar from the "Tragic Sonata" had been written while the psychic was out of the room and the folded paper had not passed out of my possession for a single instant—I had placed it between my collar and my neck (it was still there)—and yet here on the slate was a perfectly definite attempt at meeting my request. Furthermore, I had asked for the signature *after* the slates were closed and in my grasp.

I could not tell whether these two bars of music were taken from the "Tragic Sonata" or not, but I was now especially moved by the appearance of two additional bars which were clearly defined.

Thus, from the first faint marginal sketchy symbol

in which the notes were merely indicated by check marks, I had now succeeded in getting a fairly well defined staff, with a signature indicating the key of C. The notes, while still without time values, were more clearly drawn. It is also worth noting that in one of these two bars the composer used a small C and in the other, a large C. It will be seen also that progress toward a more definite use of pitch notations was being made. Each attempt yielded clearer, more intelligible results.

Now came a message which read: "I was so tired and not myself. I am well and in a world of progress."

How much the psychic knew of MacDowell's last days, I had no way of knowing; but the words thus given had very definite significance to me. They referred to the brain-lesion which ended his work and finally his life. The bars of music were a direct answer to my request for identification, but I was not able to prove at the moment their relationship to the sonata.

In one corner of the slates now appeared a script which looked like a Chinese name, and with it the singular word "Isinghere," which could be read "I sing here" but which had no relation to the other writing.

"Have you been sitting with a Chinese recently?" I asked of the psychic.

"Yes, I sat with a Chinese gentleman for two weeks," she replied. "But that was a month ago."

Here then was another mystery. This Chinese signature was due to a lingering influence, something which emanated from another sitter. Just as Henry Wallace's psychic had insisted on giving to me messages which concerned Wallace, so here a Chinese spirit had left his signature on my slate.

Now came a series of rapidly written messages which I copied each time before Mrs. Hartley cleaned the slate.

The first question, which purported to be from Edward MacDowell, was this: "Is my wife happy? Is she cared for?"

To this I replied aloud as if speaking to him, "She is not unhappy, and she is cared for."

He then wrote, *while I myself held the slate:* "I thank you for what you have done. I have been told my mind is clear."

In this I read a still more direct reference to the fact that his mind was shadowed during the last months of his life. It is possible, of course, that Mrs. Hartley had read of his condition and that I had stayed in the same hotel in order to be of service to him and his devoted wife.

No voices came during this sitting although I had expected them. I went away delighted with Mrs. Hartley's frankness and hopeful of further messages at our next séance.

II

To my sitting on the following morning, I carried a sheet of note paper on which I had written, "Edward, which would you like better, a memorial in Peterboro or a building in Manhattan?" This sheet which lies before me bears Judah's home address.

To this question I got no reply, not even a reference to it; but the music kept coming, in spite of my repeated declaration that I could not record it. The notes remained sketchy, hardly more than check marks.

A record which I made at the time reads thus:

"The forces were very strong. The psychic showed the strain. Her fingers dripped with perspiration and once she said, 'My arm is numb and as cold as ice.' She was very tense and grave."

The slates now seemed alive and determined to come over to me. They pulled away from the psychic's hands and came to rest upon my knees; but when I started to take them up they drew away. No sooner was my right hand back on the table than they returned to my knee. I asked, "Do you want the slates to remain near me?"

The invisible rapped three times, an emphatic "Yes."

At last I was permitted to hold them while the writing was going on. The action was very violent, and as I put my full strength into my grip one of the slates was broken.

On taking them out I found that two more bars of music had been sketchily written. The clef was clearly indicated, and a part of the staff was filled in; but the marks were all so hurriedly, so uncertainly drawn that they were merely symbols, suggestions of intent.

" 'Edward,' " I then said, "I want you to correct and strengthen these notes and write a word of direction above the two bars."

The psychic herself held the slates beneath the table but again they broke away from her and came to me. *While they rested on my knees, I heard the pencil at work.* On taking them out I found that the musical sketch had been remade. The line beneath the two bars had been firmly drawn, some new notes had been added

and two of them had been "sharpened." Others which
had been very dim were now clearly defined.

The notations were all signed "E. A.," which was
puzzling for I had never known him to sign his name in
that way. His middle name was Alexander. The medium, convinced that I was also a medium, now became entirely friendly.

We gave "E. A." the slates to work on again, and
additions to the musical score were made. I drew a line
above the staff and again said, " 'Edward,' give me a
word of musical direction."

In answer to this request, the abbreviation "Mod" was
written. Again holding them beneath the table, I said,
"Write it out in full."

"Andante Mod" was then written and the word
"fragment" was added with several fine lines beneath
the last syllable. The signature was again "E.A."

This was one of the most significant sittings I had ever
held, for I was practically in control of the process—
"E. A." and I worked all the later messages out together.
There was no suggestion of complicity on the part of
the psychic. She relinquished the slates to me as if
understanding that "Edward" and I were furnishing all
the power.

I heard no voices, but I now spoke to "E. A." as if
he were in the room and could hear me and respond.
This he did by means of writing on the slates.

It appeared from his questions that up to this moment
he had been unable to reach his wife or to learn of
her condition. This was very curious. Why could he
not gain knowledge of her? That he signed most of his
messages "E. A." was also strange. So far as I knew, he

had never done this when alive. Nevertheless at the moment I seemed to be in close contact with the spirit of Edward MacDowell.

About this time I began to hear a faint whisper which seemed to come from the air a foot or two above the psychic's head and to the left of her. I could distinguish only a few of the whispered words, but the psychic (who said, "They come from my guide") interpreted them to me.

Two personalities therefore stood between me and my invisible friend, and yet I must admit that all his queries and his answers were astonishingly significant in character. He was eager—painfully eager to know of his wife's health.

Under conditions which shut Mrs. Hartley entirely off from any normal participation in the phenomena, I continued to receive bars of music, each time more clearly defined in their form than before.

"These notes," the whisper declared, "are from the third movement of my 'Sonata Tragica.'"

Each written message was accompanied by that curious little device like the letter C with a line drawn through it (¢). I thought this at the time a proprietary signature like the butterfly which Whistler used on his paintings. Later it developed into the "signature" of a staff indicating the key.

During a third sitting I secured on the slates, *entirely under my own control*, another writing of the singular word "Isinghere" which the whispers said was the name of an unfinished unpublished manuscript. Later the word varied to "Isighere" and to "Unghere." I began to think it might be an ancient form of the word

"Hungaria"—a guess which the whispers confirmed. I secured two more bars of music which I copied at the moment.

Speaking to the invisible, I said, "Are these from an unpublished score?"

"Yes," was the whispered answer.

"Is it a completed composition or only a marginal note?"

"A small instrumental piece," he replied.

"Where is it?"

"Among my manuscripts in my New York home."

On the opposite side of the slate from the music were some Chinese characters.

Some of this music came while I held the slate on my side of the table. *Once the writing took place on the slate while under my foot.* I could feel the vibration of it. Some will say, "You imagined all that"— but part of the time I opened the slates myself and read the messages before the psychic did. The writing was real.

It is worth noting also that after I began calling the invisible one "E. A." the signatures were all "E. A." and not "MacDowell." I was not sure that the psychic realized that "E. A." and "MacDowell" were one and the same person for as a test I had called him "Edward Alexander."

The whispers had ceased to be uttered by "Dr. Coulter," they came directly from "E. A." himself. I must confess that I had the feeling of being in touch with him. As the whispers became more important to me, I closely observed the psychic's mouth but was unable to detect the slightest movement of her lips or throat.

Ventriloquism can not account for the music written between my hands and under my foot.

(As I write this, in 1935, I have on my desk the identical notes which I made during the sitting or immediately after it. The messages appearing on the slate I copied carefully before they were rubbed out.)

The music continued to come with more and more power, and at last I said: " 'Edward,' you've got beyond me. I can neither transcribe these musical notes nor identify them. I must have help. You remember Henry Fuller of Chicago?"

He answered "Yes."

"I am asking him to come down and join me in these tests. He can write music, and he is a good amateur pianist. With his aid I shall be able to make a clearer record of your messages."

The invisible one expressed disappointment at the delay but acquiesced. I said, "Good-bye," and the whispering ceased.

III

These sittings appeared to me to be supernormal—on their mental as well as on their physical side. The messages were all directly to the point and so intimately personal that I could not relate the psychic to them. The invisible one uttered no banal remarks, no vague philosophy, no bad poetry, and no pinchbeck rhetoric. The later whispered sentences were curt, concise, and highly characteristic of MacDowell—and yet the contents of the messages were all within the circle of my subconscious mind or that of the psychic. The musical notation was rudimentary for neither of us could write music.

To the Judahs I said: "Unless there is an unpublished manuscript among MacDowell's papers in New York, there is no convincing evidence of his identity. I need help."

Mrs. Judah, who knew and valued Fuller, said: "By all means have Henry come down. His aid should be valuable."

Among the notes which I made immediately after this sitting I find these paragraphs:

"Mrs. Hartley said: 'Sometimes in order to make anything clear I cover it with my hand.' Later she remarked: 'Sometimes the personalities brought up by a sitter linger on for a day or two after the sitter has gone. This confuses the record of the next sitter. "MacDowell" does not come to me in that way—he comes with you. People coming to me from another psychic sometimes bring bad influences.'

"She complained of being always the medium. 'I can never escape it. I get tired of my job. Wherever I go it is the only topic of conversation—and I am always expected to furnish either amusement or consolation for other guests.'

"She admitted that it was a struggle to keep her sanity. 'The spirits are always with me. They speak to me all the time. They have no regard for me or of the proper time to talk. They keep talking at night. Sometimes they prevent me from sleeping. I have had them write on my nightdress. My mother devoted me to this work when I was seven years old. She made me sit in the dark for long hours. I hated it but I could not escape it.

My mother considered me just a telephone over which she could speak to those who had passed on. I regard my work as a gift. I use it to do good in the world—and yet my mediumship is considered a disgrace. My neighbors sneer at my son, and the children call him, "Son of a medium! Son of a medium!" He will not enter this room. He calls it "The Ghost Room." Sometimes I feel like taking him with me and fleeing into some far-away country where no one would know of my mediumship.'

"She added: 'Sometimes I fear paralysis. The lower part of my body often grows numb. Sometimes my legs are useless. I can't walk. This condition lasts for hours. My hands and arms during a sitting are always cold and numb. Sometimes my arms are as rigid as marble—and yet I go on, for I believe in the work. I consider it the most helpful work I could possibly do—one of the most helpful in the world.'

"She said: 'Spirits can not see in a room as we do. "Coulter" often asks "Who is here?" Time and space don't mean anything to them.'

"She was very serious throughout all our talks. Only once did she smile. This was while telling me of a singular independent manifestation which took place one night in her home. She said: 'I heard some one walking up the stairway. I thought it a burglar. Creeping to the head of the stairs I looked down. The stairway was brightly lighted and what I saw scared me stiff. A pair of men's slippers were stepping up the stairs all by themselves, exactly as if worn by an invisible visitor.' She smiled a bit sheepishly. 'I never was so scared in my life!'

"This amused me. 'What!' I exclaimed. 'You—a

woman in constant touch with the invisible, frightened by a pair of slippers on invisible feet!'

"She admitted that she feared the evil spirits who came to her. 'I get dreadful messages from the spirits of bad men and women—spirits who use profane and vulgar words. One spirit who came said, "Tell my wife how I hate her!" He called her all the vile names he could think of. He said, "I've waited twenty years for a chance to give that woman hell and now that I have the chance, I'm going to improve it." Some of the messages I get are too awful to repeat.' "

The closer I studied my record of these sittings, the more astounding they became. "What is the meaning of the sign ϕ ? Is that column of strange words a Chinese signature? What is the significance of the word which began 'Isinghere,' changed to 'Isighere,' then to 'Unghere,' and at last to 'Ungarie'? Why should the invisible sign his name 'McDowell' and call his wife 'Mary' instead of 'Marian'? Is the music indicated by these sketchy notes taken from the 'Sonata Tragica'?"

These and a dozen other puzzlements led me to write to my friend Fuller urging him to come down and help me. "I am incapable of recording the music which 'E. A.' is so eager to have written—heed my Macedonian and come at once."

CHAPTER FIFTEEN

PHANTASMAL FINGERS

I

HENRY B. FULLER, the man to whom I now turned for help in recording these amazing manifestations, was not only a keenly observant novelist, but a man of cool, sceptical, and alert judgment. He had read widely in records of psychic research but had never witnessed any of its phenomena. I relied upon his eagerness to experiment when I requested his immediate aid. My reliance was not misplaced. He knew the Judahs well and had a very real affection for them. He did not wait to write—he wired that he would come down on the first possible train.

Upon his arrival, without a moment's delay I laid before him the results of my sittings. "My invisible composer is insistent on conveying his composition to us, and if we can secure by this supernormal method any part of an unpublished manuscript by MacDowell, we will come nearer to proof of individual survival than any psychic record known to me."

"I can't believe a word of your story," he replied, "but I look forward to a sitting with joy."

About half-past ten the following morning when we

set out for "the ghost room," as Mrs. Hartley's little son called the chamber in which we had been sitting, I stopped at a stationery store and purchased two flexible book-slates, each with two inner leaves. On their corners I wrote my initials and the date with an indelible pencil.

Fuller remarked: "Today is Friday the 13th. I hope that will not affect your composer."

"It won't. He has finished with earthly superstitions. Time does not exist for him. We'll find him waiting for us."

Mrs. Hartley received Fuller pleasantly and thanked him for coming. "Mr. Garland and I are not musicians," she explained. "We need your help in recording the music which Mr. Garland's friend insists on giving us."

I have before me at this moment the yellowed sheets of paper on which I made an immediate record of this sitting. They are dated November 13, 1908, and I would not venture to describe what happened, without the corroborative support of these notes.

"This was the most marvellous sitting of all," is the opening line of my first entry. "The psychic put powdered slate pencil between the leaves of one of my newly purchased book-slates and said, 'We will try first for a picture.'

"The 'picture' which came on the slate *under my hands and without contact by the psychic,* was an outline drawing of a girl's head with the words 'Sister Jessie.' So far as I am aware, neither Fuller nor the psychic knew that I had a sister—long ago dead—whose name was Jessie.

"On its physical sides this was literally stunning. The

method was supernormal and the writing of the name metapsychical.

"Fuller then tried and got a message on the slate *while it was under his foot,* a message which came, he declared, from a Colonial New England ancestor—a man his family had almost wholly forgotten."

Observe the definite statement made at the moment, that this message came under Fuller's foot. Also consider the improbability of the psychic knowing that Fuller had a relation named Payne. One of the slates is before me as I write. On it are the names Jimmie, Booth, Jessie. "Jimmie" meant nothing to me, and I wondered if "Booth" was Edwin Booth; but "Jessie" was the name of my sister. Another rapidly written note follows:

"The whispers now began to be heard. They appeared to come from the air just above the psychic's head and a little to her right. I could hear the utterances quite clearly but Fuller was not as keen of hearing as I, and for his benefit the psychic repeated the words which she said came from her guide, 'Coulter.' I could detect no movement of the psychic's lips or throat. However, ventriloquism does not account for the writing under Fuller's foot nor for 'Payne.' "

In his report written several days later, Fuller says:

"The psychic was not in trance at any time. She conversed throughout in ordinary voice and manner except now and then when she undertook to hasten the pace of her lagging 'controls.' Her principal guide, 'Dr. Coulter,' spoke in whispers but his words were repeated to me by the psychic herself. Later 'Coulter' seemed to withdraw altogether and Garland and I were

in apparent communication, direct, rapid and uninter-
rupted, with an intelligence which for convenience's
sake I shall call 'The Composer.' "

These whispers did indeed suddenly change in character. They became swift, concise, masterful.

"Line off one of the books for a musical staff," the
invisible speaker commanded, and as Fuller started to
do this, the composer said, "Not that way—draw it
lengthwise of the slate and cover every leaf—provide
for seven measures."

It was at once evident that Fuller's presence had
aroused the unseen musician's hope of getting his composition recorded. His sibilant directions produced in
me the impression of an eager, powerful personality—
in fact they were at the moment infilled with the character of MacDowell. I spoke to him as if he were alive
and he replied in the same manner.

Fuller, who could not hear all the words, was less
impressed with their personal quality. Nevertheless he
lent himself cheerfully to the composer's commands.
I quote now from Fuller's own report, which details
the exact method of procedure. He wrote:

"The slate was now entirely in my hands. The under-
cover of the slate, a flexible leaved affair with a bit of
slate-pencil tightly enclosed, rested on my knee with the
upper part pressed against the frame on my side of the
table. My thumb rested rather lightly on the middle of
the nearer half of the cover and my fingers assisted in
supporting the nearer half of the under-cover.

"The psychic had surrendered control of the slate
entirely to me. She had no contact with it beyond touching the edge farthest from me. Furthermore the slate

was clamped shut by the pressure of my knees. Later the slate was wholly on our side of the table. During this period, *the psychic did not touch the slate at any moment.*"

I ask the reader's careful consideration of these facts. According to records made at the time or within an hour after the sitting, Fuller and I, two men in the middle prime of life, testified that on a closed slate (under our control, in full daylight, and without contact by the psychic) certain bars of music appeared in accordance with the directions of a whispering voice, a voice which had no obvious connection with the lips and tongue of the psychic.

Even if we grant the possibility of ventriloquistic impersonation, there remains the insoluble mystery of the writing which came on the closed slates while they were lying on my knees or under Fuller's hands, wholly beyond the psychic's reach.

Leaving the content of the whispered words out of the problem for the moment, I restate the conditions:

Fuller and I were seated close together on one side of the rickety table, with the medium on the opposite side facing us. She was leaning back in her chair with her hands in her lap, a look of calm expectancy on her face. That she was pleased by Fuller's ability to receive and record the music, was evident, and she left the task entirely to him. "I have never had a test like this before," she said. While the whispers were coming out of the air, I observed that her lips were tightly closed but lifted slightly at the corners.

As the whispers increased in power they became more and more characteristic of MacDowell. The construction of the sentences was wonderfully like his speech, concise, quick-spoken, imperious. He became humorous. Once when correcting a mistake, he called it "a slip of the tongue." Each moment his musical instructions became more highly technical, passing entirely outside my knowledge and that of the psychic.

Note after note was added to the score while the closed slates rested entirely under our hands. The composer from time to time indicated mistakes, and dictated corrections *as if he saw the writing*. All his energy seemed directed toward the recording of an unpublished score which he called "Ungarie," and which he declared could be found among his manuscripts.

As I heard all the whispered words very clearly while Fuller could not, I came to the conclusion that my perception was partly subjective. I spoke to the Invisible precisely as if he were in the flesh, hidden behind a cloud. At the moment I had no doubts. I called him "Edward" and he at last began to call me "Garland." Fuller addressed him as "MacDowell."

At noon, while in the midst of this highly exciting dictation, a whisper from the guide (apparently) said, "Break off now and come again at three."

II

As we walked away I said: "Spooks are very considerate. It is a bit of a shock, however, to find that a process so marvellous as this can be turned off and on so easily. Nevertheless, I feel that we are getting into the upper air of psychic research. If you can obtain the score of that fragment, we will have one of the most interesting and convincing records in all psychic literature. I felt MacDowell in those whispers."

"So did I," Fuller replied. "Whether that music came from him or not, it is distinctly out of Mrs. Hartley's comprehension. Furthermore she had nothing to do with putting it on the slate, for it was in our control."

At Judah's we made our report and during our luncheon hour discussed every phase of our incredible experience.

I said: "That is the third time that my sister Jessie's name has appeared on the slates or been spoken from the trumpet, but neither my mother's name nor that of my older sister has ever been indicated. Why should Jessie say, 'I died from a fall,' and make no mention of her mother or father? I don't know what caused her death, but it was in childbirth. It is possible that a fall brought on premature birth."

Fuller remarked: "My case is still more difficult. Why should one of my New England Colonial ancestors write his name while all my near relatives, recently translated, make no sign?"

Mrs. Judah was enormously impressed by the musical part of our communications. "I don't believe Mrs. Hartley knows a thing about MacDowell. She may have heard some one play the 'Wild Rose,' but she could not possibly dictate a bar out of a sonata. Either MacDowell was there or Mr. Fuller is himself the composer."

This amused Fuller. "I never sat before. All I know of psychic research is what I have read."

At three we returned to our seats in the séance chamber, and almost immediately the composer began to dictate the composition of the score from the point where he had left off. Fuller had some difficulty with one bar, and the composer said: "Sing it, Fuller. The sound will help."

Fuller protested. "I can't sing. I have no voice."

"Very well," retorted the composer with decisive inflection. "Take the table to the piano. I want you to play the score."

The piano, a small upright instrument, was in the parlor on the street floor and so, while Fuller retained control of the slates, I picked up the decrepit table and carried it carefully down the stairs and placed it with one end near the keyboard of the piano.

The psychic then took a seat in an easy-chair on the opposite side of the table and settled into place as if she were to be merely an observer. Fuller drew out the bench which served as piano stool, and took a seat on the end nearest the keys whilst I sat on the same stool close beside him.

For two hours we sat there with Fuller alternately recording and playing the notes which the composer dictated, while the score grew into a weirdly sweet melody. At times while Fuller played it, I felt a singular thrill, something like an electric shock. At the moment "MacDowell" seemed in the air before me and almost visible.

During these hours the psychic sat leaning back in her chair, with an expression of indifference, almost of boredom on her face. Her hands were limply folded in her lap. She had nothing to do—in any normal way —with the writing, and I could detect no connection between her organs of speech and the whispers which became stronger as the sitting went on. In fact Fuller ceased to regard her as an active factor in the game.

His own report reads:

"The psychic had surrendered control of the slates to me. She could have had no contact beyond touching the edge farthest from me. For the most part she had no contact with it at all. I could hear and feel the writing. It was a combination of light and very rapid scratching and pecking while the slate twitched and moved slightly from side to side."

At times the psychic appeared mystified by Fuller's highly technical comment. Whether she was weary or not did not concern "MacDowell," but he said to me, "Garland, I hope *you* are not bored," and his emphasis made plain his understanding of Mrs. Hartley's indifference.

In his report Fuller says:

"The composer throughout was most patient, persevering, courteous. Toward the end he showed some confusion and uncertainty. 'Wait a moment,' he would say; and once as an aid to his perception he said, 'Cover that slate with your hand.' This I did and he said 'I see it now.' As the work of correction progressed he asked for the opportunity to make the changes in notation himself.

"Thereafter I folded the slates on a bit of pencil and held them on my knees or laid them between Garland's hip and my own, and the corrections were made by the composer himself on the inside of the closed slates. Even the most minute notes were placed precisely on the lines and in the spaces of the staff. With inconceivable skill the tiny flags were added to the stems of half-notes or quarter-notes."

Another inexplicable phenomenon must be noticed at this point. While Fuller was making these changes in the notes, the slates were not only entirely out of Mrs. Hartley's reach but out of the range of her vision. That the composer could see the slates was evident, for he not only gave minute directions as to what should be set down or corrected but said once or twice as Fuller was adding a note, "Not there, Fuller." When Fuller had changed the position of his pencil, the whisper added "Yes, there"—as if he had pointed out the precise place.

He appeared to be looking over Fuller's shoulder, seeing every stroke of the pencil, and yet his voice came from the air before us.

Only when the slate was closed could he himself use the pencil.

When Fuller asked, "Shall I make this an eighth note?" the whispered "Yes, if you please" showed not only his knowledge of the score but his courtesy.

In some instances he put the little flags on the stems of the notes himself—but only when the slates were closed. He could perceive equally well whether the score was in the light or in the dark of the closed slates.

Fuller says:

"On these occasions when the composer directed my pencil the slate was four feet from the psychic and practically out of her sight. I held the slate on a slant, so that *the writing was not only invisible to her but upside down.* She could not possibly read it normally."

The corrections which the composer himself made on the closed slates became more and more astonishing.

Notes were changed from one value to another while musical directions were placed exactly in their proper places. As for the music itself, it became the kind of composition which the psychic could not understand. It was elliptical, touched with emotional subtlety.

"I find it very difficult to play," Fuller confessed.

The composer whispered, "I am surprised, Fuller, that you find anything so simple—difficult."

Slowly, very slowly, after two hours of close co-operation between Fuller and the composer, the score became a strange little melody with a bass accompaniment which the composer called a fragment. He said " 'Unghere' means 'Hungary.' "

The first bar of the composition went through me like the sound of his voice. At the moment it appeared the identification I had been seeking. Nothing I had ever experienced in a séance brought the emotional stir which at this moment I acknowledged.

After another half-hour of intense application, the control suggested that we stop for the day and resume the following afternoon. "Leave everything just as it is and the composer will resume control exactly where he left off."

Deeply as I regretted this postponement, I recognized the need of it, for Fuller and the psychic were both very tired and the composer showed signs of weakness. We took away our slates, for the Judahs were eager to see them.

III

On the table I had placed a small pad, on which, from time to time while the sitting was going on, I made hasty notes—recording what the Invisible whispered to me. These are before me at this moment, and I quote them, for even in their fragmentary shape they are valuable:

"Edward said: 'Tell Marian I didn't mean what I said. Tell her I love her with all my heart. Tell her I knew her—my girl—I knew her when she called me. I heard her—when she called but I couldn't answer.'"

This was, perhaps, a reference to his last moment of life.

"He was quick as light in correcting the score. He asked for me every few moments. He began to call me by my first name. He said, 'Hamlin, I want my lectures published at once.'"

This was not in character; he had always called me "Garland."

"Someone else, 'Coulter' perhaps, whispered, 'They don't know what you do this slate-writing for.'"

"Fuller and the composer were in full control for more than an hour. Each moment the composition became less sketchy, more exact— The composer insisted on filling in the bass and treble. 'It is only a melody now.'"

"I felt Edward's presence—I had a sense of his nearness."

As I compared notes with Fuller, I came to the conclusion that I had for the moment a keener ear than he, for the whispered words were not only audible, they gave me the effect of a voice. My normal hearing was better than Fuller's. Whether ventriloquism can account for these whispers, I do not know; but that the musical composition on the closed slates in Fuller's hands was beyond the psychic's normal powers, I am very certain.

On a sheet of yellow paper in my files I find these lines written in pencil *immediately after* this astounding séance:

"Fuller and I walked away fairly stunned by the significance of this beautiful test. 'If this melody, so like MacDowell, can be found among his manuscripts, it will be a marvellous case of mind reading. Either MacDowell knows it or the psychic is able to take it from the manuscript,' I said.

"To this Fuller replied, 'If it can't be found this composition must stand on its musical significance. It is beyond the psychic's normal skill.'

"In this sitting were several absolute tests of the genuine supernormal character of the writing; but aside from that, the quality of the melody, so singular and sweet, was above Fuller's powers of composition. He found it difficult to play."

To the Judahs I remarked:

"I have always said that I would follow the evidence, and I am ready to do so now. If Edward MacDowell can manifest himself in this unmistakable fashion, I'm ready to welcome him. The next thing is to lay this all before Marian and get her confirmation."

That night for the first time in my life, I heard raps on my bed. They came on my pillow and kept me awake for an hour or two. When I awoke at daylight, I was surprised to find my notebook on the floor and my glasses missing. I searched all about the stand and among the pillows. At last I found them under the bed, halfway to the wall and nicely set up, with the lenses down and the bows on top.

This amused Fuller immensely. "I heard no raps, but I saw musical scores all night long."

IV

Although conditions were quite perfect at Mrs. Hartley's home, I felt that my report would be more convincing if I could test her powers in some other room, and as the Judahs were eager to hear a séance, I suggested that we hold one in John's study.

Judah at once agreed: "That's a good idea. You can say that she has never been in our house."

"I'll invite her to luncheon," said Mrs. Judah, "and we'll have the sitting immediately afterward. We'll have no one else at the table."

On the following day Mrs. Hartley came in a few minutes before one. Mrs. Judah met her in the reception room and led her almost immediately to the dining room. She brought nothing with her but a handbag about six inches long.

At the close of our luncheon, we all entered Judah's library together. It was a large room with a bay-window fronting the west. It contained an upright piano and a man's desk, and the walls were lined with books.

According to my notes, the psychic took her seat at a small table in the bay-window. The sun was shining in almost upon her head and she remained in this position during most of the tests.

"She began by giving us all slate-writing tests. At one time *four slates were being written upon at once.* Judah got a message from Aaron Burr while the slate was under his foot; and Mrs. Judah while holding her slate in her lap received a greeting from 'Newton Booth.' She reported, 'I heard the pencil write.' "

This message was most significant for me. It answered my question concerning the name "Booth" which I had received the day before on my flexible slate. I had wondered at the time whether or not this was intended to be a message from Edwin Booth. This question was answered by the message to Mrs. Judah. Newton Booth was a family name, and is the name of Booth Tarkington, whose full name is Newton Booth Tarkington. I ask my reader to ponder this fact which, apparently trivial, has very great value as evidence. Why should "Newton Booth" come to me when Mrs. Judah was not present? What was the influence which produced his name on a closed slate in Mrs. Hartley's séance room? By what magic was he now able to give his full name while writing was going on between two other slates held by Fuller and Judah? Why should Aaron Burr write his name on Judah's slates? How could he do so while it was under Judah's foot?

My notes go on:

"Judah and I then joined in holding a pad under the table. Writing came on several leaves and on one leaf came a bar of music. Apparently 'Edward' was with us. The number of the page where I had inserted a pencil was written with a pencil."

I then said to the psychic in pretended complaining, "I am neglected. I had no writing on my slate."

She smiled genially and said, "Bring another pad, one that has not been used by any one."

At Judah's suggestion I followed him to the other end of the room where stood a large roll-top desk. He opened a bottom drawer and showed me a pile of ten or more Manila pads of legal size, all new and untouched. He did not handle the pad, he merely drew the drawer open. I took up and examined one of these pads. It had no writing in it and contained some sixty or seventy leaves—perhaps more.

Mrs. Hartley, who remained standing behind the table, then said, "Place a pencil between the leaves."

The pencil I had was at least six inches long. Placing it at about the center of the pad, crosswise of the pages, I approached the table and presented to her the closed end of the pad, maintaining a firm grasp on the corners of the open end. As I did this a whisper in my ear said, *"Have the others leave the room."* I repeated this command to the Judahs, and they all went out into the hall, leaving me standing before the medium holding the pad firmly by the corners of the open end.

The psychic then put one palm below the pad and one above, and in this position we stood for a minute or two. I both *heard* and *felt* the writing as I gripped the pad. I heard a whisper say, "It is done."

Backing away from the psychic, I opened the pad myself, and hunting through the sixty or seventy pages, I found three pages in the middle written upon. On one was the name "Jessie," on another "Burr," and on the third the words, "have Schubert—E. A."

Drawing a line around each of these messages, I closed the pad, gripped the open end and again presented the book to the psychic. The closed end was toward her and while I stood holding it thus, I received several other messages. One was for Fuller signed "Payne." The singular word "Singhere" was again repeated.

Believing that the words "have Schubert" were part of a sentence—"have" being written without a capital letter—I said, " 'E. A.' wants Fuller to play a selection from Schubert." I called to Fuller who was in the hall. "Come in. 'E. A.' wants you to play a Schubert selection for him."

The reader will soon discover that this is a very significant action.

When Fuller came back into the room I told him what had happened and showed him the written words "have Schubert." Taking my view of it he went to the piano and began to play very softly. The Judahs now came in and took seats. They also agreed that it was a request from "MacDowell" to have something from Schubert played for him. Let the reader bear this in mind. We all thought along these lines.

The psychic was moved to do something more for me. She said:

"Go to the shelf and select a book—any book—and put a pencil in it."

Walking along the shelves which lined one side of the room, I selected a thick, neutral-colored volume. In this, without looking at the pages, I laid a long pencil lengthwise, and with the book held by the corners I approached the psychic. While we both stood, closely watched by Fuller and the Judahs, she put the tips of her fingers on the closed end of the book, *which did not leave my hands*. At last a tapping indicated the completed task.

When I withdrew and opened the book, I found that

a sentence from the right-hand page where the pencil lay had been written along the margin of the *left-hand* page—a most amazing "stunt."

Fuller said, "Why should my ancestor 'Payne' and 'Aaron Burr' intrude themselves?"

The psychic now attempted to dematerialize a key. "I am sometimes able to introduce a coin into a locked box," she said. That she failed in this made the wonders she had previously wrought still more wonderful.

Fuller and I assumed that the message signed "E. A." was a continuation of the influence which had been speaking and writing to us, and yet, so far as I knew, MacDowell had never signed his letters in that way. I related the use of "E. A." to the fact that I had addressed one of my questions to "Edward Alexander."

The important fact for the reader to remember is this: Fuller and I both accepted the words "have Schubert" as a request for a musical selection.

As for the writing in the pad, I offer no explanation of its appearance. I am using it at this moment (September 1, 1935) for verification. Each of the first signatures or messages is encircled by my pencil marks— exactly as I have described them. The writing is apparently in lead pencil lightly applied. They are all on the middle leaves of the thick pad of Manila paper, legal size. Two of my questions, heading certain leaves, one addressed to "Don Carlos Taft" and another to "MacDowell," were unanswered. The pages are blank.

Slight as these phenomena may seem to some scientific men, they are so tremendous in their implications that they would not believe them if they saw them. What would Einstein think if while holding a closed book in his hands he should receive a message written in the middle of the volume?

These problems must be met.

Neither Fuller nor I was a man of science, but we were in our prime and were keen observers. In addition to my realistic habit, I had been educated by seventeen years in psychic research. Judah, a lawyer, while of theosophic trend of thought was a business man, humorous and clear-sighted, and Mrs. Judah too, though predisposed to believe in these phenomena for the reason that psychic power had discovered itself in her family, was a realist. We all agreed that these tests were evidential. "A singular power resides in Mrs. Hartley."

She came into a house strange to her and sat in a room which she had never before seen. Without a particle of apparatus other than the slates and books which I and the Judahs furnished, she produced phenomena which equal in value those witnessed by Crookes and Zöllner.

That they were all in the nature of stunts, I admit, but stunts of extraordinary interest to me. The forces, whatever they were, seemed determined to prove to me the existence of the fourth dimension.

Later Comment

Let us go over this performance again with a little more minuteness of analysis. The psychic had never been in the room before. She knew nothing of the books on the shelves. At random, guided only by a desire to make identification more difficult, I chose a volume in neutral binding. The book did not leave my hand at any moment, and I held it tightly gripped with the pencil lying lengthwise in the closed side which I held to the psychic. I did not consciously note the pages where I inserted the pencil; certainly I did not read the line which was transferred.

Now leaving out the question of spirit agency, let us meet the argument that I was guided in my choice of a book by the mind of the psychic, and that the number of the page was set by her, and that from my mind she had somehow derived the words of the line which she transcribed.

These are preposterous assumptions, but suppose we allow them: how was the writing done? It was apparently made in lead as if with a pencil, but the pencil was six inches long and laid across the lines of print and tightly held in the back of the book.

Nevertheless, the psychic appeared confident that she could do the trick. In her voice was a note of calm authority. She directed the test with quiet assurance. She commanded her guide "Coulter" to give the test. It was not a consoling message, it was a stunt—there is no other word for it; but it was a miraculous stunt. It was as if the invisible agent wished to prove to me that he was not hedged in by material walls nor confined to our third dimension. He wrought, swiftly, silently, with no bewildering smoke and no magic formula.

If human testimony is of any value, this astounding phenomenon went to its end exactly as I have described it, for I wrote a report of it at once, and I had the Judahs and Henry Fuller as witnesses. It remains to say that they were under no emotional tension. They watched me in silence, interested and curious but in no sense bemused. Fuller and Judah were both standing near me when I stepped forward with the book in my hands. The psychic remained on the farther side of the table through it all. The event at the time seemed perfectly *natural*, but its method remains inexplicable to this day.

In the message written in the Manila pad, I sensed a personality, and one whose mind ran in opposition to mine; but this writing in the book was addressed to no one and meant nothing except to prove that it could be written under conditions impossible to mortal hands. I leave the puzzle to my reader, who may have a clearer notion than I of the existence of a fourth dimension.

CHAPTER SIXTEEN

WEIRD MUSIC

Upon entering the psychic's little parlor the following morning, we found the table, the stool, and the easy-chair just as we had left them, close beside the piano; and I again took my seat on Fuller's right, leaving to him the end of the bench nearest the keyboard. This was in anticipation of the composer's wish to have additional bars of his composition played from time to time.

It is the influence of the habitual and the normal which makes belief in the supernormal so difficult. In this pleasant commonplace little room spirits of any sort seemed incredible, and yet whispers began almost immediately, so strong and so distinct that Fuller was able to converse with the invisible composer quite as if he were present in the flesh. "Edward" again assumed control. Mrs. Hartley and her guide "Coulter" retired, leaving Fuller in full charge of the proceedings.

"Play it as it stands, Fuller," the composer said.

Fuller played the melody again—eight measures of it —and the composer said: "That is right. Now go over it, adding the bass."

Fuller complied as well as he could, but the difficulties involved in holding the slate and reading the scattered notation made it difficult. However, two or three brief passages were written in, and when he took them to the piano and played them with both hands the composer expressed pleasure.

"The treble and bass are correct separately," he said, "but they are not played together in correct time."

"I am aware of that," replied Fuller. "I find it very difficult."

"I am surprised that anything so simple should be considered difficult," the invisible one remarked. "I want you to fill in the treble and the bass. As it stands it is nothing but a bare melody."

"I'm not qualified to do that," protested Fuller. "You're getting beyond me."

"You're too modest," the composer replied with an effect of genial comradeship.

This dialogue, which I recorded later, shows how far beyond the psychic's dramatizing skill these interchanges were. I had the feeling that she had not yet learned that "E. A.," "Edward Alexander," and "MacDowell" were all designations of one and the same person. I do not think she knew that he spelled his name *Mac*Dowell instead of *Mc*Dowell. However, this is not vital, and I pass it.

At this point an amazing episode began. I had been leaning forward on the table while Fuller was busily receiving and recording the musical notation; and now, feeling a little cramped, I took my arms from the table and settled back in my chair. Instantly, and with a note of anxiety in his voice, the invisible composer whispered: "Where's Garland? I can't see him! Garland, where are you?"

"Here I am," I replied, replacing my arms upon the table.

With a sigh of relief the invisible one said, "I see you now—don't go away."

It was as if for the moment I had moved out of his *ectoplasmic spotlight*. It was evident that the withdrawal of my arms for a few inches took me completely out of his perception.

The narrow range of his perception appeared later in several forms. Two or three times while in the midst of his dictation to Fuller, he paused, to ask, "Is Garland here?" He could see Fuller, and he could minutely follow the musical notation; but he could not at the same moment perceive me—and yet I was less than three feet away. At times he could see my hand or elbow but not my head.

On the table were pencils and some sheets of paper; and in order to record from moment to moment these immensely significant and mysterious happenings I was hastily pencilling words and phrases to assist my memory in reviewing the séance, when the composer, interrupting his composition, sharply whispered: "What is Garland doing? I see his hand moving."

I replied, "I'm making notes, Edward."

"Don't do it," he protested. "It worries me."

This gave me much thought then and thereafter. Why did he not say, "Garland, what are you doing?" Why did he ask Fuller? If he could see the slates, why could he not see me? Why did my moving hand worry him? . . . I don't know. Some will say it was a clever play of the psychic. I do not think so.

I wish to emphasize once more the fact that the slates which Fuller held and upon which he was receiving the music, were at least four feet away from the psychic across a table and directly in front of her. The writing on the slate was wholly out of her sight *and upside down.* She could see only the back of the slates. There was no discernible mirror on the walls, and even if there had been she could not have checked the subtle points of the composition.

We now tried to get the name of the composition. On the slate the word "Isinghere" was again written, varied in spelling; and as Fuller spoke several Slavic and Italian words which meant "Gypsy," the written word changed *in accordance with each suggestion* and was finally spelled "Zingere" or "Zingara." This would seem to argue that Fuller's mind dominated the writer.

On other points, however, the composer's will was *opposed* to Fuller's. Once after recording some dictation, Fuller said, "That can't be right."

"It can be and it *is* right," retorted the composer.

Fuller persisted. "But it is very unusual to begin a measure in that way."

Quick, imperious, exactly like MacDowell as I knew him, came the retort, "It is a liberty I permit myself."

He spoke as the master, one who makes rules. Later he seemed to weaken—to suffer a loss of memory as well as of skill.

Once he said: "That final note is wrong. It should be an eighth note, and not a quarter note."

Thereupon Fuller closed the slates and laid them on the stool between us. A few moments later he opened them and showed me that the minute flag had been put with miraculous precision, exactly on the stem of the disputed note!

Again and again we tested this incredible skill. Notes

that had been sketched were touched up; others were set exactly on extra lines drawn above or below the staff. There was no indecision or fumbling.

Supernormal in fact, these changes were supernormal in execution.

Fuller once said, "That bar, number seven, is not properly filled."

"You are right," the composer replied, and directed that a curved line be drawn connecting the three notes and that a figure 2 be written above the curve.

"I don't understand that," said Fuller.

"Never mind," replied "E. A." with kindly tone. "I will write it differently. You may cancel the figure 2 and complete the measure with a rest."

This is but one of the many subtleties which were entirely outside my knowledge and over the head of the psychic, I am sure. In some cases Fuller confessed that he was puzzled.

At this point the composer reverted to the uncompleted message that I had received on the Manila pad in Judah's library.

According to my notes (made at the moment) he said: "Garland, there is a certain *étude* which I took to Schuberth. I want you to regain it and take it to Schmidt. Mary will know about it." He then added with an effect of sadness and confusion: "I meant to take it away—but did I? I was so badly off mentally that I don't know whether I did or not."

Fuller asked, "Do you mean Schuberth the music publisher?"

"Yes."

I then said, "And you want this manuscript recovered from Schuberth and given to your regular publisher, Schmidt?"

"Yes."

All of this, the reader will recall, was wholly in opposition to our thought when the message first came on the pad in Judah's library. It is evident that our minds had *not* given rise to this later request. Furthermore, the composer's confession of his brain-trouble a year before his death must be reckoned with. The psychic could have known nothing of that, for no one knew of it except his closest friends.

Fuller then said, "What shall be done with this fragment 'Unghere'—shall we publish it?"

His reply was curt. "That is what it is for."

"How many bars are in it?" asked Fuller. And as the composer was silent, he added, "Are there as many as forty?"

"More."

"Are there as many as sixty?" Fuller persisted with intent to *suggest* an answer.

"Yes, sixty or seventy," was the reply; and to me this reply was like a mental echo. For a moment, Fuller's mind appeared to dominate the composer's thought. I felt that if he had said, "Are there eighty bars?" the answer would have been, "Yes."

It is significant also to note that "Edward" continued to speak of his wife as "Mary," whereas her name is Marian.

[Later, I asked Mrs. MacDowell if he ever called her "Mary." She replied, "Never."]

Let the reader ponder the fact that we now had the completed message (of which I had received only a fragment on the Manila pad, and which I had taken, at the moment, to be a request for the playing of a Schubert selection—with a totally different meaning); that the composer's wish had persisted for two days *against* my concept of his meaning—and in opposition to all our thought—is evident. "Have Schubert . . ." I now understood to be part of a sentence which when completed would have read "Have Schuberth return that piece of musical composition which I forgot to bring away from his office."

It is only fair to say that this argues the action of an independent personal discarnate intelligence. To say that it all came from Mrs. Hartley argues too much subtlety. Furthermore, it was conveyed to us by a voice independent of her lips and tongue and by writing without contact. At the end of this sitting, I felt like one who had walked the verge of a new dimension.

Fuller in his final report, which is precise, orderly, and scientific, arranged the phenomena of this sitting in three divisions. He says:

"We had: First: phenomena *with the composer in co-operation.*

"Second: the composer *in wholly independent action.*

"Third: the composer *in direct opposition to our thought.*"

He also emphasized the fact that the psychic and her guides had finally withdrawn, quite unconcerned apparently with what went on. The sittings came to be a matter of Fuller, Garland, and "MacDowell."

For the benefit of those with musical education, I copy the following paragraphs from Fuller's report:

"Two further examples of the composer's independ-

ence from our influence will perhaps suffice. In the sixth
measure there was a run of three eighth-notes in the
treble, exactly above a corresponding run of three
eighth-notes in the bass. In making a revision the invisible composer directed that each of these three pairs
of notes should be joined by stems. This took the treble
notes down to the bass and left the last half of the treble
bar empty—a fact unnoticed by me and *wholly beyond
the purview of the psychic or of Garland*. The composer, however, observed the hiatus.and himself directed
the insertion of two rests. . . .

"A curious point to finish with. On the first day I
inquired of certain doubtful notes by name as 'A,' 'C
sharp,' 'D' and the like, while the composer indicated
their positions by specifying lines and spaces as 'third
space,' 'second line,' and so on. The next day when I
made my inquiries on the basis of lines and spaces, the
composer oftenest named the notes by letter—an entire
change of action."

One explanation of this might be that the composer,
knowing that I had no knowledge of music, adapted
himself to my ignorance by naming spaces and lines,
but when Fuller, entirely competent to follow his musical nomenclature, came into the case he naturally re-
acted to the use of letters.

We both felt, for the hour, that we were in actual
mental contact with Edward MacDowell, and that the
psychic was not uttering the whispers ventriloquially.
In proof of this I record the following colloquy:

Toward the end as we were holding the slate between
us, the composer whispered to me: "Fuller is a fine
fellow. I met him, twice."

Fuller heard this and said, "Can you tell me where?"

Without hesitation the composer spoke. "Yes, it was in New York City." Then after a moment he added, "It was at dinner both times."

"You are right," replied Fuller. "Can you tell me exactly where?"

"Once it was at a dinner on Fifth Avenue. The other was—I can't tell the location precisely, but it was down cellar, down a short flight of steps."

"That is correct," I said, "for I was there. Can you tell us who the other guests were?"

His voice grew hesitant. "Well, Mary was there, and John Lane—and you, of course, and Fuller and—" Again he hesitated, and his voice weakened, he seemed to sigh. "I can't be sure of the others."

Fuller looked at me in amazement. How could this information come from Mrs. Hartley's mind? Granted that she was a ventriloquist—how could she know of that down-cellar dinner on Sixth Avenue?

There was something touching and convincing in the sigh of regret with which the composer confessed his lapse of memory. This meant more to me than it did to Fuller, for I first detected MacDowell's disease at this dinner. It was the beginning of his nervous breakdown.

From whatever angle it is viewed, this proves the power of the psychic to acquire facts which were in our minds but unuttered. Ventriloquism could not account for the knowledge she put into words, and yet "Edward" still spoke of his wife as Mary instead of Marian, her real name; and equally puzzling was the fact that while he spoke from the air in front of Fuller, he continued to see and direct his pencil from *behind* him.

Throughout this sitting, which was long and tiresome, the composer remained courteous; but in expression he grew more and more the master. His talk with Fuller became highly technical. When he asked that a dot be added to a note, Fuller placed it after the note. The composer instantly detected this and protested: "No—no! Put it *over* the note—above the staff."

In his formal report Fuller states:

"As the work of the correction progressed, the composer several times asked for opportunity to make the changes himself. Thereupon I would enclose a pencil-tip in the slate, and the proper correction would be made. In cases where I made the changes which he desired *he watched the progress of the pencil,* a larger pencil than the one we used between the lines. He gave directions as to its use. 'Not there!' he would say as I started to make a change. Changing my pencil point to another place I would ask, 'Shall I put it here?' He would reply, 'Yes, here!' He often acknowledged a correction by saying, 'Thank you'; and when I made a suggestion he would say, 'Yes, if you please.' On all these occasions the slate was four feet from the psychic and the writing out of her sight, and upside down to her eyes."

This was completely baffling. It made absolutely certain that she could not and did not guide that pencil in any normal way.

At the end of the sitting the control "Dr. Coulter" came back to confuse the situation by saying, "The music you have obtained is not the reproduction of one of the composer's manuscripts but a mental picture of the composition."

Thereafter the composer himself used the word "scattered" in describing this composition. He seemed to imply that he had sketched out his musical ideas on various detached bits of paper. "Mary will know," he said.

"No more music today," whispered the control, and the sitting ended. This statement by the psychic's guide sounded to me like "hedging." It was as if he were preparing me for disappointment.

Fuller in his report absolved the psychic, as I did, of any complicity in the composition. I quote his report on this point:

"On the second day, during which the bass of the composition was produced, the slate was exclusively in my control—the psychic not touching it at all. The progress of the writing was both *felt* and heard. It was a combination of light and rapid scratching, pecking and twitching, with an occasional slight waving motion of the slate up and down."

Of the deep-reaching, scientific implications of these phenomena on their physical side alone, I was especially aware, for while Fuller was acting as amanuensis I had long hours in which to observe the psychic; and I repeat: "Whatever share Mrs. Hartley might have had in the mental side of this composition, she had nothing whatever to do in any normal way with the process of recording."

In appearance she was as much the onlooker as I. She said, "I never had anything like this happen before." During most of this final hour Fuller and the composer worked intently on their problems, seemingly without our aid, certainly without my interference.

As I have elsewhere recounted, some of the corrections were made on the closed slates by the composer's phantasmal fingers with inconceivable precision. Flags were added to the stems of notes, and notes were placed exactly on extra lines drawn at his request above or below the staff; and these purely physical effects absorbed my attention. As for the quality of the melody, it was manifestly not the kind of music which the psychic could analyze, much less write. It was elliptical, subtle, and touched with wistful melancholy. "Although simple in appearance," said Fuller, "it is absolutely not commonplace."

So far as we could judge by his voice, the composer at the end of the séance was unwearied and intensely eager to go on; but the psychic was manifestly tired, and so was Fuller. Reluctantly he said: "Good-bye, 'E. A.' I am obliged to leave for Chicago this afternoon."

With a promise to return the following morning, I, too, bade "Edward" good night, with an apology for our failure to carry out his wishes.

I did not record the exact words of his reply, and my memory is that he made no direct plea for our return.

That night was another uneasy night. I suffered the conviction that "Edward," in his mysterious place of being, was longing to go on with his composition. He had been so joyously active, so glad of our aid—now we who had created his only channel of expression were about to fail him. He had seemed so real—so alive—that to disappoint him was a kind of treachery.

My remorseful feeling was justified, for on going back to Mrs. Hartley's the next morning I found him waiting for me, eager to proceed. He pleaded with me to go on, but I again protested: "It is of no use, 'Edward.' I can't receive your musical dictation, and Fuller has gone home. I can take down any other messages you care to give, but I am utterly unable to record your music."

The hour was as unsatisfactory to me as it was to him. Nothing new developed, and I made no record of the sitting. I merely set it down briefly as a failure. The fact is, Fuller's departure weakened our battery. That he gave definiteness as well as power to the manifesting intelligence was evident. The composer appeared bewildered by my action. Sadly and reluctantly I said good-bye and came away.

CHAPTER SEVENTEEN

THERE WAS NO SUCH MUSIC

I

UPON reaching my home in Chicago, I had Fuller come to dinner, and together we reviewed our "spirit" music, comparing it with the score of MacDowell's published piano pieces. We found that all the technical peculiarities which the invisible composer had used were employed in "Sea Pieces" and "New England Idyls." We found the device of tying three notes with a curved line with a figure 2 above it.

Fuller said: "If Mrs. Hartley has been a student of MacDowell, or if she is familiar with his music, she may be able supernormally to reproduce one of his pages, or out of my own subconscious mind. As for the melody itself, it seems to me to be a mixture of your memory of certain Ute and Cheyenne songs with my knowledge of the work of MacDowell's compositions."

"Granting that she is familiar with the MacDowell music, you must admit that the method of communication was supernormal?"

"Yes, the process remains inexplicable. My control of the slates was absolute. She did not once touch them during our last sitting. She could not even *see* them while the corrections were being made."

"Suppose we say that the voice was ventriloquistic. How can you explain the fact that our invisible speaker not only described the place but the personnel of a dinner party at which you and I and MacDowell were guests?"

"I can't explain it—except to say that it was a clear case of mind-reading. She couldn't possibly have known of that dinner party and its make-up."

Fuller had transcribed the melody in regular form upon music paper, and when my wife saw it she asked him to play it. He declined. "No, no! Last night, after I had finished copying it, I played it several times with the result that I could not get it out of my mind. It ran in my head all night. It is a weird little tune. I will not play it again."

We urged him so strongly that at last he complied, and as that wistful melody, utterly unlike anything else I had ever heard, entered my ears, the same shudder which had seized me at the final sitting came back upon me. It was as if MacDowell had laid his hand on my shoulder. For several months I felt this singular electrical shiver whenever I heard any of his music. Gradually this emotion lessened and died away.

The report which Fuller wrote at my request gives in detail his share in our most remarkable sittings; and in order that the reader may get a little closer to the mysteries of the process, I quote again, at the risk of repetition, his summing up of the evidence. He did this under three heads:

"1. *The composer as coöperator.* The piece in three

sharps opened on the tonic, yet the first note in the bass was G-sharp. The following colloquy ensued:

"FULLER: Does the piece begin with the tonic chord of A?

"COMPOSER: Of course. That makes it right. How could it be otherwise?

"Here is another example. In the second bar a note which I had taken for an eighth-note, was explained by the composer as being a grace-note. I pointed out that this left only five eighth-notes to fill a six-eight measure. The composer then directed the insertion of an eighth rest at the beginning of the bar. In the fourth bar there was a partial chord E–B—a fifth. I drew the composer's attention to this blemish and he requested the insertion of a G-sharp between, thus completing his triad."

Fuller significantly interpolated this remark: "These and other examples are not without resemblance to thought transference."

"2. *The composer in independence.* Under this head may be placed his various instructions relative to tempo, expression and the like. The signature was set down by myself as the result of an inquiry, but the time, six-eight, was written by the composer at my request. It was a distinct and separate effort, for which the pencil was put in the slate and the slate placed beneath the table. The time was set down before the notes themselves were secured. The six-eight sign was clearly and neatly written on the proper staff, in correct relation to the G-clef and to the signature, and the two figures were in correct relation to each other."

All of this was done while Fuller held the slates entirely out of reach and out of sight of the psychic.

"The word *Moderate* was written in by the composer's direction *without* my request. Later the words 'with feeling' and the marks of expression 'p.p.' were obtained in the same way. Ties, grace-notes and staccato-marks were insisted upon by the composer with great vigor and earnestness.

"3. *The composer in opposition.* I have said that some of the phenomena of Division One resembled thought transference but numerous examples of cross-purposes between the composer and our circle now developed.

"On the first opening of the slate at our last sitting, I found that the seventh measure of the treble contained but two notes which the composer presently declared vocally to be quarter-notes. This left the first third of the measure vacant. I called the composer's attention to this and he said, 'Insert a quarter-rest.' I objected to this. 'It gives the measure a three-quarter look, instead of a proper six-eighth look.' Quick as a flash in a sharp whisper came his answer, 'That is a liberty I permit myself!'

"At another stage, he requested that a certain note should have a 'dot' added. I put the dot to the right of the note—thus lengthening its value one-half. 'No, no,' he whispered. 'Put it on top—above the staff.' (This made it evident that he could *see* the correction. *This the psychic was wholly unable to do.*)

"In the eighth and last measure which did not appear to be satisfactorily completed, the composer directed me to insert a figure 2. I did not understand this and said so. The composer graciously replied, 'Never mind. I will write it differently.' He cancelled the

figure 2 and completed the measure with a rest. Later
I learned that he wished two quarter-notes to receive
the value of three eighth-notes.

"A similar instance occurred in the fifth measure,
when the composer called insistently for a double
sharp (x). I ventured to object and he replied, 'Try it
on the piano.' I did so. The double sharp was felt by
him to be unsatisfactory. 'Take it out,' he whispered.
'It won't make much difference anyway.' "

With Fuller's technical report supplementing mine,
I felt certain that I had obtained one of the most complete and highly intellectual records of identity as well
as of supernormal physical phenomena in the whole
range of psychic research.

"The next step," I said, "is to lay all this before Mrs.
MacDowell. If she can find a musical fragment called
'Ungarie' among his papers, we score a triumphant
finale."

"What if she can not find such a manuscript?"

"Well, we shall still have the inexplicable physical
phenomena to ponder upon. Supernormal methods of
transmission do not argue the truth of a message, but
they suggest it."

II

As soon as I was able to leave Chicago, I took these
slates and other records of our sittings with me and
started for New York, eager to secure Marian Mac-
Dowell's comment upon them. I am willing to confess that I was a bit apprehensive of the effect of my
story upon her. She was not recovered from her bereave-

ment, and my demand was exciting. I especially hoped
that she would identify the very sketchy two bars of
music which I had secured before Fuller joined me, and
that they might prove to be from the opening movement of the "Sonata Tragica." I was more excited,
more expectant than I had ever been during my previous twenty years of experience with psychic phenomena.

My interview was a disappointment. She listened
while I described in detail the method of recording this
music and these messages. "The method was supernormal, but the proof of identification must come from
you," I declared. I told her of the whispers, I drama-
tized the masterly technique of the invisible composer.
"The speaker was like Edward," I went on, describing
how his message, misread at first, had persisted even
against our contrary concept of its meaning. "At last
he whispered to me. He asked about you. He was
anxious about you. He *told* me of this manuscript and
said you would know about it. 'I want it recovered
from Schuberth and handed over to Schmidt for immediate publication,' he said."

I had expected, almost feared, that she would be
greatly moved by my story—but she was not! On the
contrary she smiled, as if amused. "There's nothing to
it," she briskly declared. "There *is* no fragment called
'Ungarie.' There never was. I know every bar that
Edward ever wrote. There never was such a composition."

"What about the message asking us to recover a
manuscript in the hands of Schuberth?"

"That is especially absurd. Edward never dealt with

Schuberth. All his music went to Schmidt. Your 'composer' was fooling you. He was impersonating Edward."

"Let us be quite sure," I urged. "Let's ask the Schuberth company. This is a most important test. This invisible composer addressed me exactly as Edward used to do, and the process of the composition was supernormal."

She yielded. "I will ask—but I know that I am right."

She was! No trace of such a manuscript could be discovered, but I insisted that the mystery of that request remained. "There is no explanation of it on any normal basis. The writer of those words 'have Schuberth' was eager to have it carried out, for he returned to it several times the following day. His will persisted in opposition to my concept. He seemed a very real and determined personality."

In the midst of my disappointment Mrs. MacDowell, while examining one of the slates, suddenly flashed into keen interest. Pointing to the signature "Edward McDowell" which remained on one of the leaves, she sharply asked, "Where did you get that?"

"It came along with the other messages while the slate was in my hands. It came without contact by the psychic; but I gave no special thought to it, for it is not Edward's signature."

"Oh, yes, it is!" she replied. "It is exactly as he signed his name when I first knew him in Leipsic."

"But it is wrongly spelled. It is 'Edward McDowell' instead of 'Edward A. MacDowell'—and it has a lot of absurd flourishes beneath it."

"That also is right. At that time he spelled his name McDowell and he used a boyish flourish under his name, just as it is here."

As she spoke a light broke upon me. I recalled seeing that signature—but where? Where? I raised my eyes to a letter in a small frame on the wall. "There it is!" I exclaimed. "There it is in that frame, exactly as it is on the slate!"

She took the frame down from its hook and handed it to me in order that I might compare the signatures. The letter was a certificate stating that Miss Marian Nevins was a capable pianist, and it was signed "Edward McDowell"—with the same flourishes which underlined the signature I had supernormally received on the slates.

"How could that woman, who has never been in your home, duplicate a signature which she had never seen and which I had forgotten?" I asked. "Conceding for the sake of argument that it was *not* supernormally written, how shall we account for the psychic's reproduction of it? If she took it from my subconscious mind and reproduced it by sleight of hand, it is sufficiently wonderful; but the fact that it was written on closed slates held in my own hands shakes my concept of the material universe. The spiritist would say that Edward sent it as a convincing sign to you."

Mrs. MacDowell's indifference to the musical messages of "E. A." was a setback, I willingly admit. She would not play the music, nor did she attempt to authenticate the bars which "E. A." said were from the "Tragic Sonata."

I have never since heard "Edward's" voice.

One other confession remains to be made. I never
had the pigment of the writing chemically analyzed.
I should have done so, but I didn't. I studied it under a
microscope and was able to perceive that it was laid
on rather than pressed into the surface of the slate.
The writing, although I have carefully preserved these
slates, in the course of time has faded out. Some of it is
still legible, but none of it appears to have the permanent quality of the pencilled initials which I put in
the corners of the new slates for identification. There
is a difference in the pigment. As for the book of
Judah's in which the supernormal transcription was
made, I have not had recent opportunity to examine
that. This should have been especially analyzed while
its supernormal characteristics could have been attested
by Fuller and the Judahs. I confess my negligence. Today they are all gone, and John's books are scattered.
The score of "Ungarie" was lost during the removal of
my own library, but most of my notes remain.

As I reëxamine the records in the light of later
knowledge, they gain rather than lose in significance.

From time to time I experienced a pang of remorse.
"I ought to go on with it," I said to Fuller. " 'Edward'
may be waiting for us."

Had I been a little more certain of those whispers,
I might have returned to push investigations forward;
I never did. Something in my mind, some barrier, could
not be overcome. I wished to be convinced, but my
desire was not strong enough to lead to further action.

Hawthorne in one of his pages on Florence states
with masterly brevity and poise the character of this
mental barrier: "What most astonishes me is the indiffer-

ence with which I listen to these [spiritualistic] marvels. They . . . are absolutely proved to be sober facts by evidence that would satisfy us of any other alleged realities; and yet I cannot force my mind to interest myself in them. They are facts to my understanding, . . . but they seem not to be facts to my intuitions and deeper perceptions. My inner soul does not in the least admit them; there is a mistake somewhere."

So with me at the close of this amazing series of happenings. My intuitions would not allow me to surrender my faith in the scientific concept of the universe around me.

CHAPTER EIGHTEEN

SOLDIERS IN THE SKY

I

MAURICE MAETERLINCK in commenting on the post-war world-wide wave of interest in spiritism, made a very curious statement concerning the effect of military slaughter on this revival. After remarking (as many others have done) upon the passionate search for consolation in which millions of bereaved fathers and mothers were engaged he said:

"Our memories are peopled with a multitude of heroes struck down in the flower of their youth, a very different host from the pale and languid cohorts of the past, composed almost entirely of the sick and the old, and upon this fact I base my belief that from this numerous and powerful throng of young spirits there must result an immense and immediate gain in our positive knowledge of the world beyond the grave."

The singular part of this statement, to me, lies in the frank admission on the part of the Belgian mystic, that the body's weakness or age can profoundly affect the soul, and that the spirit of a young man is a more powerful agency for intercommunication between our plane and theirs than that of an aged philosopher. I am loth to grant that a man's soul is conditioned by his body. That the war gave an enormous impetus to the study of psychic phenomena, I admit; but a simple explanation of it lies in the force of world-wide unnatural bereavement. The desire to bring back the dead was strongly increased by the millions of sons, husbands, and fathers who were slain.

This was made evident in my small world by the increasing number of those who came to me seeking a source of comfort. "Do you know of a reliable medium to whom I can go for consolation?" each mourner demanded of me. In this lies the strength of the spirit hypothesis—it offers something audible and tangible to the mourner.

There is another angle to Maeterlinck's statement. Not only were the slain soldiers mostly young, but their fathers and mothers were still in the full tide of life, subject to intenser emotions than the aged, and as seekers they undoubtedly added their forces to the wave of spiritism which went round the earth. Along with this passionate hope went a loss of faith in the wisdom of the ancients. The demand was for experiment, for proof.

"All that the Greeks or Romans had, we have," they said. "We must find our answers to our own questions. Socrates and Plato knew no more about death than we do. The problem is one of today—our day. We must solve it for ourselves. Do our dead still live?"

In this attitude I profoundly sympathized. I did not believe the report of those who saw "the soldiers in the sky" at the battle of Mons, but I shared the conviction that if the souls of those soldiers had outlived their mangled bodies, there should be a way of proving it. Quoting ancient script, whether Greek, Roman, Hebrew, or Chinese, was of no value to me. I remained wholly sympathetic with the scientific method of inquiry.

"When the body dies, does the soul persist?" is the question, and I believed it to be a legitimate problem for science.

Sir Oliver Lodge is the most outstanding illustration of the effect of the war on a father. Although one of the most eminent of our physicists, he published in 1916 a book called "Raymond," in the preface of which he writes of the appalling amount of "premature and unnatural bereavement" caused by the war and bravely proclaims his belief in the fact of survival after death and invites the reader to follow his argument.

Raymond was his son, slain in France, and the book is a statement of the evidence on which he was willing to stake his great reputation as chemist, physicist, and philosopher. He says, "Death is not a serious matter, it is only a moment of change like birth," and one section of his book is filled with the records of Raymond's communications, conversations which convinced Sir Oliver of his son's lively existence and led to his publicly proclaiming it on the platform in America as well as in England.

Another great advocate to whom "the soldiers in the sky" were not wholly a fantastic vision was Sir Arthur Conan Doyle, who, when similarly bereaved by the war, became an unfaltering evangelist. He toured Australia, Canada, and the United States proclaiming his faith. He wrote incessantly. He financed spiritualist organizations for experiment, and aided magazines for the promulgation of his faith. He turned his almost unequalled popularity as a novelist into channels of propaganda whose persuasiveness gave new power to the spiritualistic hypothesis.

He came to America in 1922 and proved himself to be the most eloquent of all modern advocates of spirit communication. He addressed enormous audiences wherever he went, putting into plain words what Lodge had cautiously clothed in scientific phrase. His influence was immeasurable.

As an old friend and fellow craftsman, I presented him to his first audience in America, an audience such as I had never before faced; and in his home in Sussex I afterward listened to his experiences in a most intimate way. No comment on the post-war revival of interest in matters psychical can leave out the testimony of this beloved author, who was a soldier as well as a physician.

During the actual period of strife European experiment naturally languished; but in the four or five years immediately following the war, books on psychic research multiplied. Geley, Richet, Osty, and many other European scientific men issued reports which summed up their experiments.

Among the most valuable of these books is Schrenck-Notzing's amazing record of four years' experiment with two young psychics in Paris: a careful, systematic, relentless study of the phenomena of materialization. It is one of the most searching investigations ever made; for at every stage of his tests skilful photographs were taken, and the reader can follow step by step the proc-

ess by which he reached his conclusions. It is an appalling record.

As I read the thick volume I found confirmations
of my own belief that a luminous substance does veritably emerge from the body of a psychic, streaming
from her lips, her cheeks, and her bosom, for in the
book this substance is pictured—photographed in the
act of condensing into hands, faces,-heads, and even
into male forms of giant size.

In these photographs can be seen the distorted faces
of the mediums, whose expressions of pain and effort
gave indubitable evidence of the destructive physical
process of mediumship. In some of the pictures the
psychic's head appears to be melting away to form a
"spirit" face. Others of these phantoms, small at first
and delicate as a rose, are shown expanding like an
opening flower or vanishing like mist. Keen, bright,
beautiful faces peer from the cabinet while the psychic
with bowed head and a look of agony on her face en-
dures the light of the magnesium torch.

"Her pain resembled childbirth," the author bluntly
states. "At times she seemed to sleep, at others she was
alert and wholly normal in mood."

These photographs were of especial interest to me,
for I had seen similar forms in shadowy actions and
had longed to picture them. I had felt such hands. I
had seen this mist rise and develop what appeared to
be a vague human figure; but I had never been able
to use a flashlight camera. Looking back over my experiences, I recalled scores of test materializations, of
which similar pictures should have been taken by myself or some other.

"Suppose we had operated a modern camera when, in Flower's home, invisible fingers picked up the scattered sheets of paper on the table, thrust a pin through them and laid them aside on a sofa? We might have caught the form of the 'ghost' who worked this miracle. In the case of Daniel Peters we might have secured a picture of the hand which clasped my wrist and lifted the glass of water to the psychic's lips."

If Schrenck-Notzing's report stood alone, it would mark an epoch in the study of spiritualistic phenomena; but it does not stand alone. In January, 1918, while the war was still going on Dr. Gustave Geley read before the General Psychologic Institute of Paris a paper in which he substantiated all that Schrenck-Notzing had observed. He showed the Institute scores of flashlight photographs and stated that his findings had been verified and checked by nearly one hundred experts, mostly doctors.

He says of the ectoplasm: "It is variable in color, white, gray, black. It is mobile and timid, retreating to the medium as if for protection. It is sensitive to the light, and strong rays cast upon it give pain to the psychic. It has an immediate, irresistible tendency to organize itself. It remains but a moment in its original shape. It forms hands, limbs, faces, complete bodies. It has no means of defending itself. It is like a timid animal. It is ephemeral, yet capable of appearing solid and permanent."

He adds: "I have seen the complete process. I have seen the substance coming from the fingers of the medium, like a fringe, a veil, to become finally a hand or a visage. Sometimes it exudes from the body of the psychic and settles like hoar-frost upon her clothing forming a sort of apron out of which a head or face appears."

There are no qualifications in this statement. It is bold, definite, and inclusive.

The working hypothesis of all these later investigations seems to be this: Some human organisms are able to throw off a physical substance which tends to take shape in obedience to the thought of the psychic or to the thought of the sitter. This substance is capable of being modelled by the mind of the psychic or sitter as wax is modelled by a sculptor. That is to say, it is *ideoplastic*; and this is proven by the fact that inanimate objects, portraits, dream-pictures, cats, dogs, and even imaginary animals are materialized.

In conclusion Geley says: "In my opinion metaphysical science involves inferences which will revolutionize biology and psychology. I abstain from all theory, and from all attempt to explain these facts."

When one reads these two cold-blooded reports, the stories of "the soldiers in the sky" are less fantastical than they appeared at first to be. If they were not there, imagination could put them there.

In my long experience up to this date I had never seen the materialization of any animal, but I had argued thus: "If the shapes which 'ectoplasm' takes are controlled by the thought of the sitters, I see no reason why a pet poodle or a parrot should not be 'materialized.' "

It is recorded of an Italian medium that one evening after a long sitting, one which she could scarcely bring to a close, she went for relaxation to a café with some friends; and that while seated at the table something, some anomalous form, developed beneath the dining table.

One of the party remarked, "There's a dog under the table." Upon examination no dog was visible but a moment later another of the group said: "It is a cat. I felt a paw with sharp claws on my knee." Again the space was examined, but no animal was visible. "Thinking created it, and thinking took it away."

This theory also accounts for the curious and suspicious fact that many of the "spirit" photographs I have seen appear to be copies of family portraits. If these are ideographs it is natural that they should resemble the sitter's memory of a family portrait. If I were called upon to describe my father or mother, I should perceive them as sitting for their portraits. It is easier to recall them in some one fixed position than in action. There is no reason to cry "fraud" because these spirit portraits look like copies of pictures on the wall. The ideographic theory may also be taken to explain why so many materialized forms are dressed as Orientals. "They are forms born of the psychic's belief in East Indian magic and wisdom."

In the desire to hold an even hand over this discussion I present the spiritualists' rejoinder: "Very well. We accept the ectoplasmic theory. We grant these forms are ideoplastic. But why limit the creative force to the psychic and her sitters? We say the modelling can be done and *is* done by discarnate minds—that is to say, by spirits: these materializations are a mixture of forms shaped not only by the minds of the medium and the sitters but by beings who are acting from another plane. Your ideoplastic theory does not exclude spirit return."

There is enough logic in this retort to give me pause. I am not prepared to deny the *possibility* of discarnate action, but I am not convinced of it. I shall continue to experiment until the weight of evidence is on one side of the scales—giving full weight to all evidence pointing to the identity of the manifesting spirit.

II

Granting the objectivity of all the phenomena detailed by Ochorowicz, Schrenck-Notzing, and Lodge, I continued to press the question, "Are these human shapes in any way related to the spirits of the dead? Or are they only 'soldiers in the sky'?"

In partial answer to this Dr. Geley says: "In all mediumistic phenomena, one observes a marked tendency toward personation, but the mediumistic personality is insignificant and ephemeral. Nevertheless it declares itself a true individual separate from the medium. I consider it as probable that the action of these entities is distinct from the medium. In a word, the phenomena induced by the medium appear to indicate, to require and to proclaim a knowledge, a power surpassing even the subconscious faculties of the medium."

This appeared to be the case of the "Composer" in my experiments in recording his music.

CHAPTER NINETEEN

IMPERSONATION WITHOUT TRANCE

I

IN the years following the World War, I continued my occasional addresses on psychical subjects, always on the lookout for "sensitives" willing to share with me their experience. I was willing to leave their beliefs undisturbed if they would assist me in further analysis of the method.

Several of those with whom I experimented were publishing books whose composition, so they said, was the work of personalities outside themselves, and higher than themselves. Naturally they could not permit a searching analysis of the sources of their inspiration. Others were preachers, leaders of congregations, and very naturally opposed to scientific research.

Scores of books and manuscripts composed "under spirit control" came to me for approval—not for judgment. Not one of them expected me to say—as I was forced to do—that such writing was, in my opinion, merely the product of their own subconscious minds. "Granting the marvel of the process," I replied in several such cases, "the product has small literary or philosophic value."

These manuscripts were all deeply religious in tone and biblical in phraseology. One of the most curious—I might almost say monumental—books of this sort is the romance "Patience Worth," written "under inspiration" by a Kansas woman, who was aided, so she declared, by the spirit of an English girl of the sixteenth century.

Patience Worth, this invisible author, not only wrote her own story but ventured upon a voluminous "Sorry Tale of the Time of Christ." Relying on this guide, Mrs. Curran came at last to a stage of mediumship in which she was able to extemporize poems without a moment's hesitation upon any subject named by a visitor. This she did without going into trance.

I have in my files the record of my first sitting with Mrs. Curran. During our talk she told me that her literary career began with the Ouija board, but that she had gradually grown free from it. "I still keep it under my hand," she said, "but I no longer spell out the messages from 'Patience.' I am able to speak them."

Placing me in a chair opposite her, she held one side of the lettered board whilst I held the other. Her husband, a St. Louis newspaper man (I believe), sat beside her with pencil poised over a notebook ready to make a record of the test.

Thereupon with no hint of abnormal psychology, Mrs. Curran composed and spoke, without hesitation or blunder, a poem on "A Cup of Tea," a subject named by the hostess. I observed that when Mrs. Curran outran her husband's pencil, and he called "Wait!" she stopped even in the midst of a line—and later took it up again precisely as if she were repeating something from memory. She did this when the subject was suggested by me. I observed, however, that "Patience" used words which belonged to Kansas and not to the England of 1600; and that she was inclined to be impudent in her replies.

In other later tests I heard Mrs. Curran dictate many similar poems while standing before a throng of guests, and I had opportunity afterward to read typed stenographic record of these improvisations. My estimate of their literary value was not high. The poems were clever—astonishingly so—but they ran to fixed phrases and in accordance with a formula. They were all below, some of them considerably below, publishing level. They were graceful, thoughtful and quaint but failed to win the approval of austere literary critics.

Most automatic writing is gravely philosophical in subject, and sets forth a highly moral interpretation of the universe. All religious and scientific problems are solved by these invisible sages. Sometimes the inspiring spirit is an "ancient," sometimes a famous modern philosopher; but in all cases the mediums are confident of their value as teachers. I do not pass final judgment on these books—I merely say that they do not interest me.

Two of the most distinguished authors of my acquaintance make use of subconscious "inspiration"; in fact I myself once depended upon it, but I controlled and directed it. I still joke about "Old Subconscious Mind" with my daughters. It is a faithful servant, but I keep close watch upon it. I accept its suggestions, but I ruthlessly revise and correct them.

I have many times induced automatic writing in my friends. Sometimes it is back-handed and upside

down, and can be read only in a mirror. This is what
is called mirror writing. In my first experiment with my
friend Mrs. Judah, her hand wrote in mirror script these
words: "My name is John Smith. I was drowned in
this lake on August tenth, 1888."

This so startled Mrs. Judah that she sprang up from
her chair and fled. I could never get her to sit again.

In two other cases of these impromptu after-dinner
experiments I have apparently caused trance and automatic writing, with curious impersonations. In one case
the spirit impersonated seemed to be that of a famous
murderess who had recently been hanged, and while the
lovely psychic was pleading, "I didnt do it—I saw it
done but I didnt kill him," she held her hands behind
her back as if manacled, and her face became hideously
contorted as though she were being strangled by a rope.
All this could be simulated, of course; but some of her
communications were true—so members of the circle
asserted.

These trances appeared genuine, but I regarded them
as entertainment for the guests who had requested
them. I mention them here as leading up to communications without trance.

II

One day in New York City an old friend, Edwin
Winter, invited me to lunch with him at the Bankers'
Club; and when I entered the grand reception room
thirty stories above Wall Street, he met me with
another guest whom he presented as Mr. Traynor.
"Traynor," he said, "has had the gift of second sight,

ever since he was a child, and I think will interest you."

The clairvoyant was so normal in appearance and so candid of expression that I could not relate him to any distinctive phase of mediumship; and during our luncheon, surrounded as we were by hundreds of hilarious business men, no observer would have distinguished our table as one given over to "spooks."

Nevertheless our talk was of the occult. Traynor told us that he had all his life been able to see forms invisible to others and to report their words to his friends and relatives.

Winter interrupted to say, "He often does this at my home, without going into a trance, and without laying down his cigar."

"What seems to be the process?" I asked of Traynor.

"It seems to be a negative process," he thoughtfully replied. "I have only to throw my eyes out of focus and render my mind as blank as possible. In this negative state I wait till a figure, a portrait, or a message comes into my mind—then I report what I see or hear. I have no power to distinguish the false from the true. I am like a wireless receiving station. I get messages and give them for what they are worth to my listeners."

Winter said: "The truth of his messages is astounding. I was a railway president for many years, and Traynor gets hold, in some way, of my old cronies in the Northwest and they talk to me through him for hours while we are seated beside my fire. I can't account for this, but it is a fact. You and Mrs. Garland must come to dinner soon. I'll have Traynor in and we'll see what happens."

Traynor interested me. He was intelligent and candid, not irritated nor alarmed by my sceptical attitude, and most reasonable in his claims. "I am willing to try anything," he said.

Winter, a widower and a man of seventy, lived in one of the huge apartment houses on Park Avenue, and when my wife and I entered his reception room, a few days later, we did not in the least suggest the members of a spiritistic circle. The apartment was a long way from the Boston back-parlors in which I had begun my investigations some thirty years before. It was a handsome room, and Traynor in dinner dress looked less like a medium than at our luncheon in the Bankers' Club.

Augustus Thomas came in later, and I was especially glad of his presence, for he had made a special study of mind reading and clairvoyance. "It is in these directions that Traynor's power moves," Winter explained.

Nothing was said of his mediumship during dinner; but an hour later as we were all sitting before the fire, with our coffee and cigars, Winter turned to Traynor and said, "Well, Tom, do you see any 'spooks' in the room?"

Traynor, holding his cigar in his fingers, slowly replied, "Yes, I see a young woman standing beside Mrs. Garland."

This startled my wife, for she not only disbelieved such phenomena but heartily disliked all discussion of them. She said nothing to encourage Traynor, and neither did I. We both waited in silence.

Without going into trance but with glance "out of focus" Traynor went on: "She says her name is Scales —'Carrie L. Scales.' She is about thirty-five. She is tall, with brown hair combed up in a roll above her brow. She says to you, Mrs. Garland, that you were not with her when she passed out—neither was her husband."

This name and this description amazed my wife, so exactly true were they; but she remained silent.

As he went on, he began to impersonate the dead woman. He spoke as if she were using his organs of speech. Addressing my wife directly, "Carrie" entered into most intimate personal details. "For a time I resented my husband's second marriage, but I am resigned to it now," she said.

She described events of which my wife had no knowledge, and of which Traynor could not have read, and my wife was deeply moved by them. "He could not have known of these family conditions," she declared, "but every relationship and every description was exactly true."

Turning abruptly to our host, Traynor said: "There is a man here who says he has known you ever since you were a boy. He says: 'I used to see you on the platform of the station at Beloit, Wisconsin. You used to come down to the train with pails of berries to sell to the passengers.'"

"That's right," said Winter. "So I did."

Traynor now impersonated this man. "You remember me?" he said to Winter. "I was conductor on the local which ran from Chicago to Madison. I wore a fancy vest—you'll remember that vest—and it was my habit to wait till the last car came along before swinging on. You liked to see me do it. You admired me." Here he changed his tone. "After you became a big man in the railway business you made me a division superintendent. That was a mistake. I wasn't big enough for the job."

Amused and excited, Winter turned to me. "I recall that man perfectly, but I haven't thought of him for years. All that he says is true. I *did* sell berries on the station platform, and I *did* watch him swing onto the rear car platform. I recall his fancy vest. It is true also that after I became general manager of the Northern Railway I promoted him. He proved a failure as superintendent and I put him back as conductor on a train. It is impossible for Traynor to know these details except by some occult process; for those details about the berries, the fancy vest, and my admiration for the man are not on record anywhere. They exist only in my own mind—in fact I had entirely forgotten them."

He then told us that "Jim Hill" and many others of his old railway companions often came to him through Traynor. "They talk to me by the hour. As a spook, Hill is just as loquacious as he was in my office in St. Paul."

Turning to Thomas, Traynor now began to talk of an old-time actor with whom Augustus had once been intimately associated, bringing to light certain facts of which Augustus himself had no knowledge. "I'll have to look into the records," he said. "My case is not so clear as yours, Winter, for this spirit friend of mine was an actor well known on Broadway for twenty years. Nevertheless, Traynor has made some very startling statements. At their lowest terms they are clairvoyant. I didn't know that this actor's real name was Dempsey, and I didn't know that my employer, Washington Bishop, the mind-reader, had a brother."

This is a brief outline of an astonishing performance. For Traynor brought up several other personalities—in fact all his messages bore on the question of identity. Seated in the light of the fire and smoking a cigar, he suggested nothing of the medium in his action or speech; and yet he had some unexplained power.

It appeared that he could turn this power off and on like twisting a key. He stopped as abruptly as he began. "They are all gone," he said.

Winter then said to me: "I like Traynor's attitude toward this thing. You can deal with him as frankly as you please. I frequently interrupt and go over my cases with him."

Traynor confirmed this by saying: "I don't know how I do these things. Some say I get my facts out of newspapers and encyclopedias. If I did, I would have no time for anything else."

"I don't quite see how you could get the facts about my wife's sister-in-law, for they are not in any biography or encyclopedia."

"Where did he get that conductor's fancy vest and my pails of berries?" demanded Winter.

"It is clearly a case of mind-reading," said Thomas. "I travelled with Washington Irving Bishop for two years, and so far as I can now recall, I never met his brother or heard him speak of his brother; and yet I might have had the fact registered somewhere deep in my subconscious memory."

"It is rather significant," I here remarked, "that Traynor had almost nothing for me—although I am the one man whose family history is detailed in 'A Son of the Middle Border' and other volumes of reminiscences.

This has been my experience all along: no psychic has brought me details of my dead relatives such as Traynor has given to you and Mrs. Garland. Where did you find the name 'Carrie L. Scales'?"

"I don't know," he frankly replied. "It came into my mind with the form. I've seen these forms which are invisible to others, ever since I was a child. My father used to punish me for 'lying,' as he called it. This mediumistic faculty has been a serious handicap to me in business. Bankers don't like to deal with 'mediums,' and so I keep still about this power when in my office."

As we were going away, Winter placed in my hands a packet of papers and said, "Read these at your leisure and let me know what you think of the case they present."

This I did the following day, and the story which these records presented is so strong a brief for personal survival that I think it should be given here in some detail, although I heard only a part of the "spirit" confession. I read the letters carefully, but I did not copy them; and I am now dependent upon my memory although the leading facts are recorded in my diary.

Winter presented, in substance, this revelation:

"One night Traynor, while spending the evening with me, abruptly said, 'There is a man here, a queer, seedy old chap, who says that he is a kind of uncle of yours.'

" 'A *kind* of uncle?' I said. 'What does he mean by that?'

" 'He says you never saw him but that he married your Aunt Sarah when you were a child. He says his name is Milton K. Smalley.'

"I thought a moment. 'I faintly recall that there

was such a marriage, but the man was only a name. I never saw him. The marriage was not often alluded to. I had forgotten him completely. What does he want?'

" 'He doesn't seem to want anything—just wishes to say that he didn't appreciate your aunt. He would like to identify himself and clear his record. He says: "I left your aunt and went down to Lowell just before the Civil War broke out. I enlisted in one of the first Massachusetts regiments to go South, and I was killed in the Baltimore riot along with four other men." '

" 'That can be easily verified,' I said. 'The records on file at the State House in Boston will show your name and the date of your death.' "

In the bundle of papers which he had given me was a letter to the Adjutant General in Boston. In his reply the Adjutant General said, "There is no such name on the rolls of that regiment, and no such man was killed as the regiment was marching through Baltimore."

Winter's report went on:

"The next time Traynor came, I told him what the Adjutant had written. He then became silent, and that fixed look came into his eyes. When he spoke he impersonated Smalley: 'Of course you didn't find me under that name. I enlisted under another name altogether. You see I'd been living with another woman since, leaving your aunt, and I enlisted as Jackson Turner.' "

This was as far as Winter's records carried me; but a few weeks later, while my wife and I were again dining with him, Winter took a letter from his pocket and handed it to me. "Here is the concluding document in that curious case of 'Smalley's.' "

The letter was from the Adjutant and confirmed

Smalley's story in every detail. A man named "Jackson Turner" *had* enlisted in that regiment and *had* been killed in the streets of Baltimore along with three other men.

Winter then said: "I wrote my sister, and here is a letter confirming the story of Sarah's marriage; so that 'Smalley' was, as he says, 'a kind of uncle' of mine. Now what are we to do about that? How could Traynor know what I did not know, what the war office didn't know, and what none of my family knew?"

I couldn't answer these questions then, and I cannot answer them now. I am willing to grant that these facts strengthen the case for personal survival, although I must add that Traynor was never able to give me any similar proof.

Not long after these evenings at Winter's home, I arranged to have Traynor lunch with me and meet an old friend who had lately lost his wife and was eager to see if she could speak to him.

My friend, whom I shall call Brown, was living in a hotel near Times Square, and our luncheon was served in his own private suite. We had hardly finished eating, and the waiter was busily clearing away the dishes, when our host turned to Traynor and said, "Have you anything for us?"

Conditions could scarcely have been more unfavorable to any mediumistic action. We had all eaten heartily, the two men were smoking, and I was sipping my coffee. But almost immediately, Traynor began to impersonate "Jane Brown," the dead wife. From his lips came words which indicated that the dying woman had twice left the body and that she had visited friends during her first flight. "I heard your voice," she said, "and returned to my body. I heard you, but I could not answer."

Traynor turned to me and spoke in "Jane's" character. "I wanted to see you before you went home, but I was not able to do so. I was too weak."

This was the fact. I had been staying with Brown to help him bear the anxiety of his wife's illness but was at last obliged to fill some lecture dates. The apparent death of "Mrs. Brown" and her revival a few hours later, was true, and so was her reported appearance at the bedside of a friend, as I afterward learned.

Brown, though much moved by this singular drama, continued to smoke while it was going on, and so did Traynor. It remains the most unconventional of all my sittings and in some ways the most impressive.

At a later sitting, one very illogical communication came to me. Traynor said: "There is a Southern man here who says his name is 'Kingman.' He says: 'You knew my son. He's been a failure from my point of view.' "

"Do you mean 'Edward Kingman'?"

"Yes, he's my son. You know him well."

"Yes, he was my agent at one time. Why? What can I do for him or for you?"

Nothing really came out of this talk except a wonder on my part that "Kingman" should come to me. I never knew him—but I dimly recalled that he manufactured pianos somewhere in the West.

I was equally puzzled when "John G. Shedd," the former partner of Marshall Field, complained to me that Chicago was not managing his public aquarium properly. I did not know "Shedd," and I knew nothing of the management of his aquarium. There was no logic in his addressing me.

In all these experiments with Traynor the question of *identity* was uppermost, the method of communication was subordinated and proof was difficult. All the messages were open to the mind-reading charge. *Somebody* knew these facts and faces, and Traynor appeared to be able to seize upon them, no matter how deep-laid his sitter's unconscious thought might be.

This phase of public mediumship, practiced on hundreds of platforms throughout the country, is sought by many thousands of eager auditors. Messages are given by the lecturer (at the close of his address) in swift alternation from left to right of his audience. He appears to select each recipient by some inner suggestion, and hits the mark each time—if one may judge from the applause.

I have listened to many such exhibitions but always with a feeling of doubt, for the messages are so swift and so consolingly stereotyped that they fail of convincing me. My experiences in private investigation have been tedious and painful, floundering and confused. All those who came before my committee were manifestly "fishing" for names.

At a public meeting of the branch society in Los Angeles, however, an Englishwoman gave an exhibition of this sort which had elements of proof in it. First of all, she was a complete stranger to her audience, and had been in the city but a day or two. She had hardly been seen out of her room, and she was surrounded by the officers of the society, including the honorary chairman, myself. Despite these facts, she gave a most convincing demonstration of mind-reading, or some other occult perception.

Among other test messages, she addressed a tall, blonde young girl entirely Nordic in appearance and said: "There is a Spanish woman standing beside you, an elderly woman in Spanish dress with a mantilla over her head. Her name is 'Carmelita.' She says she is your grandmother."

As she gave the message the girl appeared moved by its truth. She acknowledged that she had a Spanish grandmother and that her name was "Carmelita."

As this psychic went on describing other invisibles and giving their names and messages, she quite convinced me that, like Traynor, she had a perceptive sense which is denied the ordinary individual. It was restricted in range, and the messages were of the usual consolation type; but, given here in the blaze of electric lights to an audience of several hundred people, they were of greater value than when given under trance or in the dark.

As chairman of our research committee, I arranged several sittings for Traynor in the rooms of the New York Society, and without the slightest pretension to trance, he showed a perceptive power quite similar to that of the Englishwoman of whom I have just spoken. With the stenographic reports of these sittings before me, I am able to quote the valuable testimony of a distinguished lawyer, who declared that some of the men and lawsuits which Traynor described while impersonating "Judge Blank," an old California friend, dated back twenty years or more, and had been completely forgotten by him. It was quite impossible that Traynor could have known of them in any normal way. On its lowest terms, this performance was a reading of the lawyer's subconscious mind.

Traynor was unsuccessful in his attempt to read a sealed letter, but he succeeded in giving something of the history of two finger rings which were placed in his hand. I particularly liked his straightaway method. He did not flounder or fish about for clues. He said again: "I give you what comes into my mind. It may be true or it may not. I am only a wireless receiving station. I have no way of determining the truth or falsity of the communication. That is up to you."

Platform psychomancy is an important problem for the reason that all over America such performances are being given every Sunday, and thousands of people attend these meetings. That they get something which comforts them is evident, for they go again and again. Doubters accuse such mediums of digging into graveyards and thumbing county histories, but not all of the messages are capable of being thus explained. Some of the persons thus publicly recalled to life never rose to the dignity of being named in any biography nor of being listed in the telephone book.

Fortunately we are able to quote Dr. Alexis Carrel on this phase of mediumship. In a book just published he concedes the truth of clairvoyance, telepathy, and several other phases of the claims of psychic researchers.

CHAPTER TWENTY

PHANTASMAL FINGER–PRINTS

No one knows what the processes of mediumship precisely are. Granted that psychical phenomena exist, the questions "How are they produced?" and "What are the physical and mental strains upon the medium?" remain unanswered. Some observers consider mediumship a temporary disassociation of personality, a destructive splitting up of the psychological unity which forms an individual. Others contend that it is a species of "possession," a period of weakness which allows an alien mind—often a malevolent mind—to dominate the individual. In sanity is considered by some to be such a "possession." In their opinion the practice of mediumship is a surrender of the will, a dangerous practice not to be encouraged.

Most spiritualists, however, regard the trance as a negative state during which certain invisible entities are permitted to use the body of the sleeper in their various manifestations. Others more scientific consider the trance a condition of *conscious rest*, in which the subconscious self is free to manifest in many forms outside the body. That something material actually goes out of the psychic whether in trance or not, is made evident by instruments which register the loss of heat;

of weight, and of physical power. In its deepest phase it is a kind of death.

So far as my own experience goes, the reality of the trance has not been proven. I have never been able to convince myself of its genuineness. There is no easy way of determining whether the psychic is actually in trance or only pretending to be, for it is known that certain individuals are proof against needles and hot irons. Doctors writing on hysteria assert that they have had patients who were insensible to hot pokers and the fumes of ammonia. Hypnotists in public exhibitions give evidence of such insensibility. A young man who came before my committee was able to thrust hatpins through his cheek without wincing or drawing blood.

Furthermore I have observed that all those trance mediums with whom I have experimented have betrayed, on awakening, a very definite knowledge of what had gone on during their supposed unconsciousness. It may be argued that this knowledge was obtained through subconscious channels, but I still remain doubtful of the trance. I have always discounted it when estimating the value of an experiment. No psychic is willing to have the veil of mystery stripped from his processes. He naturally refuses to admit shamming. He adds to the mystery, rather than takes from it.

Some of the most powerful psychics with whom I experimented did not enter into trance. They were as wide awake as I. Even Mrs. Smiley, who apparently went into deep sleep, groaning and gasping, was at other times awake and perfectly normal while the most inexplicable phenomena were going on—upsetting all my theories. Several times while thus calmly joining in the talk of the circle, she assured me that she remembered nothing of the "fuss" she had been making. Her sufferings could not have been serious, for she continued the practice for forty years.

To further illustrate this point: I have just read the report of a séance in a South American city in which an academic committee state that after a series of most astounding materializations, the medium, a scholarly man of middle age, suddenly collapsed, convulsed and nauseated; "and yet," the writer adds, "he recovered in a few minutes and showed no sign of his terrifying seizure."

Eusapia Paladino after nearly thirty years of unequalled strain (not to call it torture) showed little signs of it in face or figure; and, so far as reported, all the famous psychics studied by Richet, Schrenck-Notzing, and Geley, while frequently convulsed during experiment, suffered little lasting injury. Apparently the practice of mediumship, whether in trance or out, does not necessarily shorten the life of the practitioner.

Nevertheless, all the mediums I have known agree in saying, "Something goes out of me"; and they all at the close of a sitting showed weariness and a distinct numbness, a condition which persisted for several hours afterward. Daniel Peters said: "On the day following a sitting I am not much good at the office. It is nothing serious. I'm just tired as if I had been up after midnight playing chess."

It thus appears that the various phases of mediumship differ in their effects on the mind and body of the practitioner. In my experience it was evident that clairvoyance, clairaudience, slate writing, and even the direct voice did not make the demand upon the body and brain which the use of the trumpet and the production of ectoplastic forms undoubtedly do. They all admit, however, that they must allow time between sittings for recuperation. A slate-writer on the contrary can sit for phenomena several times each day without injury, and trumpet mediums can enter a circle several times a week.

All this points to the biodynamic character of the process. The practitioner is something more than a sensitive, a passive instrument; she is an engine, whose occult powers are more or less under control of her will. Just how much or how little she directs them is our problem. Some mediums following in the footsteps of Home and Fay boast of their ability to perform difficult feats at will. Peters when about to produce a certain result said, "*I* will do so and so." Botazzi taught Paladino's hands to do *his* will. In some cases I myself have wrought the psychic out of her method into mine.

In most instances, however, individuals who possess these powers treat their séances as rituals whose order, set by a higher intelligence, can not be changed. Of unquestioning faith themselves, they have no patience with conscientious enquirers. Their sittings remain inconclusive and repetitious. Insisting on darkness, they refuse to have their limbs controlled, and the scientific investigator remains a mere listener—in most séances he is not even an onlooker. Such programs are worthless to an investigator of the process.

For these reasons the spiritualistic performances of today are almost identical with those of sixty years ago.

Several meetings that I have recently attended presented the same credulous, awed circle, the same ringing of bells by invisible hands, the same voices declaring themselves to be "Mother" or "John" or "Big Thunder"— and all this traditional business continues while Geley, Morselli, and other Europeans of precise knowledge are seeking to prove the supranormal processes of mediumship by bringing to bear mechanical and electric control.

With intent to prove the identity of these "spirit" hands, prints of them have been obtained in flour and on sheets of paper; and Dr. Geley in 1919 obtained plaster casts of these "supernumerary limbs" by requesting the invisibles to dip their hands in melted paraffin. Gloves of wax were thus formed, and when plaster of Paris was poured into these molds, exact models of the "spirit" hands resulted. Expert witnesses (sculptors) stated that the wrists of these gloves were so small that the hand on which they were formed could not have been normally withdrawn, and that the ectoplasmic hand must have dematerialized.

Artists and medical men united in declaring that these molds exhibited joint and skin peculiarities which in no particular related to the joints and skin markings of the psychic, who was thus cleared of all complicity in their making. The hands belonged to some other person than the medium.

Dr. Gustave Geley, Director of the International Metapsychic Institute, in his latest volume (published in 1919) details these experiments and definitely says: "I saw the spectral hands in the process of making these wax moulds." He also declares that he saw the ectoplasmic lips from which the direct voice came, and that they were not those of the psychic. He makes the very curious observation that the words from these lips appeared to be formed on an *inhaled* and not an exhaled breath.

This was a new thought to me, and after reading his statement I experimented and came to the conclusion that he was correct. It may be that it is this use of the indrawn breath which so often gives to the "spirit" voice its indistinct, impersonal quality.

Dr. Geley makes another most important statement. He says, "The materialization of animals is no longer in doubt." He asserts that in the presence of Sir Oliver Lodge, in a locked room with all of the sitters chained, he felt a hairy animal moving about. Lodge also touched this creature and called it an ape, but the spirit of his son "Raymond" who was present said, "It is not an ape but a primitive man."

Geley adds, "Dog forms also came in to the circle"; and a spectral bird was photographed while seated on the shoulders of the medium.

Here again the medium must be cleared of all deception. No sleight-of-hand, no trick can produce a spectral bird or an ape-man in a circle of physicists in a locked room, with all observers chained together. I quite agree with Geley when he says: "In my opinion metapsychic science involves inferences which will revolutionize biology and psychology. It is not a question of religion or philosophy but of fact." But I do not find in these materialized animal forms proof of the spirit hypothesis.

II

Nothing like these European proofs of identity was carried on in America till 1924, when a group of Boston investigators set out to repeat Geley's experiments with paraffin gloves and plaster of Paris molds. The medium in this case was Margery Crandon, the young wife of Dr. L. R. G. Crandon, a well-known surgeon connected with one of the principal hospitals of the city.

I first learned of these experiments through the usual newspaper "exposé" of the medium, and from time to time I read articles attacking or defending the Crandons; but I knew little of the actual facts concerning them till in 1927 I accepted membership on the board of directors of the American Society for Psychical Research.

At the very first meeting which I attended, "the Margery mediumship," as it was called, came up for discussion and I learned that two of the directors were bitterly opposed to the Crandons and that a resolution instructing the editor of the society's journal to print no more articles or letters concerning the Lime Street sittings was being formulated. One or two members asserted that a recent report by an academic committee had exposed the medium, but others who had taken part in several experiments at Dr. Crandon's house were not so ready to vote for the resolution: "We should keep an open mind and publish the arguments for as well as against the Lime Street findings," they said.

In speaking in support of this position I said: "I have no direct knowledge of Mrs. Crandon's mediumship, but after thirty years of personal experimentation, I do not assume to pass judgment on her performance without seeing it. Prejudiced reports by a newspaper man have no decisive value with me. Scientific investigators in Europe have worked patiently for many years upon problems which these critics claim to have solved in one or two hours of observation.

"We should approach every new séance as a chemist approaches an experiment with new chemicals. Every circle is a different combination of creative elements. The problem is human as well as psychical. We should share many sittings with the Crandons before passing judgment upon them. In such wise the scientists of France and Italy have proceeded. Geley and Richet gave many years to the study of mediumship.

"As I understand it, we are neither a spiritualistic society nor an organization to expose mediums. Our task is to patiently investigate and report fairly on what we see. I am eager to witness the novel phenomena which credible witnesses declare Crandon and his wife have developed. I welcome news from them."

It was at this meeting, perhaps as a result of my talk, that Mr. Bristol, the president, asked me to become the chairman of his research committee. "Select your associates," he said, "and make such tests of the Crandons and their phenomena as you see fit."

Riding home in the car of John R. Gordon, vice president of the Society, I learned more in detail of the Crandons.

"The two most valuable of their contributions to the records of psychic research," he said, "are these: taking a leaf out of police records they have secured prints on wax of a man's thumb, prints differing from those of any thumb in the circle. This clears Mrs. Crandon from the charge of fraud in the use of her hands. Their next advance was along the line of proving that she had no normal connection with the spirit voice. They have devised a machine to that end. I hope you'll go to Boston and take these important claims into immediate consideration."

This use of thumb-prints as a test of identity interested me. "That is a very real contribution to the science," I said, "and I shall at once get in touch with the Crandons."

III

The facts concerning the Crandons, as I now assembled them, were these:

Beginning in 1924, a group of amateur investigators (who had been meeting at Dr. Crandon's home in Boston with intent to develop the mediumship of his wife Margery) attempted to secure paraffin molds of the ectoplastic hands of "Walter," their guide. Following the methods which Dr. Geley had used in Paris, they requested Walter to immerse his ectoplasmic hand in a pot of warm wax and to let it cool in the air. In this way they obtained "gloves" into which plaster was poured and the exact features of the invisible hand reproduced. Several such gloves were secured by the Crandon circle. "The hands were all masculine," their historian reported, "and none of them showed any of the characteristics of Dr. Crandon's hands." Some of these molds were of the doubled fist.

Out of this series of experiments came a still more

original suggestion: Why not obtain thumb-prints of the manifesting spirit?

"No one of us had any definite belief that finger-print patterns of a dead man's hand could be reproduced through the power of a medium; but Dr. Crandon had faith in 'Walter,' the control, who claimed to be the dead brother of the psychic. He promised to lend his best efforts to such an experiment. To him was referred the problem: 'How can we best secure and record the pattern of your thumb?'"

At "Walter's" suggestion various media were tried. Ink, paraffin smeared on glass, and other methods were employed; but none of them was satisfactory. At last one of the group, a dentist, suggested the use of wax, the material used in taking impressions of teeth. This substance, known as "kerr," was adopted as the best medium for taking and retaining impressions, and for nearly two years experiments of this sort were tried with complete success. Thumb-prints had been obtained which were neither those of the psychic nor those of Dr. Crandon.

"Meanwhile 'Walter's' voice had become amazingly lifelike, and his speech fluent and characteristic," reported one of my associates. "He told Dr. Crandon where to find some of his own finger-prints. 'They are on a razor I used,' he said. These prints were found but proved so fragmentary that they were inconclusive. 'Walter' has been dead some fifteen years but he is coöperating in all these experiments with cheerful readiness and notable skill."

So much I learned from Gordon and other of my fellow members on the board of directors, and I said to Mr. Bristol: "I am convinced that Mrs. Crandon is the most interesting psychic in America, and as chairman of your Research Committee I shall write to Dr. Crandon requesting the privilege of testing for myself some of his wife's marvellous phenomena."

Bristol and Gordon agreed that I should go to Boston and arrange if possible a series of sittings for my committee.

This was in February of 1927, but it was not till May that I wrote to Dr. Crandon asking the privilege of sitting in at one of his séances.

He replied: "I shall be delighted to have you join our circle. Come to dinner. We should be especially pleased to have you as our guest for the night."

From certain of my Boston friends, I learned that Crandon was well connected in the city. One friend wrote: "He is a charming host and entertains many distinguished guests. His wife, the medium, is young, vivacious and pretty."

On the strength of this letter I accepted Crandon's invitation to dinner and clothed myself accordingly.

Although in my youth I lived ten years in Boston, I had never set foot in Lime Street and had no notion of its location; but the driver of my cab took off across the Common, turned to the left just where the Back Bay meets Beacon Street, and a few minutes later drew up before a substantial three-story brick house on a clean and quiet street.

It was with something more than ordinary curiosity that I approached the door of Number 10. "If one quarter of the marvels reported from here are true, this is the most important psychical laboratory in America."

The maid who received me led me up a flight of stairs into a handsome library where Dr. Crandon, an attractive man just under middle age, received me. I was most favorably impressed by him. He was scholarly in appearance, slender, low-voiced, and graceful, entirely in keeping with his book-walled study.

He was in dinner dress, and so were the two men whom he introduced to me as Dr. Richardson and Mr. Butler. Neither of these men could be called eccentric in speech or dress. I saw nothing in any of them to warrant the bitter attacks which had been made upon them.

A few minutes later our hostess, the widely celebrated Margery, came in—a lovely young woman charmingly gowned. She was much younger than I had expected her to be. She was indeed hardly more than a girl.

In the belief that my readers will be interested in the human side of this problem, I frankly confess that I was surprised as well as pleased by the tasteful dining room to which the hostess led the way. The guests who took their seats about her ample table were equally surprising. They impressed me as a group of cultivated people who were seriously pursuing an investigation of occult forces, while remaining quite normal in their social relationships. I saw nothing in them resembling the "cranks," "dupes," and "tricksters" which newspaper men had reported them to be.

Mrs. Crandon had given me a seat beside her, and as soon as courtesy permitted I said: "I hope you won't mind my asking you a great many questions. I hate to be a bore, but I am eager to know more about you. I must improve my opportunities."

"Proceed," she said. "I'll answer as best I can."

She showed no signs of the many gruelling tests to which she had been subjected for nearly four years. She was not only smilingly at ease but humorous in her replies; and yet, beneath her gay mood, I caught now and then a hint of serious purpose.

"I am willing to undergo any test you care to make," she said toward the close of the dinner. "I take a special interest in having you study my case, for I know you in your books."

She did not argue for the spirit hypothesis, but she spoke of her brother as if he were alive. " 'Walter' is a good deal of a tyrant. He insists that our sittings shall begin at exactly nine."

At a quarter to nine she rose, and following her husband's lead we mounted to the third story of the house, where one by one we entered a small chamber in which a faint electric globe was burning. The room was so dark that I could see only a few strange machines and a tall cabinet of glass which stood against the wall.

Dr. Richardson, a member of the group who had charge of the psychic, called my attention to this three-sided cabinet and explained its use. "These two small apertures cut through the solid glass sides are so placed that Margery's hands can be thrust through them and wired or padlocked on the outside."

He then showed me an instrument composed of a long glass tube bent to form two upright vessels, filled with water on which rested two small balls of pith. To one of these tubes a rubber hose several feet in length was attached. Presenting this small tube for my inspection, he said: "This is the voice cut-out machine invented by one of our group. It renders the psychic absolutely speechless while 'Walter's' voice is heard. Place this glass mouthpiece between your lips. You will find that it fills your mouth to the corners so completely that you can not utter a sound."

With this flat mouthpiece between my lips, I tried to speak but could only utter a low moan through my nose.

Dr. Richardson went on: "As you will see, this mouthpiece is attached to a rubber tube which connects with these two glass tubes. So long as you blow, the two pith balls floating on the liquid within these tubes are out of equilibrium. If you fail to keep up the pressure, they approach each other's level. Now blow."

I blew, and the two balls moved to unbalanced position. I ceased to blow, and they fell to a common level. I could see no way in which the machine could fail to act as a cut-out of the medium's voice.

Dr. Richardson then said: "At first we used a round glass tube as the mouthpiece; but we found that an experimenter could make sounds from the corners of his mouth. We then designed this flat mouthpiece. In spite of it, however, 'Walter,' our invisible, while the psychic is blowing into the tubes always whistles, which is, of course, especially difficult—in fact it is impossible as you will find so long as this glass instrument fills your mouth."

Meanwhile Mrs. Crandon had cheerfully taken her place in the glass cabinet, and my attention was called to her hands, which had been locked outside the cabinet. The light was then lowered and almost immediately "Walter" manifested himself by voice and movement.

The room became his veritable workshop. Dr. Crandon, Richardson, and Butler moved about at his suggestion like attendants in a physical laboratory. The proceedings were in no sense religious. The spirit of the circle was wholly scientific. No hymns were sung, and no invocations voiced.

At an early stage of the program they put into my hands a box with a series of partitions so arranged that an electric bell installed therein could not be reached by any outside agent. The bell rang when I took it up, and at Dr. Richardson's suggestion I turned completely round, while holding it, thus proving that no wire connection existed. It might have been rung by some wireless arrangement, but not otherwise. They then showed me a pair of scales which balanced even when weights were piled on one pan while the other remained empty. Certainly the psychic had no hand in this.

Now came the test of the cut-out machine. With the mouthpiece of the tube placed between the psychic's lips, while I stood near enough to witness it, she was told to blow. As she did so—holding the pith balls at unequal heights—"Walter's" voice rang out in a jocular remark. Her complicity in the production of that voice seemed disproved. She had no normal part in it. Of its supernormal production she may be considered the cause, for it took place only in her presence.

In a group of this kind, I failed of the close grapple with the phenomena which my committee desired; but I was given opportunity for testing this and that instrument, and the light was fairly strong. I could not forget, however, that this was a circle of the psychic's friends meeting in a prepared séance room, and at the close of the sitting, while Dr. Crandon and I were alone in his library, I frankly confessed to a feeling that it was all inconclusive.

"To a sceptical outsider your prepared room and your machinery savor of commercial magic. They suggest wires, dictaphones, trick handcuffs, and all the rest of it. That these phenomena were genuine, I am inclined to grant; but as chairman of a research committee I should like to have a sitting with Mrs. Crandon in some other place, in New York City if possible, without you or any of your friends in the circle. I am asking this in the friendliest spirit. Only in some such way can we meet the criticism of those who say, 'Nothing can happen except in a prepared room and with Dr. Crandon present.' I grant that your room is a laboratory and that more and stronger phenomena can be produced here than elsewhere; but in my judgment a few phenomena on neutral ground and under the control of my committee would have far more value to the public than all the marvels produced here."

He replied that the medium was not seeking endorsement and that he was reluctant to turn her over to the control of a committee.

"With that I sympathize," I responded; "but I have had many such test séances with women psychics, and you may be assured of the fullest consideration for Mrs. Crandon. I shall ask Mrs. Derieux, the secretary of my committee, and Mrs. Garland to be present."

As I rose to go he said: "I am favorably impressed with your plan, but I must take time to discuss it with my wife and Dr. Richardson. I shall write you our decision in a few days."

To Bristol and Gordon, I reported the results of my visit to the Crandons. "I was favorably impressed by them and shall not permit newspaper criticism to prejudice their case. I shall draw my own conclusions in this instance as I have in many others during my long experience."

CHAPTER TWENTY–ONE

THE VOICES OF THE DEAD

On May 26, 1927, I received a letter from Dr. Crandon in which he agreed to have me conduct a test séance with Mrs. Crandon anywhere in Boston provided her physician Dr. Richardson and Mrs. Richardson were present.

"Mrs. Crandon can not go to New York. First, because it would not mean any more than a sitting in any house not ours in Boston, and second, the mediumship is entirely amateur and not seeking endorsement. In fact, after our experience we are inclined to believe that endorsement is a bad thing to have."

Shortly after this I received a letter from Dr. Richardson, to whom apparently the whole matter had been referred. He wrote that Mrs. Crandon was willing to sit with me in any room in or near Boston provided Mrs. Richardson were present.

In reply I suggested bringing Mrs. Derieux, who was not only acting as secretary of my committee but was chairman of the Society's Publications Committee. "In case she can not come I will bring Mrs. Garland. I grant the justice of your request that a woman should be in the circle, but to cover disputed points, we should have Mrs. Crandon sit without a cabinet and under entirely different methods of control. In this way," I concluded, "we shall negative the reports of certain scientific critics and render my own official report the more valuable. I particularly wish to have your 'voice cut-out' test applied. I think it entirely admirable.

"In order to meet the charge of untying knots it is my practice to employ tape in confining the psychic's wrists and to nail this tape to the chair and also to the floor. In many cases I have used dental floss as an added precaution."

Dr. Richardson promptly sent me his acceptance of my conditions.

"There will be no difficulty, I am sure, about your methods of control. Anything that causes no discomfort to the psychic will be acceptable. The place of meeting, you can yourself select, anywhere in greater Boston. As regards the time, about 9 P.M. has become almost the official time for 'Walter's' appearance and he goes away quite promptly at half past ten. As regards the cabinet, we generally use at such sittings a three-way screen. This can easily be secured.

"As regards the phenomena to be tested, we expect to try at first only those which have become thoroughly familiar to 'Walter.' In this connection it might be desirable to get some of 'Walter's' finger-prints in a locality removed at some distance from Lime Street. In such a case, would you mind having present Captain Fife, the finger-print expert from the United States Navy, who has this entire matter in charge?"

To this I replied: "I shall be very willing to have Captain Fife present. If we can get finger-prints of all of us including the finger-prints of 'Walter,' we will gain something very much worth while, and I shall report on them in detail. The three-way screen will be entirely acceptable to me. A system of control such as I have suggested would do away with all talk of 'trick' screw-eyes, 'slip-anklets,' and the like. Mrs. Crandon can be assured that I will ask for nothing which may prove painful to her. We should, of course, have a stenographer.

"I realize that we must not try too many things, but it might not be a bad policy to be prepared with the balances, and the voice cut-out machine. I should like to make it as conclusive as a single sitting can be. I am unable, however, to name a room in which we could meet. Most of my Boston friends, I regret to say, are in opposition, and it would not be well to have the sitting in the home of any of the known partisans of the psychic. Mrs. Derieux is disposed to think that a room in a hotel would solve our difficulty, but this is distasteful to me."

As a compromise Dr. Richardson then suggested that Mrs. Derieux and I come to dinner at his house and use his dining room for the séance. As he lived in Newton Center, several miles from Lime Street, and as Dr. Crandon was not even to enter the house, I saw no reason for declining this arrangement. An entirely neutral roof would have been preferable, but none such offered.

The house I found to be a plain suburban cottage, entirely free of any spiritualistic suggestion. It was indeed pleasingly commonplace, and Dr. and Mrs. Richardson were cordial and attractive hosts.

Mrs. Derieux and I were the only guests, and we discussed quite frankly the character of the Crandons and the mediumship with which Dr. Richardson had been associated from the first. "I approve of your plan to test the psychic in extemporized conditions and in the absence of her husband," he said. "The doctor will drive Margery out at eight but we will see that he does not put a foot inside the door."

As soon as dinner was over, I set about transforming the room into a laboratory. The long table being cleared, I shoved it against the kitchen door and then helped Mrs. Richardson to darken the windows whilst Dr. Richardson brought in the voice cut-out machine and the material for the thumb-print experiments.

A three-wing screen was set up as a cabinet. Over this I threw a robe, and in it I placed a chair with wooden arms. "I want to drive nails into those arms," I explained to Captain Fife, who came in at this time. Fife was introduced to me as "a finger-print expert connected with the Naval Station."

At eight-thirty Margery came. Mrs. Derieux and Mrs. Richardson met her and took her to an upper chamber where they disrobed and examined her. When she entered the séance room she wore a loose-sleeved robe, but under my direction Mrs. Richardson drew these sleeves tight about Margery's wrists and *stitched around them* a fold of the long tape which I had provided for that purpose. I then nailed her folded sleeves and the doubled tape to the arms of her chair, as I had so often done with Mrs. Smiley.

The reader will see that all talk of hidden wires and machinery, all question of trick knots, all remarks about prearranged devices of any kind, must be ruled out of this sitting.

With the aid of Mrs. Derieux loops of tape were next passed around the psychic's ankles, and after joining the two ends of this tape with the ends of those which confined the psychic's hands, I nailed them securely to the floor behind the screen.

"The simplicity of this control is its recommendation," I said to Fife. "If there is any virtue in tapes and tacks, this psychic will be found here, after the sitting, exactly as she is now."

The heat of the room was intense, and the psychic's position sadly uncomfortable; but she submitted cheerfully to her bonds. She made no objection to having a ribbon tied close about her neck and knotted to the high back of her chair. "We must be able to say that you could not stoop and could not lift your wrists from your chair," I said, and in the spirit of a martyr she granted the need of all these precautions.

Fife had brought with him several sheets of paper especially prepared to receive finger-prints and also several cakes of wax to be used for thumb-prints. After taking impressions of all our thumbs he asked that a kettle of hot water, a cloth, and a long flat dish be in readiness.

The door into the kitchen was barred by the heavy dining table, and the door into the lighted hall was closed. The girl who served as stenographer was placed in a small china closet at the corner of the séance room. This closet had no outside door. A red light and a small table enabled the girl to make a stenographic record of proceedings.

Fife took his seat at the psychic's right hand whilst I controlled her left hand, and when I say I *controlled*,

I mean just that. I held it so closely that it could not and it did not participate in any of the phenomena which followed. Fife's control of her right hand was equally unrelenting—according to his report.

Furthermore Crandon, the "arch conspirator" according to several highly critical reports by university men, must be counted out. He did not enter the house and had no part in the proceedings. Dr. Richardson, who sat directly opposite the psychic and hence at the farthest point from her, was in charge of the lamp which had been fitted with a soft red bulb. Mrs. Derieux, my assistant, controlled Fife's right hand while his left hand was clasping the psychic's right wrist.

Almost immediately after the light went out, I heard a loud merry whistle, like that of a boy signalling to his fellows; and a moment later a curious guttural voice was heard that might have come from deep in a man's throat. It had nothing feminine in it.

From where I sat, this voice appeared to come from the corner of the room beyond the improvised cabinet in which the psychic sat. It could have been caused by the stenographer or by Fife, but I could not refer it to the lips of the psychic. Dr. and Mrs. Richardson declared it to be the voice of the psychic's brother "Walter," and they greeted him cordially. "Good evening, 'Walter.'"

As he answered in slangy humorous phrases his voice cleared. He addressed me in a rather more serious tone, promising to meet my requirements. All of this, I will admit, might have come from Fife or the psychic, although I did not think so then or at any other stage of the proceedings.

"Walter" now took entire charge of the experimentation. He was direct, positive, not to say impudent at times. He did not regard it as a religious ceremony: it was a laboratory experiment. His utterance became fluent.

On the floor at my right a basket containing ten or fifteen wooden letters had been placed. I was careful not to handle these letters or even look at them; and when "Walter" ordered me to place the basket in front of the psychic's feet, I readily complied, for I knew that the psychic could not pick them up with her slippered foot.

"Is your control perfect, Captain Fife?" I asked.

"It is," he replied. The others also declared control complete.

With my right hand gripping the psychic's left wrist and Fife professedly controlling her right, I waited for "Walter" to demonstrate his freedom of action. I heard a fumbling in the basket. Something fell upon the floor. "Walter" said, "That is a Z."

I picked the letter up and held it to the red light. "That is right: it is a Z."

One by one, five or six letters were tossed from the basket toward me, and correctly named in every case but one. "Walter" was mistaken in calling an M a W— a natural mistake even by a spook.

So far as the psychic's left hand was concerned, she had nothing to do with these simple but momentous happenings. Granting that she might have uttered the words ascribed to "Walter," I am certain that she could not pick those letters from the basket with her toes; much less could she identify them. She could not stoop in any degree, for her head was bound to the back of her chair. She could not move her hands one inch from the arms of her chair, for they were circled with tape and nailed to the wooden arms, and in addition they were held by Captain Fife and myself.

This perception of small objects in black darkness, the reader will recall, had many times aroused my wonder and led to experiment, and I regarded this as just another supranormal stunt with which the psychic had nothing to do *in any normal way*. Richardson could not have reached the basket even with his foot, and Fife would have had to do both the handling of the letters and the ventriloquism necessary to perform the trick. Furthermore, he could not reach the basket with his right hand. I could have picked up the basket; but I could not have produced the voice, and I could not have differentiated the letters.

Whoever did the trick—it was *not* Margery.

In my previous séances, I had many times seen ectoplasmic hands and felt the grip of ectoplasmic fingers; but I had never witnessed the production of an ectoplasmic thumb-print. Fife and "Walter" had both promised it, and as all our thumb-prints had been taken at the beginning of the sitting, any impressions made during the hour must either accuse or exonerate us all.

On the table was a packet of white paper specially treated for the reception of finger-prints, and on this "Walter" now promised to lay his hands. "I'll give you a print of all the fingers on both my hands," he said. "Turn the paper over, Fife."

Fife rose and reshaped the pile of sheets on the table and returned to his seat. We then heard a rustling of the papers, and "Walter" called out in a tone of jocular challenge, "You'll find I've placed both my hands on the two top sheets of the pile."

At this point Richardson lit the red lamp and Fife removed the top sheets and put them on one side. (I pause here to say that at the close of the sitting Fife developed these prints with powdered charcoal while I looked on. I saw the prints develop. They were of two large strong hands—a man's hands, both right and left, with fingers widely spread. They were absolutely not those of the psychic.)

Fife said, "They are 'Walter's,' " and I let it go at that. I had no way of proving that they were not.

Let the reader reflect with me for a moment on this unexpected demonstration of "Walter's" power. He had shown not only that the spread hands were masculine but that they were left and right hands laid on the paper at the same time. They had not the precise value of proving any identity, but they cleared the psychic of any normal complicity in their production.

"Walter" was a busy sprite. Something was doing every moment of time. He seemed to be in several places at once, but his voice came from a point, apparently, beyond the psychic. He never seemed to be at my shoulder or at my side, but he operated at my knee and on the floor at my right utterly out of Fife's reach.

He wished us to understand that the prints of his hands were in no sense a substitute for thumb-prints, and he now called on Fife and Richardson to coöperate with him in the attempt to get an impression of his thumb on the tablet of wax which had been given me at the beginning of the sitting and which I had marked for identification.

Richardson now placed on the table a shallow dish filled with hot water and in this Fife laid a strip of cloth and my tablet of wax.

" 'Walter' will take this wax out when it is soft enough, and he will press his thumb upon it," Richardson declared.

Immediately after the light was dimmed, "Walter" set to work. We could hear him as he busied himself. He exclaimed boyishly, "Gee, that water's hot," and a moment later he added, "It's *too* hot!" His voice was now quite clear.

When the red light was turned on, *the cloth was outside the dish with the wax tablet partly mashed and rolled lying upon it.* Two hands must have been used in this act. Here again the critical reader can accuse Dr. Richardson or Fife, but he can not accuse the psychic. She had nothing to do with the handling of that wax or with lifting the hot wet cloth.

The resulting print was imperfect, but Fife said, "It was made by 'Walter.' "

I saw the print, but I was not qualified to say whether it was a right or left thumb. Fife was disappointed, but I was not. I was not concerned with proving "Walter's" identity. I was testing the medium's power.

In foregoing chapters the reader will recall my attempts to verify the spirit voices by covering the mouth of Mrs. Smiley with a cloth, and later with my hand. At my request Richardson now brought his voice cut-out machine into action.

"When the psychic blows into the tube, the two pith balls take different levels," said Fife, "and so remain as long as the psychic continues to blow."

It was an ingenious and apparently infallible test. Margery could not speak while she blew into it. I had never before been able to wholly satisfy myself that the "independent voice" *was* independent of the medium, but now, according to Fife and Richardson, I was about to have it proven.

The red light was now on and I could see the psychic quite plainly. She was leaning back in her chair, limp and still half asleep. Taking position beside her, I placed the mouthpiece in her lips with my own hands while Mrs. Derieux, my assistant, rose and held her palm above the open end of the taller tube, to prevent any outside interference.

As the psychic blew into the mouthpiece and the two pith balls took unstable equilibrium, "Walter" (as if to double the value of the test) uttered a clear and powerful whistle. He then sang, and his voice rang out more powerfully and with clearer utterance than at any other moment of the séance.

Some may say that the stenographer was the whistler and Fife the singer. I can not swear that he was not, but I affirm that Margery's lips had nothing to do with the production of these sounds.

Furthermore, the "Walter" voice heard while Margery's mouth was stopped was that of a vigorous, humorous, rough-and-ready man of twenty-five or thirty, with such intonation as a Canadian youth working as a conductor on a street car would use.

He had not much respect for me or for the other sitters except as our action bore upon the character of the psychic. He called me "Garland" in a friendly tone and spoke to me as if I were a man of his own age and walk of life. Death had not increased his reverence for age. He was shrewd, unrefined, resourceful and combative. His dominant motive was to prove that the psychic had no hand or voice in the proceedings.

The net results of this sitting can be concisely stated:

1. Crandon, the "arch conspirator" of the academic committee, was entirely eliminated. He was ten miles away and had absolutely nothing to do with what took place.

2. Margery had nothing to do, normally, with the production of the hand-print or thumb-print phenomena. Her hands were rigidly controlled by Fife and myself while "Walter" was tossing out the letters and also when working among the dishes. Her organs of speech were under mechanical control while "Walter" sang.

3. The prints of *two* large hands, not those of any member of the circle, were left upon a sheet of paper. I affirm that so far as her left hand is concerned, she had no normal part in that print, and the right-hand print was of corresponding size.

4. Small objects were moved without possible contact by the psychic.

5. Small objects were handled and identified in the dark, actions entirely outside the normal activity of the psychic.

This telekinetic handling of small objects and their supranormal perception, I had many times witnessed. But the prints of hands on sheets of paper, the thumb-prints on the wax, and the elimination of the psychic's speech organs from any share in the production of the voice, were all new and of deep significance. I put the mouthpiece between the psychic's lips—and I watched her closely as she blew into it, while "Walter" whistled.

Finally I ask the reader to note that the sitting had none of the customary spiritualistic coloring. It had no ritual, and none of my dead relatives or friends spoke to me. The only invisible in attendance was "Walter," and he brought no message. None of us regarded the hour as one of consolation and reunion, and neither did "Walter." He was in effect an inventor, providing new evidences of spirit power. In demonstrating his supranormal ability to see and feel, he was definitely exonerating his sister from all charges of deceit.

In truth he completely ignored her at times.

It was all highly dramatic—an amazing exhibition of a highly developed ectoplasmic organism. While he could not be *seen,* he was to my other senses as much a personality as the "Katie King" of Sir William Crookes. He presented himself as a youth, humorous, powerful, impudent, and testy. He ordered us about like children. He assumed the tone of a master as though by the mere act of dying he had become possessed of all the wisdom of Lodge and Edison, and yet he busied himself with tricks to astonish us like a boy of twelve!

To accuse me or Captain Fife of fraud has no value except that by so doing the charge of deceit is shifted from the psychic. Some of the feats Fife could have done, but others were impossible to him or to me. I could have carried out some of the phenomena, but neither of us could have produced all of them. I leave the doubter to draw his own conclusions from this plain tale.

It was a hot, uncomfortable confinement, but Mrs.

Crandon met every demand cheerfully and without the slightest complaint.

In scores of sittings hitherto, I had seen ectoplasmic hands, I had felt them, I had seen them write—now here I had their imprint. To whom did they belong? The lines of these thumb-prints would ultimately tell us. They were precise, mechanical records, not vague memories which may be only mind-readings.

Only one objection remained. The scene of the sitting was not neutral ground. I determined to ask for this as a further step in advance.

CHAPTER TWENTY-TWO

ON NEUTRAL TERRITORY

I

Despite the fact that I had been given full opportunity to test Mrs. Crandon's powers in a room twelve miles from Lime Street and in the voluntary absence of her husband, I was not entirely armored against criticism. I wished to make another test in a room which the psychic and her friends had never entered. "This will forestall all charges of complicity on your part," I wrote to Crandon, "and also on the part of those who have shared in the Lime Street séances. Furthermore, the test would be more convincing if none of Mrs. Crandon's friends were in the circle."

Crandon recognized the justice of this contention and readily agreed to all my requests except the last. He insisted that Captain Fife should be included in the circle. He urged Captain Fife because of his position as finger-print expert for the Naval Station in Boston. "He is essential if you wish to secure such evidence."

This I granted, for I was intending to try for a left thumb-print.

The more carefully I studied the history of Mrs. Crandon's mediumship, the more inclined I was to call

313

her the bravest living psychic, so numerous and so severe had been the tests to which she had submitted. For four years, scores of critics had practiced the most painful methods of control upon her with intent to prove her guilty of deceit or of lending herself to deceit. With this controversy I had no concern. This volume is a record of my personal experiences. I came to a study of Mrs. Crandon after nearly forty years of study and experiment—as my readers are aware. I had tested most of the phases she exhibited, but others were new to me and most important as evidence.

Among my fellow directors of the Psychical Society was a very distinguished specialist in nervous diseases, Dr. Frederick Peterson. He was a member of the Century Club, and we often met there at luncheon time. With no expectation that he would consent to act, I asked him to come on my committee and share my third sitting with Mrs. Crandon.

Much to my surprise and pleasure he consented, and I told him that one of my oldest friends, Joseph Edgar Chamberlin of the *Boston Transcript,* had offered his library as the "neutral ground" of my test séance. "He knows nothing of the Crandons except what he has read, and is entirely sceptical of all spirit phenomena. He and his wife live alone in an apartment on Commonwealth Avenue and would like to share in our experiment. There will be only the Chamberlins, ourselves, and Captain Fife the thumb-print expert present."

"Admirable," said Peterson. "Mrs. Peterson would like to go with us, if you don't mind."

Thus it happened that the test circle included only Mr. and Mrs. Chamberlin, Dr. and Mrs. Peterson, Captain Fife, and myself. This suited me well, for the smaller the circle the closer our study and the more valuable the resulting phenomena.

On the day appointed, Dr. Peterson met me at the Copley Square Hotel late in the afternoon and I took him to call upon Dr. Crandon, whom he had never met. We found Crandon in his handsome library taking his ease after a busy day at the hospital. He was tired but mentally alert and made a most favorable impression on Dr. Peterson as well as upon me.

He said: "I was just where you gentlemen are when, in 1924, my wife began to develop her occult powers. The phenomena, increasing month by month in reality and variety, at last convinced me of their truth and of the personality of 'Walter,' who claimed to be her brother. His knowledge and resource are astonishing. Each week he devises something new in our tests. He is, in a sense, our chief engineer."

He then showed us a series of enlarged thumb-prints and described how they were received. He indicated the points of similarity between them and a thumb-print which "Walter" declared was made while he was alive. I listened in silence. It was all too technical and too intricate for me to follow, and I suspect Peterson felt the same lack of information.

After describing the room at Chamberlin's in which we were to sit, I explained to Crandon that Dr. Peterson was a member of my committee, and that the circle would be small.

He was plainly relieved. "I shall deliver the psychic at Mr. Chamberlin's door at the hour named," he said.

Just as we were about to leave, Mrs. Crandon came

in, and we had a few moments' chat with her. She was a gay and charming figure, smartly gowned and graceful, the farthest remove from the conventionalized picture of a medium; and Dr. Peterson's grave face relaxed as he listened to her laughing remarks about the possibilities of the coming test. " 'Walter' will do his best, I am sure," she said.

While walking away Peterson said, "She seems entirely normal—not in the least the kind of person I expected to meet."

II

It was not easy to darken the Chamberlin library, which was large, with several windows and doors; but we succeeded in doing so, and when Margery arrived her chair was ready for her. At my request Mrs. Chamberlin *stitched* the tape to the psychic's sleeves, and in my usual way I drew the doubled tape and her sleeves close to her wrists and nailed them to the arms of her chair with long tacks.

In addition I tied a second tape tightly about her wrists and nailed its two ends to the floor. The knots were in the middle of the tape.

We then placed the library table in the center of the room, and at a little distance from it we set a small table at which the stenographer was to sit. A red lamp provided light for her task. Fife was on hand with his wax tablets, illuminated basket, and other tools for the carrying out of our experiment. I would have preferred to have Dr. Peterson at the psychic's right hand, but as I was in full control otherwise I made no protest.

I am aware that all this is boresome repetition, but it is a necessary part of every report. I condense it to the point of saying, *I made it impossible for Mrs. Crandon to have any hand in what was to take place.*

Mrs. Chamberlin and Mrs. Peterson, who had met the psychic and witnessed her disrobing, agreed that she brought nothing into the room.

The official stenographer took her seat at her table, which was behind me and a little to my left. The small shaded red lamp which she used remained alight throughout the sitting. Her notes and the report which I wrote immediately after the séance are the basis of this report.

Almost immediately after the turning out of the lights, "Walter" announced himself by whistling merrily. He then greeted us all in a breezy not to say rowdy style.

As I had satisfied myself at a previous sitting that this voice did not issue from the lips of the psychic, I replied to it as a separate personality. Peterson and Chamberlin, I've no doubt, considered this merely ventriloquism on the part of the psychic. In this case I could affirm that the sound did not come from the stenographer—she was not the culprit; it came rather from Captain Fife's side of the table.

If this voice was "independent," as I believe it was, these first four minutes were worth all the trouble we had made the Chamberlins; but I read disbelief in their wondering silence. Fife and I were in "key" positions and less concerned about their attitude.

"Walter's" voice was quite as vigorous and much less guttural than at the former sitting. In fact his utterance had all the variety and dramatic force of a distinct personality. For example, he said to me, "Mr. Garland, what can I do for you tonight?" And when I replied with a challenge in my tone, "I want a *left* thumb-print," he whistled as if in dismay. "You don't want much, do you?" he retorted.

"No," I replied. "Just a left thumb-print."

He made some remark to the effect that he would see what he could do. I think he knew why I wanted a left thumb-print. I wanted to grasp the nailed and leashed and taped left wrist of the psychic while the impression was being made. Fife was at her right hand, and while I did not distrust his vigilance, I knew that my official report would have much more value if I received the print of a left-hand thumb.

Conditions were, in truth, quite ideal. Crandon and Richardson were both eliminated. Aside from Fife, the members of the circle had my complete confidence and control. To meet all charges against the psychic no sensational or spectacular phenomena were essential under these conditions. The slightest supranormal movement of an object on the table would exonerate her.

"Walter" treated me almost as a member of the family. Notwithstanding my years he addressed me as "Garland, my boy," his tone indicating that he regarded me indeed as a "reg'lar feller."

The stenographer's notes read: " 'Walter' then called for the basket in which were a score or more letters cut out of wood. This basket was behind Garland and at 'Walter's' command Garland reached back, caught the basket by its handle and set it down under the edge of the table and near the psychic's feet."

I had no notion of the number of the letters or of their character, and I made sure that they were out of reach of every one but Fife.

" 'Walter' then moved the basket saying, 'Hello, Garland, how are you tonight?' He then threw a letter out on the floor near Garland saying, 'This is an M.' Garland picked it up and said, 'I think it is a W.' 'Walter' then said, 'Hold it up and I'll tell you.'

"Garland held the letter up. [It was so dark that no one could even see my arm much less the difference between an M and a W.]

" 'You're right, my boy,' said 'Walter.' 'It is a W.'

"He threw out another letter on Fife's side saying, 'That is a Z.'

"Fife examined it and said, 'Z is right.' "

Four or five other letters and one number, 8, were thrown out of the basket and correctly named. I don't know what Chamberlin and Peterson thought, but my conviction at the moment was that these were not only genuine telekinetic phenomena but clear-cut examples of perception in the dark.

The psychic could not touch these letters with her hands, and to pick them out with her stockinged feet and correctly name them was not in the range of her normal powers.

Trivial as this stunt may seem at first sight, it became enormously significant when linked up with my previous experiments. I must repeat and repeat that her wrists were bound with tape and nailed to her chair.

"Walter" now said something about "passing the contribution box" and immediately the smaller illuminated basket rose in the air and moved about the table. "Drop something into it—some object to be identified and returned later."

This we all did. As the basket came to me I dropped into it a poker chip, a most unlikely object to have in one's pocket, and a most difficult object to pick up with a stockinged foot. I then placed the basket under the table as before, some distance from the psychic's feet, and resumed control of her left hand.

Again I quote the stenographer's report:

" 'Walter' is heard to move the basket. The first object identified and thrown on the table was a spectacle case belonging to Mrs. Chamberlin. The second a bottle of pills, confirmed by Fife. The third a pair of scissors in a little case confirmed by Chamberlin. The fourth a poker chip belonging to Garland."

Now all these articles would be difficult to lift out of a basket with one's toes, but my poker chip would be especially elusive. I regarded this as an admirable test. However, I was determined to push the experiment further. I said, " 'Walter,' I'm going to stump you. I'm putting something into the basket which will try your powers."

He replied jocosely, "Shoot!"

I dropped into the basket a minute object which no toe could possibly lift or define. A rustling of the basket followed, and for a few seconds "Walter" was silent as if *feeling* of the object. At last he said in a puzzled way, "It's a coin about the size of a Canadian five-cent piece." Then after another pause he added, "It has a hole in it—something like a Chinese coin."

"Bravo, 'Walter'!" I called out. "You've almost got

it. If you'll tell me what that hole in the middle of the coin means, you'll win a grand victory."

After another pause he said: "It seems to have a couple of slits. I can't make it out."

I then said to the other sitters: "The coin is a token such as the railway company in Washington uses. The rough place which 'Walter' feels is the letter W cut out of the coin."

In an injured tone "Walter" asked, "How could you expect me to know that? I never was in Washington."

A moment later the coin was deftly dropped into my hand. The precision of this movement was in line with all the many similar observations I had made. There was no searching, no fumbling. It came to my invisible palm as though darkness did not exist for the agent. Will the doubter say that the psychic picked up that minute coin with her toe?

I had in my pocket another small metal object still more difficult to handle and identify in the dark. With another jovial challenge to "Walter" I dropped this object into the basket.

This he at once fingered—to judge from the rustling sound—and presently threw it out on the floor, saying, "It resembles the bar on a watch chain."

"Fine!" I exclaimed. "Now feel of the two ends and tell me what you find on them."

"Lay it in the dish on the table," he replied. A moment later I felt it being pushed into my half-closed right hand.

Having laid it in the dish I resumed firm control of the psychic's wrist and waited.

"Walter" then said, "One end is rough and the

other smooth—and there is a groove in the middle of it."

Again I applauded him. "If you can tell me what is on the end of that bar, it will be one of the finest tests ever made."

He gave further attention to it, then said: "I give it up. It's too fine for me."

I then explained to the circle that the object was a large-size printer's quad. One end was smooth, but on the other end the Lord's Prayer was molded in microscopic form. On one side was a notch which "Walter" had called a groove. It was an astonishing feat of perception in the dark. To say that the psychic put that minute object into my hand is absurd.

Again I quote the stenographic notes: "Fife then broke his control in order to pour some hot water into the dish which had been placed on the table in preparation for the making of finger-prints. Garland repeated his request for a left thumb-print and 'Walter' said, 'I will give you one.' The hot water was put in the dish with the cold water dish beside it. 'Walter' asked Fife to break the piece of wax in half. This he did and resumed control of the psychic's right hand."

A few moments later I heard something drop into the dish and "Walter" said, "Garland, put your hand in the cold-water dish and take out the wax."

This I did, placing the wax on the table near me. Fife then turned on the red light.

The cloth was outside the dish and neatly folded. There was no wax in the hot-water dish. It had been crushed into a wad, and on it I could see a roughly outlined thumb-print. Whether it was a left thumb-print or not, I can not say; but it was nearly twice the size of the psychic's thumb. Fife declared it to be a right thumb-print and that it was "Walter's."

The psychic had no normal part in this stunt. The thumb-print may have been Fife's or Peterson's or Chamberlin's. It was not mine, and it was not Mrs. Crandon's. Furthermore *two* hands must have been employed in removing that cloth and folding it. If it was a trick, the psychic must be counted out.

At the request of "Walter" I then moved the illuminated basket to the middle of the table. The lights were again turned out, and immediately the basket began to move.

"Are all hands controlled?" I asked.

All responded "Yes." The basket then rose and swung in a circle above the table, performing some rather intricate movements. There was nothing in this which was new to me, but the character of the members of our small circle made these movements of great value.

One of the playthings hitherto had been an illuminated perforated cardboard disk about five inches in diameter which "Walter" had named "the doughnut." Taking it from the basket, he passed it to me, saying, "Lay it on the table before you."

This I did. He then took it up and flourished it above my head. This was out of Fife's reach. He then carried it down nearly to the floor, and held it there at my right knee—*a position impossible to Fife.*

From that point it rose slowly and came toward my face. Afterward I learned that "Walter" wished me to take it from his hand. Why did he not speak to me at the time, I can not imagine. I did not think of this, for I was maintaining rigid control of the psychic's left wrist. The disk dropped to the floor near my feet. Picking it up with my right hand, I placed it on the table again.

"Walter" then directed me to draw the disk closer to my side of the table. "Put your nose on it," he said.

As I bent my head over the disk I felt fingers touching my head. "Somebody pulled a lock of my hair."

"Walter" said, "I'm the guilty party."

I then said, "Show me your hand above the dough-nut." While gazing down at the disk I plainly saw a large hand, a left hand, a clumsy black silhouette moving with a circular motion just above the faintly glowing disk. It was not the psychic's left hand, and I do not believe it was Fife's. I had seen and felt such hands several times before under test conditions, and I am willing to call it phantasmal. I did not touch it, but it touched me.

This practically ended the sitting, which must be called a success in so far as it eliminated Crandon and Richardson from the group of suspects. That it was more convincing to me than to Chamberlin or Peterson was natural, for I was closer to the psychic. In my judgment it confirmed the reality of Mrs. Crandon's supra-normal powers.

As a further detail I may add that, to free her from her bonds at the close of the sitting, I was forced to use a tack hammer. I had driven the nails down through the doubled tape and the folds of her sleeve so deep into the chair-arm that they had to be pried out.

The handling and identification of the coin and the quad by "Walter" evidenced the most delicate perception, a perception which had the effect of seeing but which must have been nearer to a sense of feeling. His hesitation in speech and the rustling of the basket would indicate that he was fingering the coin, feeling of it, puzzled by it. If the reader is disposed to accuse Fife of doing the trick, I must continue to state that certain of the movements of the disk were wholly beyond *his* reach.

Such accusations will not do. Critics began by accusing Margery of fraud. Then they shifted the guilt upon her husband. Crandon being out of my circle, suspicion fell upon Richardson. Now here in this circle Richardson was eliminated. Charges of fraud can lie only against me or Fife.

This process is absurd. As Richet says, "The moment you begin shifting the cry of fraud from the psychic to the sitters, you enter upon an endless chain of foolish evasions." Furthermore this sitting was merely one of a long series of tests many of which I have detailed in the foregoing pages. If it stood alone, it would be convincing, but it is only one of hundreds.

All these phenomena, trivial in themselves, are important as telekinetic evidence. The hands which picked those small objects from the waste basket and put the coin in my hand, were not the psychic's. The hand which moved between my eyes and the illuminated disk was not hers. Her fingers did not pull my hair. The doubter is at liberty to say that I imagined it all or that somebody cheated me.

As for "Walter" himself, I sensed him as an entity but not as an entirely separate entity. He impressed me at all times as a personality which had grown out of a long series of similar sittings. Like "Wilbur" and

"Mitchel" in the case of Mrs. Smiley, and "Katie King" in the famous case of Florence Cook, "Walter" was a powerful, busy, slangy and combative personality; but I could not entirely admit the claims of his friend. I am willing to grant that his voice was not normally produced by the psychic, and yet there was something in his tone which related him to her.

Some of my readers may complain that *all these happenings were stunts,* and this is true. They had nothing to do with religious precept or consolation. Like the "spirits" of many other of my sittings, "Walter" was definitely working to astound me by meeting my most difficult test. He brought no messages from my beloved dead, and I did not ask for such messages. In all that he did he remained the shrewd and competent workman.

I will go further and say that he was moved by a desire to prove the honesty of his sister's mediumship, and with this he succeeded without establishing his own identity.

His chief disappointment, his only failure, was in the thumb-print, which was a right thumb (so Fife declared) and not very clear at that. At this time, so far as I knew, no left thumb-print had been secured. However, the psychic's right wrist was as securely nailed to her chair-arm as her left wrist, and I ask the reader to recall that at the previous sittings we got both right and left hands on a sheet of paper in the middle of the table.

In short, we are concerned with Margery's supranormal physical phenomena as based in the realm of unexplored biology.

If any one sort of phenomena in these two sittings under my control can be said to be more inexplicable than any other, I should instance those in which "Walter" whistled and sang while the medium was blowing into a tube which filled her mouth, and while I stood beside her watching her lips.

In many previous tests I had secured these voices in the light, and in the middle of a horn while holding it in my own hands. I had conversed with these invisibles for hours at a time, and yet I had never before been able to convince myself that they were wholly independent of the psychic.

Whence came this voice? How can a voice be produced out of the air without tongue, teeth, lips, air passages, or lungs? How is it possible for these invisibles to whistle, sing, joke, chuckle, sigh, utter characteristic tones, all without tangible heads and diaphragms?

The spiritualist is ready with his answer: "They *have* bodies, the exact counterparts of their bodies while on this plane." Geley declares: "I saw the lips form while the whisper came."

My mind is open to argument. I remain curious about the mechanism which produces these voices. My *feeling* at this sitting was that it all sprang from the medium in some extra-normal way, and I was deeply interested when Dr. Crandon told me that they had seen and photographed this "ectoplasmic structure."

In a more recent report he writes of it in this way:

"As the voice of 'Walter,' the dead brother of Margery, was of the greatest value in our investigations, it became important to establish its reality. This we did, apparently—by mechanical means. We proved this voice to be independent of the normal use of the anatomy and physiology of the medium. But so far as we know, to form the words there must be developed a teleplasmic structure in some way similar to the human organism. To confirm this we have many times seen and photographed a structure which 'Walter' says the medium uses for the production of the human voice.

"There is almost no similarity, however, between this structure as we see it, and the human voice-producing mechanism. It is a small mass, either gray or white in color, resembling in size and shape a potato. At times as we look at it, it seems to simulate a small face much like the dried heads of the head-hunters of the South Seas.

"From the small mouth of this potato-like face comes a structure like the human umbilical cord, from one-fourth to one-half an inch wide. It is twisted and from eight to twelve inches long. This cord enters the right nostril of the psychic. We have many photographs of this structure and our photographs confirm what our eyes see.

"This small head has been seen and its voices heard while several scientific investigators were permitted one by one to put a hand over the mouth of the medium."

All this does not clear up the mystery. It is not possible for me to link the robust voice of "Walter" with a mouth in a small face no larger than a potato. In many dark séances I have heard voices of booming sonorousness. Did they come from a small mouth in an ideoplastic structure no larger than my fist?

Furthermore these voices have individual characteristics. They resemble the voices of our dead. How can this be unless the lips, teeth, head, and air passages are similar to those of the man or woman we knew? "Insoluble mystery!" as a Frenchman would exclaim. All these mysteries are solved only by calling to our aid other still more insoluble mysteries.

While writing this chapter I have received Volume III of the proceedings of the American Society for Psychical Research, in which I read that a conclusive test of the independence of the "Walter" voice has been made. I quote a paragraph in description of it:

"We took a sensitive microphone similar to those used in radio broadcasting and placed it in a closed and sealed box which was mechanically, electrically, acoustically and magnetically shielded from external physical influences. We then connected this microphone electrically with a loud speaker located in a distant part of the building, all connections and equipment being likewise shielded from external influence."

Notwithstanding all these precautions, "Walter" spoke through the microphone in this sound-proof box! His voice was heard in a distant room, while not a sound could be heard by those who sat about the box in the séance chamber.

"Under these controlled conditions there was no possibility that the microphone and loud speaker could have been made to function by any normal means whatsoever."

I am willing to grant that this application of laboratory methods of isolation demonstrates that Mrs. Crandon had no normal physical part in the production of the voice. My doubts begin when the identity of the speaker is declared.

It remains to say that "Walter," according to recent report, has been able to function in the absence of both Margery and her husband. He has been able to read cards held up in the darkness of the séance room, and to move small objects; but thus far he has not been able to speak to the circle while she is out of the room. Perhaps he may be able, soon, to overcome this inhibition, for he has been able to use the microphone in a locked box while his sister was in another part of the house.

However, I do not hold myself responsible for anything beyond my personal test. As I have repeatedly said, this is a plain narrative of facts personally witnessed. My experiments must justify themselves.

CHAPTER TWENTY-THREE

A GROUP OF LITERARY GHOSTS

AFTER these rigidly controlled sittings with Mrs. Crandon, I was less inclined than ever to sit with commonplace mediums in dark circles, no matter how intelligent and sincere they might appear to be, and for several years I encountered no other novel phases of mediumship.

"There is but one more advance for me to make," I told my friends, "and that is to have the phenomena of my sittings with Mrs. Crandon, Mrs. Hartley, and Daniel Peters duplicated in my own library with no one present but the members of my family." And to this end, I sought for a psychic willing to coöperate with me.

In 1930—three years after my meeting with the Crandons—I found myself a resident of Los Angeles, in whose genial air all varieties of religious devotees find refuge. The city swarmed with clairvoyants, crystal-gazers, seers, psychometrists, trumpet mediums, yogis, and astrologers. In such a welter of wonder-workers I had the hope of finding one or two who would be willing to lend themselves to my purpose.

Alas! No such individual could be found, and I well

understood the reason. Most of these practitioners of occult rites regarded their mysterious powers either as a means of grace or as an endowment to be used for the consolation of the bereaved. Some had made their gifts a source of profit as preachers or as adepts. None of them were keenly interested in a scientific analysis of the nature and origin of their gifts; and I suspect that those who had joined the branch of the American Society for Psychical Research had done so in the belief that it was, at bottom, a spiritualistic body.

I did not blame these practitioners then, and I do not blame them now. Why should a minister step down from his rostrum and submit his powers to the cold-steel and electrochemical control of investigators? What would the materializing medium or the public psychometrist gain by meeting with a research committee? The martyrdom involved in a series of tests such as I had repeatedly carried out with others, was not alluring. I could not blame them; I should refuse if I were in their places.

The séances in Los Angeles to which I was occasionally led, opened with prayer and ended with the doxology, and were held in dark chambers. In no case were the psychics or sitters subject to control. Faith ruled, and the happenings were all of the good old sort. The voices, the caressing hands, the sound of bells—all the phenomena common since the Fox sisters, were still taking place. These meetings were not merely stereotyped, they were traditional.

I do not accuse any of these mediums of deceit; I think they were sincere in considering their circles essentially devotional. They were consolers and healers. What had they to do with thumb-prints and voice cut-out machines? Several of them were elderly ladies who had been dispensing comfort in this way for half a long lifetime, and who were surrounded by clouds of witnesses, earlier devotees who, having themselves become spirits, now returned to augment the invisible ranks of supporters.

Among these who held private séances, wholly without pay and for their friends, was Delia Drake, an old acquaintance who, by sitting devotedly and regularly for more than a year, had developed definite mediumistic powers. Her phases, as reported to me, were feeble, consisting of the movement of a trumpet in the dark, and raps on near-by objects—all very rudimentary; but in the belief that I could develop her into stronger phases, she consented to sit with me, at my convenience. I consented to try her out.

As she was an old friend, a woman whom my wife had known for thirty years, I could not ask her to submit to control; and so I must ask the reader to value the phenomena (as I do) on their amusing literary character. They offer so many curious and illogical happenings that I consider them worthy of record at this point. They are interesting from the human side.

My diary fixes the date of our initial séance.

"January 22, 1933. We tested our psychic friend for two hours last night. The circle contained only my family. The windows were darkened and the lights turned off. The trumpet was about two feet in length and wore a band of luminous paint in order that we might follow its movements. After a tedious wait which we filled in by singing and telling stories, our psychic began to cough violently, as if being strangled. Immediately after this attack, the horn rose and came to me. After tapping me on the arm as if in greeting it faced me with an unwavering stare of its larger, radiant end. It seemed to wait for me to speak. I asked, 'Is it someone for me?'

"It waved up and down emphatically three times— 'Yes.'

" 'Can't you speak and tell me who you are?' I asked.

"Without answering me it went over to my wife, who said, 'Is it someone I know?'

"A faint whisper came from it, 'Yes.'

" 'Can't you give your name?'

"I could not hear the reply but my wife and my daughter Isabel both caught the word 'Fuller' and my wife cried out, 'Is it you, "Henry B"?'

"In reply the horn shook as if with joy and waved vigorously up and down in most emphatic affirmation.

"Going to my daughter, it tapped her gently on the arm, and then as if exhausted sank softly to the floor. A few moments later it rose again and returned to my wife. Upon her request for the name of this operator, a whispering voice said, 'I am "Charles Francis."' This was the name of her brother-in-law, a Chicago painter, Charles Francis Browne.

"At this moment another fit of coughing seized the psychic and the cone rising in the air addressed itself to Olive Grismer and began a whispered message broken by sobs, a singular effect. Mrs. Grismer heard the words plainly and at last said, 'It is my sister who died some months ago in France.'

"She was deeply affected by the message which she

declared was entirely evidential. I could not catch all the words but I sensed the agony in the sobbing breath of the speaker.

"At various times during this sitting, movements of the pencil and paper could be heard and I repeatedly urged 'Fuller' to write his name. At the close of the sitting I found this sentence clearly written: 'Trust us to prove all life.' Back to back with this line a short sentence was written, but so illegibly, and in such strange characters, that it was absurd. It looked like 'Root is here.' "

That this sitting will have small value to the critical, I am fully aware, but as William Stead said, I had "proved my ready reckoner" so many times that I was ready to give our guest the benefit of the doubt. Assuming the attitude of the doubter let us say, "Your psychic could have manipulated both the horn and the pencil on the paper. They were all within her reach."

This is true: she might have moved the cone and produced the whisper. But as she knew nothing concerning Mrs. Grismer's sister in France, her dramatization of a spirit suffering poignant remorse may be conceived as a case of mind reading. We all felt the emotion of this dialogue, and Mrs. Grismer was herself deeply moved by the truth of it.

This sitting led me to say to our psychic friend, "From this time on, I want you to sit in my study, with no one in the circle but my immediate family."

To this she readily consented, and I set about the preparation of my library, which is on the second floor and at the back of the house. No room could have been more favorable. It was quiet, separated from the telephone, and easily darkened. Placing a small unpainted round table in one corner, I grouped five chairs about it and laid pencil and paper on its top.

As soon as we were seated and the lights turned out, I said jocularly, addressing the invisible, " 'Fuller,' I expect to have your signature on that sheet of paper."

After a long wait our psychic again began to cough, as if choking, and immediately the trumpet rose and hovered over her head, and then came to each of us. This spirit announced herself as "Barbara," the psychic's daughter.

As the horn tapped me on the arm, I asked, "Is this 'Fuller'?"

A strong clear definite whisper came from it, "Yes."

"Fine!" I exclaimed. "I'm glad you're here. I want your full coöperation in this series of experiments."

We then conversed for a few moments quite as we used to do when he was in the flesh. The utterances from the trumpet were entirely in character, concise, humorous, keenly intellectual. I said, " 'Fuller,' do you remember our sittings with Mrs. Hartley, when we talked with 'MacDowell' and secured some of his music on closed slates?"

To this he whispered, "Certainly I do."

I went on: "I have just been going over your account of those sittings."

"How does my report read now?"

"As well as ever. Now, 'Fuller,' I don't want any mahatmas or 'Little Bright Eyes' mixing in here. You and I took the purely scientific view in 1908, and I want to continue in that attitude. Let's make this series of sittings worth while."

I ask the reader to bear in mind that while the room was almost perfectly dark no outsider was present: the sitters were my wife, my daughter Isabel and her husband, and the psychic—who was my wife's personal friend and had nothing to gain and all to lose by playing jokes upon us. She was a serious elderly woman of religious type. I ended the sitting with a feeling that our psychic's case required still more careful analysis than I had been able to give it.

The only writing on the table this time consisted of two words scrawled in the corner: "god rules." The absence of a capital letter is significant.

Toward the close of our sitting the table flopped over on its side, spilling my pencils and paper on the floor. I mention this for the reason that it led me to prepare against a similar "roughhouse" the next time.

A week later as we took our seats in the same place and in the same order, I said to "Fuller," who at once announced himself: "You tipped the table over last week and spilled our pencils and paper so that we got no writing. To prevent this, I have fastened the sheets of paper to the table with thumb-tacks and have tied the pencils to the tacks with dental floss."

This seemed to amuse him. He chuckled softly. "That's like you," he whispered, "always prepared!"

Now occurred one of those illogical manifestations which make for the honesty of our psychic. Two invisibles whispered their names to my wife. One was an elderly woman, a relative by marriage, the other was her daughter, who spoke in a wistful, eager way precisely as we remembered her. Why should these two spirits come to my wife, when she naturally expected her father and mother? The younger woman whispered as one deeply agitated, voicing a desire to send a message to her sister.

She vanished, and "Fuller" came back. After tapping me on the shoulder he spoke in a strong, full whisper, but I could not quite distinguish his words. I said, "I hear you plainly enough, 'Fuller,' but your articulation is bad. Your words all run together."

To this he replied with an effort to speak clearly: "Yes, that is our barrier. Articulation is difficult."

I then said: "I have been reading a report by Geley, who suggests that the utterance of the invisibles is often made by means of an *indrawn* rather than by an outgoing breath—and that this accounts for their defective character."

The invisible one seemed to ponder this for a moment. "There is something in that," he replied judicially. "I'll look into it."

"Now, 'Fuller,' " I went on, "let's get down to fundamentals. How do you move that horn? Do you use your ectoplasmic hands?"

To this he instantly replied, "*Bands,* not hands."

I went on: "Here is a grand chance to experiment. You are in my study with only my family present. You should be able to present many novel phenomena."

No reply came from the horn, but at the close of the sitting we found on the top sheet of paper this line: "*Plan,* and I will attempt to work it out satisfactorily." The word "plan" was underscored. The words were properly spaced, the *i*'s exactly dotted and the *t*'s crossed. The writing closely resembled "Fuller's" script.

It chanced that this sitting came only a day or two

after the Long Beach earthquake—and on the same sheet with "Fuller's" declaration were these words: "Bands of helpers were busy on this earth while your earth was shaking." At right angles with this, and in "Fuller's" handwriting, was a reply to a remark I had made to my family during the sitting, "He seemed to like 'Lily Dale' and 'Belle Mahone.'"

"I always enjoyed simple melodies," he wrote.

The question to be answered first is this: Why should "Fuller" came to me rather than my father or my mother? Was it because our psychic knew "Fuller" and did not know my parents? Or was it because "Fuller" had more power—more skill? Why should a distant relative by marriage come to my wife, rather than other and more intimate friends?

At our next sitting in which only my wife and I took part, the room was not darkened completely. To make a "dark cabinet" I spread over the low table a very large thick woolen blanket which trailed on the floor for a yard or more. On this robe I set the megaphone. We could see our psychic and the cone on the table, though dimly. My wife said, "The cone is outlined against the window." But I could see it only by reason of a pale cloud of mist which shimmered around its larger end, partially obscuring the band of radiant paint.

In spite of these conditions the cone rocked on its base without any visible hand touching it, and at the close of our sitting we found under the horn and under the robe, on the sheet of paper tacked to the top of the table, these words written in large wavering lines: "The work progresses difficult light."

At our sitting on April 9, I tried something new. I placed beneath the small table a portable typewriter, and after we were seated I said: " 'Fuller,' that machine on the floor is the one you used so often in the back room of our flat in New York City. I want you to write your name with it." No reply was spoken, but on one of the sheets of paper this message was written, also in character: "I had no idea that my going back to the typewriter would have value, but I will try it if you wish."

My record reads:

"This was a most interesting sitting. 'Fuller,' who had displaced the psychic's guide, her daughter, was in full control. He brought to me 'William James' and 'John Burroughs.' He said, 'We'll all leave our autographs this time.'

" 'James' spoke to me with a great deal of feeling in a husky whisper: 'Garland, the world is ready for this philosophy. The great thinkers are going our way.' He then compared the mystical philosophy of Eddington, Jeans, and Einstein with the materialistic tenets of the nineties. His hoarse whisper was almost a tone, but he spoke so rapidly and with such poor articulation that I could not distinguish some of his words. It was all in keeping with his thought and character.

"The content of the entire sitting was literary. 'Burroughs' surprised me by the fervor of his utterance. He spoke in a rapid whisper with deep feeling. 'Fuller' on the other hand was cool and 'nippy,' wholly in character.

"On another sheet of paper were the promised autographs. The names 'Burroughs' and 'James' were in feeble small script running sideways to the medium's position, while the initials 'C. F. B. and 'John C. V.' were at the very top of the sheet and upside down. They stood for 'Charles Francis Browne' and 'John C. Van Dyke.'

"The entire sitting was taken up by a discussion by those invisibles, of literary and philosophic subjects. Nothing but a stenographic report could set forth its lifelike character. The psychic coughed as if strangling at times, but for the most part remained quiet as if in a light trance.

"At the close of the sitting she seemed dazed and physically inert. Her hands appeared swollen and heavy, and she did not recover her normal condition till after she had taken two strong cups of coffee.

"April 19. The session tonight was again wholly literary with 'Fuller' as the dominant personality.

"One of the first whispers to come after we were settled was that of a spirit who gave his name as 'Bert'; and when I asked, ' "Bert" who?' the answer came with painful effort. I could distinguish only 'Bert—Bert,' repeated eagerly. 'Fuller' then said, 'It is a man whose quips in the *Tribune* used to amuse you. It is "Bert Taylor." '

"Here was another unexpected visitor. Why should 'Taylor' come to me rather than 'Edward Wheeler' or 'Carl Akeley,' for whom we have called? 'Taylor' was a friend but not an intimate friend.

"Now came a strong whisper from an invisible who called himself 'T. R.' And when I asked, 'Is it "Theodore Roosevelt"?' he replied vigorously, 'Yes, yes! "Roosevelt —Roosevelt." ' For several minutes I talked to him as if I believed in him—although I could not imagine 'Theodore Roosevelt' with his lips to that cone, breathing a message into my ears."

At our next sitting I said to "Fuller," "Does our singing really help you?" In reply he whispered, "Yes"; and at the close of the sitting on one sheet of the paper, and sidewise to the psychic, these words in scrawling script appeared: "Song opens windows." It was not in "Fuller's" writing, however.

On the other sheet was a message in small, admirably formed script, properly dotted, crossed, and punctuated: "Garland, we will prove to you the things you already know. J. B."

This I took to be a gentle slam at me by "John Burroughs," who always addressed me as Garland, and who had listened to several of my talks on psychics. He considered me a believer.

On the following night, true to his promise, "Fuller" came again to our sitting, in which only my wife and I took part. The "power" was weak. "Fuller" spoke, but I could not distinguish his words. His whisper had volume, but his utterances blurred into a kind of rumble. I understood him to say, " 'William James' is present."

I said: " 'Henry,' you used to visit us at West Salem, at Onteora, and in New York. I wish you could see us here in our new California home. *Can* you see us—or rather *perceive* us here?"

He did not reply to me through the cone, but at the close of our sitting we found these words in his script: "Your eyes plus your thought of us give us experience." The last word was badly jumbled, but "experience" seems to be the meaning.

There is something rather fine in this thought. Our eyes, plus thought of our dead friends, make us visible to them.

In discussing the general subject of psychic manifestations during these sittings I said to my wife: "These phenomena—these miracles—have always existed. All literature is filled with just such manifestations but under various names."

When I turned on the light I found these words written: "The greatest of all proof is in the Bible." The word which I have interpreted as "proof" was so blurred that I could not be quite sure of its meaning. "Proof" will serve. The writing resembled that which had been signed "James," and on the second sheet in the same hand was the signature "William J."

In talking to "Fuller" I had said, "I am going East and will soon be at the Century Club among our old friends." He had made no vocal answer to this, but I found a line on the second sheet of paper: "I will meet you at the Club." It was not signed, but it closely resembled Fuller's writing. The *t*'s were precisely crossed although the word "Club" was rather sketchy. It was all legible, however.

II

At this point my sittings were interrupted by a trip to Chicago and New York; and my next record is dated July 24, shortly after my return from the East:

"Only my wife and I, my daughter Isabel, her husband, and our psychic were present. The room was perfectly dark, and no control was in effect. 'Fuller' came at once, and I had a great deal of natural and humorous talk with him. I said, ' "Fuller," I am at work on the fourth volume of my literary log, and I am inclined to give a full chapter to you.'

"To this he replied with characteristic humor, 'Tread lightly!'

"I spoke of my approaching lecture for the Psychical Society. 'I am quoting from your report on our "Mac-Dowell" experience.' He said, 'Be careful.' He then asked, 'How does my report read?' I replied, 'As logical as ever.' This seemed to please him.

"I then said, ' "Fuller," now that my literary reminiscences are almost finished, I am going to take up my psychic record again.'

"To this he replied promptly, 'A good idea, but let the incidents in the book spell out something. The trouble with your "Shadow World" was the lack of sequence. It was chronologically jumbled.'

"This I admitted. 'I did that as you know for the editor of a popular magazine who wanted a series of after-dinner conversations. I shall make my new book a straight historical account of my experimentation and psychic progress. I am to address the Psychical Society here on Wednesday night, and I intend to lay all my cards on the table.'

"His reply was characteristic. 'Don't forget the ace!' he warningly whispered.

"Throughout this conversation, which was perfectly natural and unconstrained, his whisper became almost full tone. His replies were swift, whimsical, and to the point. His talk with my wife and daughter was also in character. To me he said: 'We have great plans for you. We'll help you write that last chapter.'

"At this moment the power appeared to weaken and we sang 'Loch Lomond' in rapid time, purposely pounding out the rhythm on the theory that such vibrations warmed up 'the machine' like a radio tube. When we had finished 'Fuller' asked with sarcastic intonation, 'What was that?'

"I apologized for maltreating this fine old song. 'We thought the rhythm more important than the tune.'

"He retorted, 'The rhythm is helpful, but you must also bear in mind the emotional part—the melody.'

"At the close of the sitting we found on the paper this sentence: 'It is well enough to make study if in the end you reach the desired result.'

"We had sung 'Home Sweet Home,' and on the lower sheet of paper in a totally different hand I found these words: 'Home means more than ever here and now.'

"This is significant. Does it mean that the spirit longs for his good old third-dimensional plane?"

III

Although these sittings have no scientific weight, they have indirect value by reason of the unexpected personalities who came into our circle.

For example, one night a whisper issued from the cone, a faint and tired voice which said, "I am 'Pierce.'"

None of us were acquainted with anyone named "Pierce," and I asked, "What is your full name?"

To my amazement the voice replied, "Franklin Pierce."

"Not 'President Franklin Pierce'?"

"Yes."

This was astounding. "Why should 'Franklin Pierce' come to our circle?" I asked.

My wife then dimly remembered hearing her mother say that "Franklin Pierce" was a distant relative. She spoke to "Pierce," but he did not answer. Wholly illogical, he faded away and never came again.

Another personality of especially vigorous action introduced himself as "Lee Summers." Lee was our good friend when alive, but there was no special reason why he should come.

Toward the end of the sitting "James" said, "Garland, you know Henry never believed in this—and neither did Alice. Alice used to make fun of it and laughed at my credulity."

My daughter asked, "Who was Alice—your wife?"

"No, my sister," the invisible replied; and the horn sank slowly to the floor.

I did not know that William James had a sister, but it is possible that our psychic did. I immediately wrote to James's daughter in San Francisco and confirmed the statement of the ghost.

On this same night a strong and pleasant voice spoke, and when I asked, "Who is it?" he replied, "I'm going to amuse you by saying that I don't know who I am."

"You don't know who you are?"

"Oh, yes, I know who I am, but I can't remember my name."

"Were you an author?"

"No."

"Were you an artist?"

"No."

"What *did* you do?"

"I did what I am doing now." He hesitated. "If I could only remember my town."

My wife spoke up. "Was it Chicago?"

"That's it!" the whisper joyously exclaimed. "It was in Chicago—I was an architect in Chicago."

"You are 'Pond'?" I suggested.

"That's right! I am 'Pond'—'A. B. Pond.'" He seemed overjoyed at being recognized, but did not ask for anything, did not say anything more. He too vanished and never came again.

That our psychic was acquainted with Pond, I knew, but his coming seemed illogical, nevertheless.

CHAPTER TWENTY-FOUR

DANGER SIGNALS

As the sittings went on, my wife became very much concerned over the very evident bad effect which they had upon the health of our mediumistic friend, who complained of sleeplessness after each séance: "I hear voices," she explained, "and I feel on my face something like cobwebs." Each sitting left her weaker and more apprehensive.

Our sitting on August 14 was predominantly literary. My record reads, in part:

" 'Fuller' came. He handled the horn expertly and spoke almost in a full tone. His articulation was so bad, however, that I could scarcely follow him; but we held a most significant dialogue.

"During my visit to Chicago I had learned of a very beautiful little book of notes and drawings which 'Fuller' had made during his first tour of Italy, and the owner of this book, his niece, had asked me to find a purchaser for it. I now seized upon this volume as an identification test. ' "Fuller," what shall I do about that book of drawings?'

"He appeared puzzled. 'What book of drawings?'

"I explained. At the close of my explanation he said with characteristic depreciation, 'Those drawings have no value.' He then said, 'You will be surprised when you learn who is here.'

"At this moment for no reason at all a vision of John Sargent came into my mind although I had not thought of him for many months. 'Is it "Sargent"?' I asked.

"The cone tapped a vigorous 'Yes.'

" 'Will you write your name?'

"Again the taps spelled 'Yes.'

" 'Fuller' then said, ' "Burroughs" is here also.'

"I said, 'I wish you would bring "Dr. Turck." '

" 'Fuller' chuckled. 'You'd have to convince him first.' "

This reply was especially pertinent, for "Dr. Turck," my most devoted friend as well as my physician, detested the word "psychic" and considered my experiments foolish.

"At this point the pencil could be heard busily at work, and I remarked: 'That may be "Sargent." Perhaps he'll leave a drawing.'

"A clear voice greeted us. 'This is "Doyle." I want to introduce a young man.' His name was not given, and no reason for his presence was offered. He seemed a casual companion, one who just 'came along.'

"I said to 'Fuller,' 'Did you miss our sittings while I was away? Were you lonely? Have you a sense of time?'

"He replied clearly, 'We have a sense of the continuity of events but not of Time divided into periods.'

"In reply to a question by my wife he replied with highly characteristic deprecation, 'As for me, I just let things slide.'

"A little later in reference to my sceptical attitude

he remarked, 'You should listen to what they say over here about your claim that we are only a projection of the medium.' He again said, 'You will be surprised by the friend who has just put his name on the paper.'

"At the close of the sitting I discovered that the signatures 'Sargent' and 'Burroughs' had been telescoped like this: 'John S.—Burroughs' as though my simultaneous thought had fused them.

"My 'surprise' was contained in this message, written in large script: 'Another body cast off, a new life of renewed fight begun, Walt Whitman.' Which would be something more than surprising, if I could believe it.

"August 23. Our sitting tonight was still more puzzling. 'Fuller' came in strong. He said to me, 'Did you ever see a face in the end of a trumpet?' I answered: 'No. I never thought of it.'

"He said, 'I shall soon show my face to you.'

"He urged us to ask questions. He said to me, 'You will soon be able to call the roll of your literary friends, and they will answer.'

"I said, 'How many are here tonight?'

"He replied, 'Many more than I can count.'

At the close of the sitting we found several characteristic signatures of my friend.

"August 29. Early in the sitting the cone tapped me on the back of my hand; and when I asked, 'Is it "Fuller"?' he replied in full tone, 'Yes.'

"He was in philosophical mood and we had much talk of modern science. He said, 'Time and space do not exist for us.'

"I then said: 'I can't follow that, "Fuller." I can't conceive of a personality without placing it in space. Our modern philosophers say time is the fourth dimension. What is the fourth dimension to you?'

"His reply was instant. 'It is the plane just beyond your three-dimensional plane.'

" 'I've thought of that. I have often had the concept that when you invisibles manifest to us you come from a fourth-dimensional region, and when you disappear you reënter it. Is that true? Are you living on the fourth-dimensional plane?'

"He again chuckled. 'Yes. I'm not quite worthy of the fifth or sixth dimension.'

" 'I don't understand that. I can't even grasp the concept of a fourth dimension.'

"His answer was a stunner. 'What would a two-dimensional man make of a cube?'

" 'In other words,' I pursued, 'if I were walking with you and you wished to disappear, you would merely step up into the fourth dimension?'

" 'You can explain it that way,' he jocosely replied.

"He then spoke at some length on the nature of force. 'The energy which lifts the cone or cracks an atom is all the same.'

"The spirit of Charles Francis Browne, my painter brother-in-law, now took the horn and demanded in his well-remembered argumentative tone, 'Do you know what is going on at this moment on your earth?'

" 'What do you mean—in politics?'

" 'Yes.' He then entered upon an eloquent harangue about economic changes and social growths, exactly as he used to argue while on earth. He closed by saying jovially: 'What are you waiting for, Hamlin? Come on over. It's a great lark. It's like getting on a train with a lot of your friends—flags flying, whistles blowing, and a great trip ahead of you. I tell you it's grand!'

"When he 'ran down' and the horn dropped, a new hand lifted it and someone whispered, 'Garland!'

" 'Is it "Burroughs"?' I asked.

"His answer was dryly humorous. 'And yet they say we can't put our personalities across!'

"Another invisible now intervened. 'Who am I?' it demanded as if to prove 'Burroughs' ' point.

"I named two or three of my friends, and at last the visitor laughingly said, "You are playing a guessing game. This is "Doyle." '

"After some remarks of no great importance, he turned the horn back to 'Burroughs' who spoke rapidly, almost gayly, on some very abstruse points in modern philosophical theories. In fact, the whole evening ran to political, social, and philosophical expositions—just such a talk as my daughter had often listened to in our New York home.

"Our psychic appeared to be in trance the latter part of the sitting, and when we turned on the faint red light, she lay inertly extended in her chair. Her hands were heavy and cold, and her face fevered and swollen. She came slowly back to life. 'I heard almost nothing this time,' she declared.

"On the top sheet of paper we found these words: 'A world movement begins to show itself in America. The power behind the man in Washington is the power behind the universe. Man begins to be man. Godspeed! Burroughs.'

"This message which resembled 'Burroughs'' script in some degree, was dotted and crossed and punctuated with precision. It grew smaller and sadly confused toward the end and the signature was quite feeble. That it came from 'Burroughs,' I could not believe. 'Godspeed' did not sound like him.

"On the second sheet appeared the initials 'W. W.' the first W being smaller than the second. I took this to mean 'Walt Whitman' although no message accompanied it."

The sitting which followed on September 7 was in many ways the most remarkable of all our experiences thus far:

"First 'Barbara' came but gave way to 'Fuller' who was in better voice than ever before. His utterances were quite clear.

"He was followed by someone who spoke in a loud whisper. Again I guessed right by saying, 'It is "Burroughs."'

"I then asked, 'Is "T. R." present?'

" 'Yes, he is here but much discouraged by his failure to reach his wife and sons.'

" 'Can he speak to me?'

" 'He will try.'

"A moment later our smaller unlighted parchment cone tapped me gently on the back of my hand, and when I asked, 'Is it "Roosevelt"?' it tapped out 'Yes.' My daughter then said, 'Shall we send a message to your wife?'

" 'No! No!' was the instant reply. 'She would not receive it. She thinks of me as *somewhere*, but she can't believe that I am near her.'

"There was nothing characteristic of Roosevelt in this reply. I could not imagine him hesitant or discouraged on any plane.

"At my suggestion my daughter and her husband then sang 'Onward, Christian Soldiers' which was Roosevelt's favorite hymn. (Later on the top sheet of paper we found these words: 'You sang our campaign song [1912]. Great times but these are greater. I stand behind my cousin. T. R.')

"The metal cone now began to rattle and dance upon the table, and something in its action led me to say, 'That sounds as it did when "Lee Summers" came.' This caused the cone to beat upon the table so vigorously that it came apart and the three sections rolled on the floor, one under the table, the other two under my daughter's chair.

"My daughter then said, 'You did that, "Uncle Lee." Now let's have a test of your powers as an engineer. You put it together again.'

"In the darkness we heard the pieces moving slowly toward each other across the floor, and a second later we caught the rattle and squeak as the horn reassembled itself and the three sections were twisted into one another. A moment later it rose triumphantly in the air and a clear voice said, 'There! I brought science to bear upon it.'

"I said, ' "Lee," you and I often used to discuss this subject.'

"He replied soberly: 'Yes. I believed in it more deeply than you did. You considered me a little soft on that side of my brain.'

"September 17. I brought up the fourth dimension

again tonight. I said to 'Burroughs' and 'Fuller': 'These sittings are absurd. I can't believe that you and "James" and "Doyle" are scrabbling around on the floor of my study, whispering to me through a tin horn.'

"This brought a lively blast from 'Burroughs,' who indignantly said, 'We're *not* scrabbling on your floor!'

" 'Well, that's what it seems like to me,' I persisted. 'Unless you are operating on a plane where no floor exists, that's precisely what you *are* doing. The whole performance is ridiculous, and I am unable to take it seriously. It is all mystifying but silly.'

" 'James' now took the horn and argued for the fourth dimension and the logic of his presence in my study. I could not catch all his words clearly and hence could not follow his argument. When he had finished I replied: 'I just can't believe that "James" and "Whitman" and "Roosevelt," or any other of my friends, are here speaking and writing for the edification of my family. I'd like to believe it but I can't.'

" 'Fuller' alluded to the birthday dinner which had been arranged for me by Gaylord Beaman at the University Club. 'It was a grand event. I wanted to be there but I didn't succeed. Many of your friends are now here offering congratulations.'

" 'Will they speak?'

" 'No, but they will write their greetings.' Later he said, 'Three have written but thirty wanted to write.'

"Soon after he finished speaking, I felt a light tapping on my hand. It was the unlighted cone. I sensed a new visitor. After several guesses, something prompted me to ask, 'Is it "Father"?'

"Instantly the cone rapped me on the knee. I said

aloud: 'This is the first time any message has ever come from my father. In all my sittings, neither he nor my mother has ever manifested.' 'Can you speak to me?' I asked.

"The cone feebly tapped 'No,' and sank slowly to the floor.

"After a moment's silence it rose again and with timid, caressing action crept across my knee and tapped me gently on the breast. When I asked, 'Is this "Mother"?' it rocked gently on my knee. Rising slowly it rested entirely in my arm for a minute or two, then softly went away."

Up to this sitting my long-time beloved friend Howells had not made his presence known although I had repeatedly asked for him. At our next meeting the night of October 5th a whispered greeting came to me. "I am 'Howells.'" The invisible then spoke at some length concerning his study of Swedenborg—which neither the psychic nor the members of my family regarded as characteristic of the great novelist, but I understood fully when he said, "My study of Swedenborg was a good preparation for this spirit life."

"He appeared passionately eager to clear away my doubts, but his long harangue only added to my doubts. His explosive utterances were wholly unlike Howells, whose speech was always gracefully restrained. His reference to Swedenborg was evidential, but his manner of speech and his sprawling initials 'W. D. H.,' which appeared on the sheet of paper, were not. Howells wrote a very fine, firm hand, and his initials were in keeping. I set this dialogue down for its singular mixture of truth and error.

" 'James' who followed, opened with a rapid-fire dissertation which I could not follow by reason of his failure to articulate. In his attempt to explain the conditions which surrounded him he said, 'Can a fish explain how he breathes and swims?'

" 'No,' I replied, 'and neither can a Hottentot understand skating on ice.'

" 'Fuller' attempted to explain to my daughter the fourth dimension. He said: 'You used to play cat's-cradle with your father when you were little, didn't you? Well, now put your hands in that position. She said, 'I have done so.' After a pause he began to chuckle. 'It's no use! I can't do it. "Howells" and "James" are amused at my attempting to explain the fourth dimension to you.'

"On the upper sheet of the paper I had tacked to the table appeared the signature, 'Wm. Vaughn Moody,' exact in every stroke. None of us had mentioned Moody, and I had not thought of him since writing of him two years before. He gave no message, just signed his name. *It was exact enough to pass scrutiny at a bank.*"

The effect of this séance on our psychic was alarming. She complained next morning of being unable to sleep, but was eager to go on, although my wife was disposed to forbid it.

Ten days later we sat again in the same place with this same group.

" 'Fuller' came as usual and acted as master of ceremonies. 'William James' also spoke. Then as before the parchment cone came softly over to me and nestled on my arm, giving me the impression of a timid and tender visitor. I asked, 'Is it "Mother"?' Again it tapped out assent. I then said, 'Go to Isabel and speak to her. She hears better than I.' The horn rose slowly and hung close to my daughter's face. It seemed trying to speak. I urged it on. 'Say "Isabel."'

"At last it whispered the one word, 'Isabel'; and when I said, 'I heard you!' a gentle sobbing followed as if the spirit were crying for joy at being heard.

"To the circle I said, 'If I could believe in that whisper, I would regard this as the most significant event of my life. Her whisper of a single word would mean more to me than all of Millikan's discourses or the cosmic ray.'

" 'James' returned and continued his discussion of the fourth dimension. He said, 'We use many words in order to project our personality to you.' I took this to be an apology for taking so much of the medium's strength. He added, 'We could be much more concise; but such saving of words would not be characteristic, and our personalities as speakers would fail to manifest.'

"On the sheet of paper at the close of the sitting was a single message: 'When I sang the body triumphant I referred to spirit. I speak of the body of thought. Walt Whitman.' "

Altogether this was one of the most perplexing of our experiences, but it proved disastrous to our psychic. She rose next morning feeling, she said, "very weak and dizzy." She looked sick. Her face was swollen, and her eyes bloodshot. Shortly after her breakfast as she was standing in my wife's chamber she slipped to the floor in a most terrifying catalyptic seizure. Fortunately a trained nurse who was treating my wife, caught her, and when I reached the room, she and my daughter had lifted the unconscious woman to the bed. She was rigid as stone and unable to speak. She looked like a dying woman.

While not as alarmed as my wife and daughter, I realized that this was the end of our séances. Plainly I could not ask this woman, a friend of my family, to go on sacrificing her health, not even to prove the return of the dead.

She recovered in a few hours, but some weeks later she went East to spend the winter with her daughter. "I shall not sit again until I fully recover," she declared as she said good-bye.

My final remark to her was intended to be jocose. " 'Fuller' and 'Burroughs' and 'James' will be eagerly waiting your return."

There is a puzzling sequel to the "Walt Whitman" message quoted above. Several weeks after our friend's departure, I chanced to take up from my desk a small scratch pad, and while idly thumbing its leaves I caught sight of some writing on a leaf in the middle of the pad. Recognizing it at once as "spirit" writing, similar to that which came on the paper during the sittings, I turned the pages carefully, finding these lines:

> Sing of the body triumphant
> Sing of the spirit electric.
> Too long has earth's note been sordid
> So long has flesh claimed the power.
> [Here two blank pages intervened.]
> Sing the spirit electric.
> [Two more blank leaves.]
>
> WALT WHITMAN

Evidently this message, written without my knowledge or that of the psychic, was a part of the message which had appeared on the sheet of paper pinned to the table. Whether the pad was in my desk drawer or lying on the corner between my daughter's shoulder and my own, I can not say. I set it down for what it is worth to the reader.

In summing up the evidence of these sittings I am unable to account for the dominance of "Fuller," the marvellous duplication of his signature and those of "John Burroughs," "William Vaughn Moody," and "Van Dyke." The writing beneath the blanket and the message from the woman who died in France are evidential. At a later date, I secured (with this same psychic) writing on a slate in the light. The signatures "Wm. James" and "H. B. F." were written in bright pigment. While her hands were on the top of the table a pale bluish light filled the hollows of her palms.

These slate-writing experiments were less destructive of her health, but they disturbed her; and at last my wife forbade even these trials.

In closing this chapter I ask the reader's attention to the fact that none of the customary spirit messages from "Red Thunder" or "White Fawn" wasted our time. Our circles were almost entirely literary. Most of the "spirits" claimed to be my personal friends: "Burroughs," "James," "Doyle," "Howells," "Roosevelt," "Van Dyke," "Whitman," "Moody," "Sargent," and several others, with "Fuller" as master of ceremonies. It is worthy of remark that none of my visiting authors were women. It would seem that I was the dominant factor in every performance. That my daughter possessed some supernatural power was evident, for I felt mysterious touches on the knee next to her, and she remarked that her legs were often cold and numb during the latter part of each sitting.

Whatever the scientific shortcomings of this chapter, I am of the belief that it will not be skipped!

CHAPTER TWENTY–FIVE

ANCIENT TONGUES AND ECTOPLASMIC MASKS

WHILE in the midst of this very interesting series of experiments in my study, I received an invitation to address the San Francisco branch of the Psychical Research society. This request came through my good friend Stewart Edward White, research officer of the organization.

Among the friends whom he had invited to meet me at dinner, were Judge and Mrs. Cannon, active members of the New York Society. I had met them in the East and was particularly pleased to meet them again for it was at a sitting in their apartment that Dr. Whymant, the Oriental scholar, had carried on a conversation (in archaic Chinese) with an invisible who claimed to be "Confucius"; and I hoped to hear more about it.

Mrs. Cannon during the evening told us the story in detail, and, veterans of psychic research as we all were, we agreed that this colloquy in a language which not half a dozen men in all America could speak, was one of the strongest arguments for persistent identity ever recorded by a group of sceptical observers.

The story which Mrs. Cannon related at my request ran about as follows:

"We were living on Park Avenue at this time, and

having become acquainted with the work of Valiantine the medium, we arranged a series of séances in our apartment. In these sittings we had been hearing many direct voices, some of them speaking languages which none of us could understand, and when one night someone named Dr. Whymant as a scholar who spoke many languages, I at once invited him to come and sit with us. 'We particularly want you to listen to one speaker whose words no one of us can understand.'

"Fortunately this voice was heard during Dr. Whymant's first visit, and we all listened with intense interest whilst he conversed with the invisible. 'He is speaking Chinese,' Dr. Whymant said, 'archaic Chinese. It is impossible for this medium to speak or understand this language. This speaker claims to be the ancient scholar "Kung Fu-Tzu," called "Confucius." '

"He told us that he had quoted the first lines of a most ancient Chinese poem, one that Confucius himself had edited, and that the voice took up and completed the poem, which was one whose meaning had been in dispute for centuries.

"Dr. Whymant, who came to five or six other of our sittings, declared that he heard fourteen foreign languages spoken by these voices, among them Hindu, Sanscrit, Arabic, Persian, Portuguese, and modern Greek. Valiantine is an uneducated man and knows no language but English and not very much about that."

So the story ran, and I was delighted to get it, for I had met Dr. Whymant in New York, and heard his public address on these sittings, but I had never seen anything he had written concerning them; and when Mrs. Cannon took from her bag a photostat copy of the letter which he had sent her, I asked the privilege of copying it.

"Dr. Whymant's reputation as an Oriental scholar is well established in London as well as in China," I said, "and his testimony is most valuable."

At the close of the evening, I took this letter to my room and studied it with care, comparing it with my own notes and my recollections of his address.

In it I found most of the points which I had heard him make in his talk to the Society; but here in fullest detail he recorded the dialogue between himself and the invisible sage. "There is no physical explanation which would cover all the circumstances in the case," he said. "I must leave to others the elucidation of the problem."

He reports in this letter the dialogue which occupied several minutes of each evening and gives to his part in it as well as to the part of the sage, just the proper tone of formal and flowing Chinese discourse. It was not merely a fluent use of a most ancient tongue, it was a complete characterization of an elderly scholar jealous of his high place in literary China more than two thousand years ago. I am privileged to quote from Whymant's letter to Mrs. Cannon:

"In a tremulous voice the invisible began: 'Greeting, O son of learning and reader of strange books. This unworthy servant bows humbly before such excellence.'

"WHYMANT: Peace be upon thee, O illustrious one! This uncultured menial ventures to ask thy name and illustrious style.

"CONFUCIUS: My mean name is Kung: men call me Fu-Tzu, and my lowly style is Kiu. I wasted more than three score years and reached the end of no road. Peace be on thy house! May I know thy honorable name and illustrious style?"

I have since met this man Valiantine and find him absolutely unable to comprehend such dialogue.

Later in the conversation this still more significant colloquy took place:

"WHYMANT: This stupid one would know the correct reading of a verse in the 'Shih King.' It has been hidden from understanding for long centuries and men look upon it with eyes that are blind. The passage begins thus: . . . [Here he quoted the lines in question.]

"To this Confucius then replied: 'It should be read this way: "O Master of Mysteries . . ."' "

Here the voice intoned the passage, giving the correct wording of this obscure and disputed poem, a reading which astounded Dr. Whymant. Nevertheless he persisted in his test:

" 'Shall I ask of one passage in the master's own writings? In "Lun-yu Hsia Peu" there is a passage which is wrongly written. Should it not read thus . . .' "

Here Dr. Whymant started to quote the passage, but before he could get well into it, the ancient voice took up the quotation and carried it to the end.

"The invisible sage then said: 'You were going to ask me about the two characters which end the last two phrases. You are quite right, the copyists were in error. The character which is written *se* should be written *i* and the character which is written *yeu* is an error for *fou*.' "

In his address at the Psychical Society I had heard Dr. Whymant report this test of scholarship as a "trap" to catch the medium; but in his letter, which is before me as I write, he admits his complete defeat and bewilderment.

As I pondered this letter, which was Whymant's first formal record of his tests of the medium's power, I should have been convinced of the actual presence of Confucius in that darkened room of the Cannon apartment: but I was not. I admitted the truth of Whymant's report; I absolved the medium of any part in this dialogue (he was absolutely unfitted to meet such a test of scholarship); but in Whymant that knowledge lay, and it may be that the psychic had the power to draw upon that scholarship and return it to him in the Chinese tongue.

I confess that this is going a long way around instead of cutting straight across, but my mind works that way. I grant that this dialogue is an almost perfect proof of survival and identity, as complete as any verbal test can be, for no modern scholar, not even Dr. Whymant, knew the exact meaning of those long-disputed lines. Nevertheless despite this voice from the dark, speaking with absolute authority, I was not convinced of the presence of Confucius in this circle.

II

White as research officer of the Society had arranged several meetings with psychics, among whom was a man who claimed to be able to secure voices through a megaphone in full daylight; and as this interested me White drove me into San Francisco to meet this wonder-worker.

We found him awaiting us in the office of the Society. He was a heavily built, middle-aged, vigorous man, commonplace in appearance and manner of speech. He claimed to be a retired army surgeon, and his candid statement impressed me favorably.

"I can't understand the process and I welcome your investigation. I'll coöperate with you in any way you name."

"You are the man we are looking for," I replied.

He showed us a large horn or megaphone, much larger than the one most psychics use, and explained his practice: "I hold the larger end of the horn against my solar plexus in this way." Here he placed it against his stomach with the small end extending toward me. "If you will listen at the small end you will hear voices, and perhaps music, coming through it."

"Do you mean now, in this light?"

"Yes, anywhere. In the daylight, electric light, in a public hall—anywhere. I am ready to demonstrate right now."

In the light of a clear morning, and in this office, such a claim seemed preposterous; but as he was ready to act and we were there to test him, I took the small end in my hand and put my ear to it while Stewart had an eye to the lips and throat of the man, alert for signs of ventriloquistic effort.

After a few moments I heard very distinctly the whispered words, "Uncle John." This I took to mean "John Burroughs" and though I asked for the last name, the whisper only repeated, "Uncle John—Uncle John."

White then put his ear to the small end of the megaphone whilst I gave close attention to the psychic's lips and throat. There was no apparent motion there, and yet White said: "I hear a name spoken. It is William. But it means little to me." A moment later he said, "I hear a sound as of the wind blowing through trees— and I hear a dog barking."

We got nothing more definite at this time, but Wheeler urged us to try again the following day. "I don't understand this power. Sometimes it works and sometimes it doesn't. I'd like to have you men investigate me thoroughly and tell me what it means."

We made a date for the following morning, and as we went away I said: "That's a new one to me. I am interested in this man."

In my diary I find this note:

"February 22, 1933. We met Wheeler again in the office of the Society and experimented with amazing results. At my request he took off his coat and vest and I ran my hands over his body to see that no microphone or wires were concealed under his shirt. Again while he held the horn I listened at the small end with Stewart watching for signs of ventriloquism. This time I heard the name 'John—John—John' insistently, almost pleadingly repeated.

"Again in the belief that the whisper meant John Burroughs, I asked, 'Can't you give me your last name?' To my astonishment the whisper clearly replied, 'Van Dyke. John C. Van Dyke.'

"I was careful not to repeat the name aloud but I saw White recording it in his notebook.

"I then held the cone in my own hands a foot or more from Wheeler's body, and plainly felt it vibrate with whispered words. The sounds appeared to be generated *in the middle* of the cone—not at the end.

"Getting Van Dyke's name was surprising, for I had John Burroughs in my mind all the time and fully expected to hear his name. Van Dyke was not consciously in my thought. The psychic, a non-literary, non-esthetic soul, could not possibly have known Van Dyke, certainly not as my friend.

"Furthermore, and still more singular, as I listened at the small end of this horn, I could hear voices in a whispered *conversation,* a colloquy, which had no relation to me. The speakers went on and on as if unconscious of being overheard. They sounded far off, and their words were indistinct; but I got the impression of a lively and continuous dialogue. While Stewart held the horn, I heard other names repeated over and over, as if the speakers were eager to be recognized—but these names meant nothing to me.

"I again held the cone at least two feet from Wheeler's body while White listened at the small end and conversed with a voice.

"He said, 'No, I don't remember any such man in my company. There was no Peter White in my command. Oh—you say, in my regiment, not in my company! That might be. I'll look you up. You were a sergeant —in command of a machine gun? All right. You'll be on record somewhere. I'll check up on you.'

"While this dialogue was going on I held the cone balanced on the palms of my hands and again felt in the cone the vibration of the whispered words.

"White now took the horn and held it entirely clear from the psychic's body, and as I listened I again heard voices eagerly repeating names; one sounded like 'Sam-Sam-Sam Smith.' I could not distinguish any words of the messages, some of which were full of pleading. It was with a distinct feeling of regret that I found myself unable to reach and comfort these appealing souls. I sensed a distinct, wistful plea for recognition. I gave over the attempt."

All this, be it remembered, took place in an ordinary business office in full daylight—with the psychic apparently normal throughout. He appeared quite candid and trustful. He let the horn pass into our hands without the slightest hesitation and discussed his performance with engaging frankness.

I said to him, "Your 'trick' is entirely novel. I'd like to try again to make sure I did not imagine those voices."

My use of the word "trick" did not disturb or irritate him. "You'll find no trick in it," he soberly replied. "It is all true and all a mystery to me. I hope you experts can explain it; I can't. All I know is—the voices come. Sometimes I get symphonic music that can be heard by all the people in a hall."

As we went away I said, "Stewart, what name did you catch while I was listening at the horn?"

"I got the name John C. Van Dyke. What did you get?"

"Just that—John C. Van Dyke. We must pursue this man further. His willingness to be investigated is promising, and his stunt is amusing and novel, so novel that I am eager to try him again."

It came to me afterward that the "Sam Smith" who so pleadingly repeated his name might have been intended for Samuel G. Smith, a young clergyman whom

I greatly admired as a boy in Osage, Iowa. I came away without another test, however, and I was never able to arrange another meeting with Wheeler.

III

That night Stewart, as we sat beside his fire, told me how he first became interested in psychic matters.

"While Mrs. White and I were spending the winter in New York City some ten or twelve years ago, we fell in with a group who were experimenting in a private way.

"I knew very little of psychic literature at that time. I didn't even know the 'patter' of the practitioners; but some of the members of this group I speak of had a pretty thorough understanding of it. Margaret Cameron, whose book 'The Seven Purposes' had just been published, was one of them. Others interested were John P. Gavit and his wife—you know Gavit—Harrison Lewis, Margaret Cameron's husband, and one or two others.

"Margaret, Lucy Gavit, and my wife had all done some psychic experimenting, but separately, each along her own individual line. None of us came to the subject because of bereavement or other emotional impulse, and no one of our circle had made a study of the history of the subject. I had no notion of what to expect, nor what the conventional procedure in such circumstances should be. I must explain, however, that all four of our sensitives, Betty, Joan, Lucy, and Margaret, were of the mental rather than emotional type.

"We went along gaily for a month or so, meeting two

or three times each week, and then at last we began to get results."

At this point he went to his files and brought to me a handful of typewritten manuscript. "Here is the record of our experiences."

He then read this paragraph:

"'January 28. Joan was completely covered by a piece of black cloth, and yet through this her figure was several times made distinctly visible, in rather blurred outline, by means of a glowing lucent effect. At one time the luminosity extended above her head and it seemed that an attempt was being made to show a standing figure. Shortly after a wraith-like thin mist about human size rose from the floor about two feet in front of her. D—— started to put his hand out toward the mist but "Anne," our guide, called out, "Dinna touch it."'"

Putting the manuscript down, he resumed his narration.

"This was the beginning of our ectoplasmic masks. One after another, Joan, Margaret, Lucy, and Betty fell into trance, and then I began to see and record the formation of portraits on their faces. The most remarkable of all, in a way, was a portrait of Margaret herself."

"The duplication of a living person!" I exclaimed.

"Yes, it was a portrait bust, located about a foot to the left of her normal body and between herself and Lucy. It endured as a luminous globe about the size of a head for some time. It presented a face but only for an instant."

"What were the other portraits?"

"One looked like Eugene Field—that long-faced, hairless type. Another suggested Eugene Debs, and then our guide brought me into it. I became the 'goat.'

"One night 'Anne,' our invisible guide, said to me, 'Come now, Stewart lad, take a seat on the floor in front of Joan.' Joan was the principal 'agent' that night. I did as I was told, but my sensations were not pleasant. It was like sitting in an ice-box with a trickling cold shower coming down from above. I noted afterward, however, that this did not make me shiver."

"Could you *feel* anything going on?"

"At first I had no sensation other than a sense of cold and a strong impulse to suck in my cheeks. Then I felt as if cobwebs were flung in my face. Gavit reported that an ectoplasmic mask had formed itself over my face; this mask, he declared, was the portrait of an elderly man, a man he had known. Some of the others recognized the likeness."

"What an amazing phenomenon!"

Stewart smiled. "Wasn't it? Then an old woman was pictured. She had a long face and a double chin. Her hair was smooth and parted in the middle. No one seemed to know her. Then came a figure in ecclesiastical robes, a seated figure with small, fine head. The features in this mask were not distinct, but they resembled the last Pope. Following this came a large-featured elderly man of the Roman Senator type—and that ended my performance.

" 'Anne,' our guide, then directed Gavit to take a seat on the floor in front of Joan, whose wrists were still being held by Margaret. Now John, as you know, has a round face with a nose to match; but as Joan waved her hands over his head, he was transformed into a sharp-nosed person, with a thin face and heavy black eyebrows. I was standing within three feet of him while this change took place and I made notes of it immediately afterward. You'll find them all here in this manuscript. John reported the same sensation that I had described, that of a cold shower-bath.

"Our invisible, 'Anne,' then called on Betty to take a seat before Joan, and we all drew close to her, so close as to almost touch her, eager to mark every detail of the process. I saw her face change in size and shape till it resembled a little girl of six or eight, a round-faced strongly brunette type. I tried to penetrate the features of this mask to the real Betty behind it, but I could not do so. It was not a luminous mask—it was as though her flesh and blood had been manipulated—modelled.

"Before we could recover from this performance 'Anne' said, speaking through Joan, 'Now we'll play a joke on Betty, she will not mind.' "

Here again he read from his notes:

" 'Thereupon Joan, her wrists still held by Margaret, waved her hands over Betty's head. Instantly her face lengthened and her brows became wide and low. She developed high cheek-bones—the result was a grotesque mask. "Anne" said, "Now she's a comic valentine!" Joan then waved her arms with a sudden motion and Betty reappeared in her true form.

" 'However, "Anne" was not yet finished with her. Again Joan waved her arms above Betty's head and she became, almost instantly, a very handsome girl with a large head, regular features, and cowlike eyes. This was a most astonishing transformation, especially as we all stood close to the victim while she was being rebuilt. "Anne" said, "I want to show how big little Betty can be." ' "

Stewart said: "This was not a spirit portrait: it was a 'stunt,' something done to amuse us, something to arouse our wonder. It was not a mask as some of the others plainly were—it seemed to be an actual modelling of Betty's flesh and bone. I can't account for it, I can only report it."

"It had no direct relation to the spirit hypothesis?"

"No, only so far as it demonstrated that this plasma could be shaped by the thought of those in the fourth dimension as well as by our own thinking. 'Anne' intimated that dogs, cats, and other animals could be so shaped in accordance with our memory of them."

As he paused I said: "Certainly the conditions were wholly favorable for exact observation. You were all friends, and none of you were professional mediums. I'd like to take that manuscript record home with me and quote from it. It is one of the most extraordinary and convincing documents I have ever read—outside my own, of course."

He laughed. "I don't know how convincing it is, but you are welcome to use any part of it you please. I warn you that it runs to several hundred pages of typewriting."

The reader should bear in mind that the historian in this case is a distinguished author who was less than forty years of age when he made that record. He was, moreover, a man of the open air, a big-game hunter, a keen-eyed, level-headed observer. He was not seeking consolation, and he did not regard mediumship as a sacred endowment. His candor, his integrity, and his robust manliness must be taken into account.

He then showed me the manuscript record of his

experiences with the Crandons and said: "You may take this, too. Margery gave us a wonderful demonstration up in Betty's room—a room the Crandons had never before entered. I've read your report of your special sittings with Margery, and I can substantiate everything you say of her. While 'Walter' showed his hand, played with that illuminated disk and patted us on the head, I not only held both of Margery's hands but with my leg across her knees I controlled the action of her feet.

"I am certain that she did not stir from an almost complete rigidity—at times I took both her hands in my right fist, and with the palm of my left controlled her mouth and lips. Meanwhile Betty on the other side was similarly controlling Dr. Crandon's. He did not use his hands while 'Walter' was performing.

"At times the ectoplasmic rod with which 'Walter' moved the 'doughnut' could be seen as it fumbled this object or picked it from the floor, with some difficulty. At one time this rod touched me—it felt like the poke of a finger.

"At a second sitting in the same room I had abundant time to study the stream of ectoplasm which came from the psychic at about the region of the solar plexus. It appeared as a mass about four inches in diameter. It was self-luminous and hovered just below the table top. Finally it rose above the edge of the table and spread itself over the surface of a photographic film which I had placed there. The mass remained there, taking the rough shape of a hand, for about ten minutes.

"This band or stream of plasm seemed to flow up and over the table like lava—if lava could flow uphill. It had a peculiar writhing, vibrant aliveness and pulsation throughout its entire length. After flowing about for a time, the mass of plasm stood straight up about thirty inches high and changed its shape. It attempted, apparently, to mold a small birdlike figure. It then made a rough attempt at modelling a head, and after that, a fist. Finally it withdrew into the psychic's body.

"I controlled Margery as before, and at one moment by request I again controlled her lips and mouth. Nevertheless 'Walter' picked up a half-dollar from the table and tapped the lower shelf of the table—then the under side of the top, and at last placed it in my hand.

"There is no use talking of trickery. The room was our own. There was no chance for apparatus. I did not nail her to her chair as you did, but I had her fully under control."

As I listened to his story, I found myself checking the correspondence between his experiences and my own. I recalled all the phantasms I had seen, and the voices I had heard. "Stewart, your report confirms all that Geley has written concerning the nature of ectoplasm, which he states can be modelled by the thought of sitters of the psychic 'as a sculptor models wax.' It does not convince me of spirit return, but it does confirm me in my own deductions."

White then showed me some slate-writing which he had secured under rigid test conditions. He said: "On this clean slate I drew two broad lines in the form of a cross, touching each of the four corners, so that anything appearing on that surface must be *above* these marks. All these messages in color which you see were written *over* the lines and while I held the slates. They did not pass out of my hands. I have had these pigments examined by one of our chemical firms in order to determine whether they could all be developed by some one process from invisible ink. I will show you the report."

He got from his files the report signed by the chief chemist, who said in effect that the differing pigments could not be developed by any invisible chemical, for each color had a different quality, no reagent would act on all alike.

"But the fact that the messages were written *after* you put the lines across the slates is sufficient evidence," I argued.

He went on. "The only suspicious fact connected with this medium's work is the presence in his desk of many prepared messages and designs—but even so, how does he put them across and above my lines whilst I am holding the slates? It may be that he prepares them beforehand in order to have them vividly in his mind when the time comes to reproduce them. If they are ideographs—if thought can model ectoplasm, as Geley states—it may be that thought can precipitate writing on a slate."

Going over the chemist's report, we noted these conclusions:

First, the characters were written or printed in chalks of various colors, showing no characteristics of being written with invisible colors.

Secondly, the inscriptions were each produced by the use of a solid crayon.

Thirdly, the materials were such as entered into the manufacture of commercial colored crayons.

Fourthly, the characters were placed on the slate in their existent form. Owing to the difference in their chemical constituents, producing all the chemical changes simultaneously was impossible, particularly with the condition mentioned that "no substance was applied during the four- to seventeen-minute period."

Stewart added, "I stated that the slates were clean when I took them into my hands and that I was positive that no others were substituted."

To this I added: "It is entirely credible to me, for your control was similar to that which I have many times practiced. As you will recall, I *dictated* what was to appear on the slates *after* I had them under my hand. I heard and felt the writing, but I did not see it appear. What are we to say when all the laws of matter stated by our text-books appear to be negatived in this way? How can we induce a man like Millikan to give study to such a small miracle? And yet a single word written on that slate, as you describe it, has greater interest to me than the cosmic ray. It demands explanation on a psychical plane—if there *is* such a plane.

"In a public meeting recently, Millikan is reported to have rebuked a speaker for speaking of the electron as though it were well known while the soul was an abstraction. He is reported as saying, 'We know nothing of the electron other than that it is a center for chemical forces.' Richet, you know, refuses to admit that these physical phenomena are in opposition to official science. He says: 'To admit telekinesis and the formation of ectoplasmic phantasms is not to destroy the smallest fragment of science—it is but to admit new data, to recognize that there are unknown energies. Materialization does not contradict one established fact, it merely adds new facts.' "

"That is my own way of looking at it," said Stewart, "and satisfactory so far as it goes. I put more emphasis on the messages than you do. The method is interesting, but the personal character of the communication is to me still more valuable."

"Richet says, somewhere, that mediums have an irresistible tendency to reconstruct in ectoplasmic material the forms and faces of individuals. I am asking, Why? What causes this irresistible tendency?"

"Probably because we all demand it of mediums—and that brings us right back to the method. How can our thinking cause these phantasms to take shape?"

In the end we went to bed quite as if the mystery involved were purely one of argument. The three points which stand out most sharply in this testimony are these:

First, Stewart's own statement of his feeling while the mask was being formed over his own face;

Secondly, the formation of an image of one of the women—a little to one side of her—a veritable phantasm of the living; and

Thirdly, the remodelling of Betty's face under the humorous, keenly observant eyes of her husband.

There is nothing in these entertaining feats inconsistent with the claim that our discarnate relatives are adepts in ideoplastic art, but it shows a mingling of the quick and the dead which increases our sense of the mystery of matter as well as of spirit.

CHAPTER TWENTY-SIX

SUMMING UP THE EVIDENCE

I

AT this point I should like to have the reader recapitulate with me the most significant events of the foregoing plain narrative of my experiences. They may help to a clearer understanding of a most elusive problem. Let us take them up in the order of their appearance:

First: In 1892, under test conditions, I heard the strings of a closed piano sound while my hand was on the lid. The strings were plucked in accordance with my dictation, now on the treble, now on the bass, keeping time to my whistling.

Second: A year later under rigid test conditions, Prof. Dolbear, a distinguished physicist, and I, in his own study, with a psychic under our control and with no one else present but Mrs. Dolbear, secured the movement of books and other small objects without normal contact by the psychic. While her sleeves were nailed to her chair-arms, we saw the moving of a huge shadowy hand and arm above our heads. Hands at my request thumbed a book, and a box was brought from a shelf at Mrs. Dolbear's request. Not only were the psychic's sleeves nailed to her chair, but her wrists were encircled by a silk thread of which the taut ends were held by Dolbear and myself.

Third: In the home of B. O. Flower, with no one present but Mrs. Flower, the psychic, and ourselves, we obtained telekinetic movements of a megaphone and secured independent writing on sheets of paper two yards from the utmost normal reach of the psychic; and as a final test, we secured writing on a sheet of paper while we controlled both the psychic's wrists, which were in addition bound by tape stitched to her sleeves and nailed to her chair-arms.

Fourth: *In full sunlight,* on slates *untouched by either the psychic or myself,* I received messages in varying script and signed by differing personalities; and while alone with the same psychic and rigidly controlling her hands and her feet, I saw the soaring flight of a megaphone.

Fifth: With Henry Fuller as my assistant, I secured from another medium, in a sunlit room, seven bars of music written on folded slates, while they were in my own hands or in Fuller's hands, at a distance of six feet from the psychic sitting immovably in full view, some of this music being recorded on *the slates while they were under my foot.* All of it came without contact by the psychic, and corrections were suggested by a voice which appeared to come from the air. The speaker claimed to be my friend the composer Edward Mac-Dowell.

Sixth: In a sunlit room while I held the corners of the *closed* end of a thick pad of Manila paper, with the psychic's fingers merely touching the closed end of the pad, I obtained on several pages in the middle of the pad, written messages; and later, in the center of a four-hundred-page book (selected at random from the shelves of a library which the psychic had never before entered), I obtained writing while the closed book was held in my two hands, a grasp which I never relaxed for one moment.

Seventh: In the presence of a psychic whose wrists were encircled with tape and nailed to his chair, I secured writing in the center of the table utterly out of his reach; and while he was thus nailed to his chair-arms and his right hand controlled by a sitter, I felt on my left arm the grip of a strong right hand. I *saw* this hand dart from a cloud of blue vapor before the psychic's breast and raise a glass of water to his lips. On another occasion, while the psychic's wrists were nailed to his chair and his little finger was linked with mine, his undershirt was tossed across the table. The psychic said it had been taken off his body while thus controlled.

Eighth: From a woman psychic while under my control with her sleeves nailed to the arms of her chair, I secured on a sheet of paper the print of *two large hands,* and on wax the print of a thumb which was neither that of the psychic nor that of any other member of the circle. In the red light of a lamp, I placed a gag in the mouth of this psychic, and while my hand was on her head, she produced (or helped to produce) a voice which did not issue from her lips, a voice which loudly sang.

While she was still controlled by my nails and tape, invisible hands in complete darkness picked minute objects from the floor, described them accurately, and afterward placed them in my hand. Invisible hands pulled my hair, touched my fingers, and at last a large hand showed itself under my eyes moving about above an illuminated pad.

I group these observed phenomena at this point not because they are more interesting than many others I have witnessed, but because they were secured in small circles, under my own test conditions. If they did not happen, then my testimony on any phenomenon in the world about me has not the slightest value to me or to my readers.

I shall begin my discussion of them by admitting that they, and many others I have recorded, were all in the nature of "stunts," as if the invisibles were intent upon amazing me rather than converting me. I use the word "stunt" in its popular sense, a display of skill in the execution of a difficult task; but describing these phenomena by a slang term does not lessen their essential mystery.

They should have astonished me, but in truth they did not. On the contrary they took place so naturally, so quietly, that I studied them without the slightest feeling of awe or even surprise.

Magical as they may seem, incredible as they are, they happened exactly as I have described them, and were recorded at the time without taking into account the aspects which religious beliefs had given them. In this chronicle I have attempted to present each event clearly and without prejudice for or against the spiritualistic theory. All I ask of the reader is a like dispassionate judgment of my chronicle. I repeat: If my testimony is of no value on these phenomena, it is of no value in any other of my experiences. I merely state what I saw and heard as in my "Afternoon Neighbors" I have recorded the words and faces of my fellow writers and artists.

II

While it would not be quite true to say that as an investigator I am at the point from which I started forty-five years ago, I shall no doubt disappoint some of my readers when I confess to a state of doubt. I rest my case, not for lack of other evidence but for the reason that, having brought my investigation to date, I feel the need of putting my experiences on record at this time in their proper order and in more detail than I have hitherto been able to do. I have no intention of adding to the discussion of this most vital subject. My interest will continue, indeed it will deepen with my days; but I shall leave elucidation to others.

The shadow of death, once so remote, has become a cloud across my pathway, so close that I can almost touch it with my hand. Questions which are wholly "academic" at thirty-one, become concretely personal at seventy-five. The problem of survival has for me, today, a significance which it did not have when I began my researches forty-five years ago.

With the rapidly diminishing circle of my relatives and friends, I find myself increasingly lonely, reflective. Already the larger part of my generation have become intangible, and many of those who remain on the earth are seeking, like myself, some evidence, some assurance of a life beyond the black deep whose waters they must soon cross. That I should welcome a hail from that dim other shore, is true, but the voice must be real and not imaginary.

As I bring this record of many personal experiments to a close, I am urged by my friends to state my conclusions. To them I must reply: "I have no conclusions. I am still the seeker, the questioner." I can only put into this final chapter some of my convictions along with a candid statement of the intellectual barriers which have thus far prevented me from an acceptance of the spirit hypothesis.

I do this in a mood of sincere regret. I wish I could end this book with a triumphant song of victory, but I can not do so.

That these phenomena are psychodynamic, that the communications I have recorded may be wholly due to a blending of the thought (conscious or unconscious) of the sitters and the psychic, may be true. The so-called "guides" indicate this. They speak as the medium imagines they would speak. "Lincoln" has a marked German accent when the psychic chances to be German, and "Thomas Paine" regrets his deistic utterances as the Christian medium thinks he should do.

In saying this I am not accusing any medium of fraud; quite the contrary. Most of the mediums I have studied have impressed me with their simple sincerity. Many were deeply religious, holding their gift to be sacred. With benevolent intention to console, they delivered only pleasing messages. They almost always responded to the desires of their patrons.

It is for these reasons that they continue to report in glad detail the doings of our friends "on the other side."

Sir Oliver Lodge in his book "Raymond" quotes his dead son as saying that life goes on with him very much as it did on earth.

There is in this material concept of the spirit world something of the wistful charm of "The Land of Youth" in Celtic mythology, in whose air no one grows old—the home of the Siddhi.

I should like to share this faith. I should like to believe that my father and mother, in restored youth, are walking a new and lovely country, feeding on astral fruits and grains while waiting for me to join them—but alas! I can not compass such a belief. I can not find the passage through the hillside into the changeless "realm of the Shee."

In writing of my doubts, I have no wish to weaken any other man's faith; I am merely stating the reasons which prevent me from accepting the spiritist interpretation of psychic phenomena, phenomena which I have abundantly proven to exist—I am still questioning the identity of the manifesting intelligences. My dissent is not upon the phenomena but upon their interpretation. I am seeking an explanation of their production (and their establishment as facts) before platting the fourth dimension or listing the occupations and recreations of those who inhabit it.

Another of these barriers to my acceptance of these spirit messages, is the language in which they are expressed. Caesar writing a message in English on a slate in Washington is absurd. Why should Napoleon speak to a German dentist in Detroit rather than to an Italian historian?

There is a certain logic in a colloquy between Confucius and Dr. Whymant, for Whymant understood the Chinese language of two thousand years ago; but there is no logic in a Chinese philosopher addressing himself to me, for I know nothing of his history or his tongue. It may be that this amazing dialogue with "Confucius" was only a dramatization, an episode born of Dr. Whymant's knowledge of Chinese literature drawn out by some unknown power in the medium.

I am troubled also by the problem of personal ubiquity. It is possible that Doyle could be heard by a thousand spiritualistic circles at the same moment (the radio has made that credible); but that he should be able to broadcast *differing* messages at the same identical moment, is to me unthinkable. Time may be the fourth dimension, but my dull mind can not grasp the concept of two differing messages finding expression at precisely the same moment.

Then, too, the theory of growth, of development in the spirit world gives me pause. A friend tells me that his daughter who died when a child of three, manifests her spirit return by roguishly untying his shoestrings, just as she used to do forty years ago. I listen, but it is to me a fairy story with a heartache in it.

If this spirit is now a woman of forty-three, I feel it unlikely that she would retain her childish relationship to her father, or that she would remember and practice this prank of her childhood. It is easier for me to conceive that she is a creation of his own mind.

Still other questions crowd for answer. How shall we smooth out in the spirit world the tangled relationships of this? What becomes of divorced wives and recreant husbands? To whom shall the widows and widowers belong? At what point does hope of reunion with a beloved first wife change to that of a second or third wife?

These and many other embarrassing and even humorous complications arise from the spiritualist's concept of life after death. The most baffling of all of these is the inability of science to draw a line between the lowest man and noblest animal; and I find myself unable to affirm that the African pygmy survives death while the gorilla and the lion vanish with their bones. In the long procession of life from the oyster to man, science finds no point where an immortal "soul" suddenly develops. Modern biology says there *is* no point where an immortal soul suddenly enters. One form of life shades into another. From the amoeba to man is an endless chain.

This being so, I am confronted by a still more insoluble problem. If we deny animal immortality but declare that all the men of all the ages have survived death, we are involved in a shoreless sea of human spirits. The ranks of the dead are incalculable.

Geologists estimate that man has been on this earth, in something like his present form, for a million years. During this time billions of ape-men, cave-dwellers, stone-wielders, and metal-workers have lived and died. Shall we grant that they have all survived death? Or shall we say that only those survived who possessed ethical attributes?

I am unable to draw this line. I can not define the law of survival.

If I confine the problem to humankind during what is called historic times, I am appalled. The number of intelligent human beings who have lived and died during the last ten thousand years is beyond computation. Consider the waves of men who have swept across and around this planet, hungering, mating, murdering each after his kind! What has become of these souls? these billions of individual men? Are the millions of satyrs, war-lords, assassins, rapists, murderers, cannibals, and savages who formed a large part of this innumerable host entitled to immortality? Shall we grant that the torturer survives equally with his victim? Can we say of the men of one age that they lived beyond the decay of their flesh, and of those of another age that they perished as the grass?

Unless the past is wholly imaginary, these problems remain.

Survival, as I see it, is not dependent upon good works nor upon the acceptance of any religious faith; it is based on a natural law. With me, it is not a question of the fate of an individual, not even of a race, but of all living creatures. Evolution is a continuous process. I can find no chasm between man and animals.

Survival therefore comes down to a question of the persistence of force. It is not a privilege granted to a few, it is all-embracing, a principle inherent in every form of sentient life. Many other great and clear thinkers profess and defend personal survival, but I can not achieve it. I wish I could.

Others who believe in personal survival seem not disturbed by questions which trouble me. Where do these unnumbered quadrillions of discarnate spirits dwell? Where in our universe can space be found to shelter and nourish them? What concept of heaven (or hell) is vast enough to contain them?

Admitting that our concept of space is illusory, and that our divisions of time are merely local, founded upon the movements of our planets (minute specks moving among the stars), I find no room for universal spirit persistence and growth.

Development as well as survival must be considered. It is an inescapable law of life. Nothing is static. In most of the individual lives of the myriads of men and women of recorded time, we find birth, growth, and in many cases old age—with death coming to all. Each child who lived, developed an individual character, a separate entity. He knew that he was neither a stone nor a clod. He counted himself a man, distinct from the animal world. This consciousness of self varied in clarity from a vague feeling to a defined faith.

For the most part savage races have believed in some form of life after death—their burial customs bear witness to that. But to me there is something incredible, something monstrous in this concept of universal survival. I confess that my notions of space and time are not wide enough to contain these Happy Hunting Grounds. I am not able to comprehend even the fourth dimension. "Time," some say, "is the fourth dimension." That does not enlighten me nor console me. As a three-dimensional being I can make nothing of these higher concepts.

The considerations I have thus outlined may not trouble others, but they have increasing weight with me—I acknowledge bafflement. When in the quiet of my study I converse with invisibles who claim to be my discarnate friends and relatives, occupying some other dimension, I am almost persuaded of their reality. For the moment I concede the possibility of their persistence, especially when their voices carry, movingly, characteristic tones and their messages are startlingly intimate. At such times they seem souls of the dead veritably reimbodied. They jest with me about their occupations. They laugh at my doubts, quite in character. They touch me with their hands. But after they have ceased to whisper and I recall the illimitable vistas of the stars, these phantasms of my dead, like all other human beings, barbaric or civilized, are as grains of dust in a cosmic whirlwind. In the light of the sun the fourth dimension, like the medieval maps of heaven and hell, withers to a fantastic mathematical formula.

I am aware that a great philosopher has publicly said, "Death is but an episode in life"—and this I should like to believe; but I sometimes wonder whether it would be well for us to reach a definite assurance of immortality. What effect would it have on our ethical standards? It may be that we are destined to be forever seeking that assurance. For twenty thousand years we have been asking, "If a man die shall he live again?"—and it may be that we must continue to seek an answer. It is, to me, the most vital of all subjects of research, more important to me than a demonstration of the existence of the Cosmic Ray or the cracking of an electron. Assurance if it comes will be the result not of reading but of experiment.

In conclusion therefore, I plead for a study of these phenomena without taking into account the aspects which beliefs have given them. The human organism should be studied in all its manifestations like any other form of organized matter. To say of any psychic phenomenon, "It is not subject to laboratory enquiry," is unscientific and absurd. Our Eddingtons and our Millikans should be aiding us to an understanding of the phenomena with which this volume is concerned, not as the basis for a new religion but as an extension of biological truth.

Now, finally, if you ask me bluntly, "What is the present status of your belief?" I must repeat that I am still the experimentalist, the seeker, and that I find myself most in harmony with those who say: "All these movements, voices, forms, are biodynamic in character. They are born of certain unknown powers of the human organism. They are thought-forms—resultants of mind controlling matter. They all originate in the séance room and have not been proven to go beyond it."

If you ask how it is that these ectoplastic phantasms speak thus pertinently and often in opposition to the thinking of the circle, I must answer, "I do not know." That "the composer" was a product of my own brain combined with that of Fuller, seems probable; but I can not tell you how he came to speak nor why his thought persisted in opposition to ours.

That these ectoplasmic phantasms are due to some occult power working through the medium, is possible; and it may be argued that the form thus shaped, existing and active for ten minutes outside the body, may, under favoring conditions, continue to live and act for an indefinite period. This is a fair inference, and I am willing that the reader shall make the most of it. I may come to that position myself as the evidence grows in power.

There is no farther wall in any science. Men will be discovering new facts in nature a thousand years from now just as they are finding out new natural laws to-day. The human organism will never be completely weighed, measured, and diagrammed. It is a microcosm of the universe. There will always be a field of unexplored biology. Beyond the fourth dimension other dimensions will allure men who are insatiably curious, those to whom the unknown is at once a challenge and a way of escape. We know a little now, we shall know a little more a century hence—but death will still be the ultimate insoluble mystery.